# SPORTING RIFLES
## A GUIDE TO MODERN FIREARMS

## BY PETER CARR

CONTENTS

**Co-authored, compiled and arranged by**
Peter Carr

**Contributing authors**
Nick Latus, Byron Pace, Tim Pilbeam, Mike Powell

**Design**
Matt Smith

**Editor**
Colin Fallon

**Photography**
Unless otherwise stated, photography is courtesy of the authors

**Copyright © 2014**
**Blaze Publishing Limited**
First published in the UK in 2014 by Blaze Publishing Ltd

British Library Cataloguing-in-Publication Data
A catalogue record for this book is available from the British Library

ISBN 978-1-910247-03-7

**Printed in Europe by:**
**Cliffe Enterprise Print Partnership**

**Blaze Publishing Ltd**
Lawrence House, Morrell Street,
Leamington Spa, Warwickshire
CV32 5SZ
**T:** 01926 339808
**F:** 01926 470400
**E:** info@blazepublishing.co.uk
**W:** www.blazepublishing.co.uk

# CONTENTS

# ABOUT THE AUTHORS

## PETE CARR

Peter Carr is known worldwide as an experienced stalker and big game hunter, and a sometimes controversial but always sporting writer. He has an extensive hunting pedigree, and taken most of the European species still open to the sportsman, and a respectful number of dangerous game from both the African and American continents with various rifles. He is also an award-winning editor of sporting publications, holding editor-in-chief roles on *Sporting Rifle* and *Modern Gamekeeping* magazines and a dual presenter-director role on *The Shooting Show*. He describes himself as a true hunter-conservationist.

## TIM PILBEAM

A writer since the early days of *Sporting Rifle*, Tim Pilbeam has firmly established himself as one of the magazine's two regular rifle reviewers. Readers trust him and manufacturers place him at the top of their 'test list' when they release a new model – such is his reputation. He's tested everything from rimfires to big game rifles, providing an honest, thorough and knowledgeable account of their strengths and weaknesses. An accomplished hunter in the UK and further afield, he's never far from his next rifle-shooting adventure.

## BYRON PACE

Brought up in Scotland but of Rhodesian descent, Byron is a regular deerstalker and African hunter – he spends much of his time each year hunting on the Dark Continent with clients, family and friends. A contributor to *Sporting Rifle* for five years, Byron's relaxed style has become a favourite with the magazine's readers, and he soon became one of the title's most prolific writers. As well as contributing hunting stories, he is a dedicated rifle reviewer for the publication as well as providing a monthly 'Calibre Hunter' column on rifle calibres both popular and obscure. His work behind a camera has also become well known on *The Shooting Show*.

## MIKE POWELL

Mike's early days were spent roaming the fields with an air rifle, or fishing from a little rowing dinghy in the river Teign or out at sea. Shooting predominated, however, starting a lifelong connection with guns, foxes, ferrets and rabbiting. Early retirement meant Mike was able to follow his passion for shooting, and the next 25 years were spent on keepering, beekeeping and other projects – primarily fox control. Finally retiring from keepering a couple of years ago, he now spends time writing on foxing and rabbiting. He is a member of the Devon and Cornwall firearms licensing committee, and countless rifles have passed through his hands over the years.

## NICK LATUS

A lifelong shooter and amateur stalker, Nick Latus is most often found with a rifle in hand stalking his local ground in Yorkshire or travelling to the Scottish Borders to take care of the bucks and does. A long-time writer for *Sporting Rifle*, he's contributed articles on a wide range of hunting topics – Highland stags, German driven boar hunting, and even rimfire hares. He's also a frequent tester of hunting equipment of all kinds – from rifles to ammunition, optics and even clothing. Nick is known for his honest reviews.

# PREFACE

After practising for just over 30 years as a full-time rifleman, I feel qualified to compile, arrange, and co-author this work. It has been a personal endeavour and a long time coming. I am however confident it fills a void in what is a very niche market.

The seed for this book was sown many moons ago, nurtured and fertilised through the years by a yearning to learn more about hunting rifles and their applications – especially when considering a new buy. Practical knowledge in book form of the available rifles and their uses in layman's terms was almost non-existent when I started out, and it remained that way for a very long time. Even today, though there are certainly some superb books and catalogues on sporting rifles, most of them are heavy on the technical aspects, and can quickly become bewildering if you aren't a student of physics. More of a biology man myself, I always believed there was a need for an honest no-nonsense guide on readily available factory rifles and their application in the field – the accurate, ethical killing of quarry.

I started out on my rifle hunting career one Christmas Day three decades ago with a BSA Airsporter-S. It turned out to be a bit of a rocky start – my father confiscated the rifle on Boxing Day owing to an altercation with our neighbours. I hadn't been able to wait to put my top-of-the-range Airsporter in all its walnut finery to good use, so I had decided on some opportune garden bird sport. But alas, my inaugural starling shoot, picking off the jippies (as we know them in Yorkshire) as they alighted on next door's TV aerial, ended in near disaster.

I was chalking up a respectful tally as Mrs H used to regularly feed the birdies, and I shot them as they stopped to survey the crusts laid out for them on the lawn below. Unfortunately a stray pellet hit the said TV aerial in the vitals just as Mr H was sitting down with his post-dinner sherry to watch Michael Caine miscast as a posh officer in the feature film *Zulu*. On investigating the abrupt absence of his audiovisual entertainment, he quickly discovered yours truly collecting an impressive bag of garden game (11 brace of starlings in a half-hour ain't bad going). Then the guano hit the fan.

I was quickly relieved of the rifle, not to mention given a swipe round the lug and a kick in the undercarriage from Pa Carr, who thankfully had averted the constabulary being called with a promise of payment to cover all damages and discomfort. The ban lasted until harvest when a ready supply of conies to safely have a crack at became available on the farm.

It was during this period of prohibition that I tried to digest everything I could on anything 'rifle-y'. Even then I had ambitions of owning a centrefire and progressing to greater game. But as far as reading matter went there was a dearth of it. For sure I could learn about the development of the flintlock and how it changed modern warfare, and the derring-do of Corbett, Patterson and Selous. I certainly wanted some of their kind of action, but I needed to know what rifle I would require for the particular job in hand.

After the rifle was reinstated, I soon progressed to a Ruger rimfire, and with proven good behaviour I eventually secured my first centrefire, a BSA mountain rifle in .30-06 that used to kick like the proverbial mule. When more money became available, I went from second-hand 'has-beens' to my first brand new factory rifle, but it all felt a bit of a gamble. Impartial advice was gratefully received, but it was from limited experience concerning one or at most two products. I wanted to explore my options more than that. But try as I might, there seemed to be nothing in print that contained the condensed knowledge and impartial in-the-field reviews that I was looking for. This book is the result of that want.

The project was far too big for one man to take on alone, so I have relied heavily on contributions from the best two rifle-reviewing scribes actively writing today. Tim Pilbeam and Byron Pace have been producing monthly rifle reviews for *Sporting Rifle* magazine and other journals for five years or more. The have both earned reputations for their honest, unbiased opinions in print.

Without these two stalwarts, this book would certainly not have been possible. Additionally, contributions from Mike Powell and Nick Latus have added greatly to the book's worth. It would also be remiss of me not to say a massive thank you to the indefatigable Colin Fallon, my deputy editor who has worked tirelessly without complaint to help me turn a smouldering idea into a book.

I have been fortunate to have worked with most of the great and the good in the international gun trade, but especially so at home in the UK. This isn't a comprehensive work, nor indeed was it meant to be, but it does cover a wide selection of factory-built rifles available to the would-be buyer of a centrefire rifle today. Any omission isn't deliberate, and if there are any, it is entirely my fault. In no way should an omission be seen as a non-endorsement, but rather an oversight on my part – or perhaps a restriction on the available pagination.

If in a decade of sporting writing – more than half as an editor – I have taken anything away at all, it has been the friendship of people I admire. In the gun trade and the rifle hunting fraternity, there are many such folk. Long may it continue, and I sincerely thank you all.

**Peter Carr**
**Leamington Spa**
**21 February 2014**

# INTRODUCTION

This book is aimed at sportsmen who are looking at buying a new fire-stick to continue their calling. Perhaps it is also for those of us who wistfully would like to do so, but never quite get round to it, as the old girl can still hit a 10-pence piece at a 100 yards. In fact, I suspect most of us like to have a moderate grasp of the popular sporting rifles readily available today – even those who are hunters first and riflemen second. This book has been written and compiled for those, too.

Every ethical hunter should aim for the one-shot kill. To achieve this he needs to be able to shoot, and to be able to shoot, he needs an accurate rifle to start with. All factory rifles today are capable of the consistent accuracy this prerequisite demands, but it's down to the shooter's skill and fine-tuning of his equipment to achieve it.

In this book, I have selected 37 factory-made rifles designed and produced with a sporting application in mind. The end user, whether he is a foxer, varminter, deer stalker, safari aficionado, driven specialist or dangerous game hunter, will get a lot from this publication. Whatever your individual passion, there will be a lot of cross-over between disciplines, and this guide will give you a sound knowledge of what each particular rifle can or cannot do in its many variants. The list is extensive and by no means exhaustive, but it is a fair coverage of the credible options offered for sale today.

The book is split into two sections. The first is a collection of rifle reviews arranged in alphabetical order for easy reference. It includes many standard bolt actions, some straight pulls, and a smattering of doubles to whet the appetite for those who are tempted to make a safari or try their hand at driven shooting.

Calibre choice is never an easy one, as a lot of factors have to be considered and weighed in one's mind before making the final decision. The second section of this book is devoted to just that, and hopefully the information contained will help the sportsman make more of an informed choice. I have selected most of the commonly available calibres and tended to stay away from the so-called wildcat derivatives, as the standard options are confusing enough as it is. From a sporting rifle sense, I cannot see any major advantage to the wildcat calibres. The slight edge they can give is for competitive shooting, and not strictly applicable to the sporting sense. Their main disadvantage, of course, is availability of ammunition, even if you load your own – it's hard to do it in a remote Highland lodge, worse still in the African bush. If your ammo box goes missing in transit, it is something of an insurance to have a common calibre, since securing replacement ammunition is then a much more realistic possibility.

Remember that even the best equipment is no substitute for excellent marksmanship. Practice and considered shot placement are required for consistent one-shot kills. Know your limitations, and respect your quarry by making measured decisions. Enjoy your sport, of course, but above all be safe. PC

# ANSCHÜTZ 1770

I have to declare a personal interest here: I am an unashamed fan of pretty much every one of the bolt-action rifles Anschütz has produced in the last 60 years.

I have had rifles by this maker for nearly 50 years, and without exception I have found them to be extremely well made and very accurate. Of course, Anschütz has always been known for the extremely high quality of its target rifles. In the last 40 years, over 85 per cent of Olympic small-bore rifle medals and 95 per cent of world-class biathlon medals have been won by athletes using Anschütz rifles.

When I heard a whisper that there was going to be a new model in .223, I immediately approached the distributor, who arranged for one of the earliest models to be shipped from Germany. Time passed and finally there was a call to say that the rifle was on its way and it was the one displayed at the IWA and Outdoors Classic Show in Nuremberg. I must admit I was more than a little excited as the box was opened, and my expectations were exceeded as the contents were removed. This was a very good-looking rifle indeed. The first thing that

struck me was the highly figured walnut 'Meister grade' German-style stock, with Schnabel forend, semi-oval cheekpiece, ventilated rubber butt pad and fine chequering. The wood has a smooth oiled finish, which looks and feels really high quality. Also, the 'famous' flag safety has been replaced by a conventional forward-and-back that falls easily to the right thumb.

Underneath, the three-round in-line metal magazine only protrudes about half an inch, and the rifle's overall appearance is sleek and functional. Incidentally, the rifle is supplied with high-visibility inserts to stick on the magazine, but to my mind this is unnecessary and looks a bit garish. Anschütz has told me it can also supply five-shot magazines if required.

The action and barrel are extremely well machined and finished, and the blueing is – as usual for this make – top quality. The 22in barrel is cold hammer-forged, of medium target weight, evenly tapered with no provision for iron sights, and fully floated. The crown is perfectly finished and the twist rate is one in nine – ideal for 55-grain ammo. For

the first time in over 30 years, Anschütz has decided on a new action, designed specifically for centrefire cartridges. The receiver is machined from a solid block of Chromoly steel, the 11-millimetre rail runs the full length of the receiver and has additional mounting holes drilled and tapped, and the ejection port is quite small. The scope rail is finished with what Anschütz describes as its 'wave' action, which looks a little different.

The extractor design is quite unusual: the hook lies in a slot inside one of the front lugs and is tensioned by a rod that runs through the two lugs and round the bolt. This seemed a strange approach, but in use it turned out to be highly efficient, flinging the spent case up to six feet away. There are no less than six locking lugs: three at the front and three at the back. These are designed so that there is a short bolt throw of about 60 degrees. The bolt action is extremely smooth and positive from the start, and a pleasure to use.

The trigger is very much the same as on my two 1700 series rifles – it is adjustable and comes set at about two and a half pounds. This can be brought down to two pounds or up to as much as four and a half. I normally set all my trigger pulls to about two and a half pounds. If, like me, you often change from one rifle to another, having all pull weights the same prevents premature release, or just a jerk and no bang! In use, the action is smooth and positive from the

word go. It truly is as good as any factory rifle I have ever used.

With the rifle set up, I set out to see what it would do. The manufacturers have engraved "for factory ammunition only" on the barrel, and so we took a supply of Federal Power Shok 55-grain soft points, and a supply of Prvi Partizan 55-grain soft points. I was particularly interested to see what the Anschütz would make of the latter as results from Prvi can sometimes be rather mixed!

I normally zero at 200 yards for the .223, which means being about 1¼in high at 100 yards. We put a few rounds through the rifle after bore sighting, cleaning after every two or three; initial results were promising. The rifle really took to the Prvi, which pleased me no end as this make costs considerably less than many others. After about 20 rounds, the groups of three were printing between half and three quarters of an inch – good enough for me!

To sum up, the Anschütz 1770 is one of the nicest rifles I have ever tested. The company set out to produce something different to the models of the last decade or so – a big departure for a firm that has been at the top of target rifle production for so many years. I would say Anschütz has succeeded – the whole unit is balanced and not only looks good but feels good too.

Any complaints? Just one: removing the bolt for cleaning is a bit of a fiddle, made more difficult by the proximity of the bolt to the comb when it is withdrawn. It would be a disaster to dent the wood, but with care it shouldn't be too much of a problem.

A final confession: I liked the rifle so much I went ahead and bought it. **MP**

**ANSCHÜTZ 1770**

*Model tested:* 1770 in .223, master grade walnut stock

*Price range:* £1,400

*Contact:* RUAG  01579 362319
**www.ruag.co.uk**

# ANTONIO ZOLI .243

I knew Zoli made outstanding high-end shotguns, but in the UK, that esteemed name had never really been associated with rifles – until now. There was no question of Zoli's fine craftsmanship, but it would be interesting to see how this would translate into producing a hunting rifle.

As I shouldered the Bavarian model for the first time, there was something strangely familiar. I knew I had never set eyes on an Antonio Zoli rifle before (although they were originally launched in 1989), but the lines and build of the action had most definitely crossed my path. It was a moment before it dawned on me. I was holding a Husqvarna 1900.

A quick flick through my book on rifle actions confirmed the origin – an aerial view showing bolt, safety and receiver matched meticulously the rifle I was holding. Browsing Zoli's website gave final sign-off of this fact – it described its rifles as based on the old Husqvarna actions.

Renowned for its build quality and strength, the Swedish gunmaker Husqvarna

originally built rifles designed around a modified Mauser action. It exported worldwide, providing Smith and Wesson with actions for its rifle debut in 1968. In the 70s, the design took a radical departure from its origins, building on Husqvarna's knowledge base to produce a more refined tool. The modern Zoli bolt-action rifle draws its design and construction almost entirely from these model 1900 rifles, and later series 8000 actions.

The deep blue of the metalwork was the first thing that caught my eye. With a traditional look and feel, the rifle strays from the modern trends of matt finishes, coated metalwork and synthetic stocks – but this is no bad thing. It is a rifle that has its roots firmly in the past, yet is every bit as relevant to the modern hunter as it was 40 years ago.

The stock was relatively plain, with clean chequering cut around the pistol grip and forestock, giving a crisp underhand feel with comfortable dimensions. It shouldered nicely with an endearing familiarity; I was enjoying the return to more traditional roots.

Removed from the metalwork, inletting was sealed and finished well, but unlike many new rifles to the market, there was no pillar or resin bedding. Having said that, I believe bedding can be requested on special order, along with a magazine upgrade for the factory floor plate.

The action itself is relatively simple, sporting a machined cylindrical receiver with integral recoil lug. My initial inspection led me to believe that the lug was welded on after machining, though Zoli is eager to point out that it is indeed formed from a single piece of steel. This is always my first query on any action. The modern move away from integral recoil lugs is purely on a basis of manufacturing ease and cost-cutting. It may be hard to quantify the downrange benefits of the integral lug, but there is no doubt that this is the strongest design. With this in mind, it is always my preferred choice, although it's inevitably more important in heavy recoiling rifles.

The bolt locks in place with twin fantail locking lugs, which – bar a slot for a Sako-style extractor – completely encases the case head with a recessed face, in the same way as with a Remington or Howa. Easy ejection is achieved by a commonly found sprung plunger, while the bolt glides effortlessly back

and forward along the raceways, aided by a protruding guide rib on the right-hand lug. I find the grooved lug on a Howa to be a neater solution, but this works well all the same.

I appreciated the oversized lugs, which provided a large bearing surface to oppose the explosive forces of ignition. The twin lugs are not fancy, but they work. The benefit of more than two lugs is an interesting point for debate, but many gunsmiths accept that it is incredibly difficult to achieve uniform bearing surfaces when employing multiple, stacked lugs. With just two, lapping can easily bring them close to 100 per cent contact with lug recesses – an important factor in an accurate rifle.

Cocking on the rise of the bolt, the handle itself is well positioned for fast operation, swept down and slightly backwards. My only

dislike was the unblued finish and less than refined handle-to-shaft interface – I have never been a massive fan of shiny bolts.

With the underside of the shaft recessed along its length, the bolt is removed by fully depressing the trigger with the safety off, dropping the sear through the action. This is similar in nature to Brno CZ rimfires, and although it functions perfectly, this feature could be potentially life-threatening if hunting dangerous game. If, owing to reasons Murphy is all too aware of, the sear sticks down when pulling the trigger, reloading will result with the rifle in one hand and bolt in the other. The likelihood of this happening is tiny, and this rifle is not chambered in truly big game calibres anyway. It is, however, a worthy observation in any case, as this would not be a new story if it happened tomorrow.

Finished with a chunky shroud, the bolt sits nicely in the action, tapering down from the full diameter of the receiver to a narrower rounded end. The only aspect that differs from the original Husqvarna is that the old rifles sported aesthetically pleasing bolt jewelling. It was not just for looks – the process helps to hold oil on the surface, which in turn facilitates smoother cycling.

A set trigger comes as standard, with the non-set option breaking reasonably, while the set trigger was very light indeed. When not cocked, there was a little more play in the trigger unit than I would like, but this locked up when loaded. Since the sear engagement doubles as a bolt stop, it does take a lot of punishment, but I think it is substantial enough to withstand anything thrown at it. I did find that where the sear notch married with the trigger, the edges were a little rougher than I expected. This didn't appear to have any major effect on trigger performance.

The safety catch is located to the right of the bolt, in the same place as a Sako, with a simple forward-and-back arrangement. With the rifle on safe, the bolt can be removed by depressing a small tab just in front, essentially providing the same feature as many modern three-position safeties. Comfortable and quiet to operate, the long, grippy surface rocks firmly back and forward. It won't be winning any

prizes for looks, though – the slightly cheap appearance isn't really in keeping with the rest of the rifle, which is a shame. To ensure safe functionality of the set-trigger, the design also ensures that it cannot be operated when on 'safe', and will automatically disengage if the safety is applied.

Joining the likes of Steyr Mannlicher, Zoli fits cold hammer-forged barrels to its rifles, following a nice slender profile and well-formed crown. The receiver is drilled and tapped for mounts, which may be all but

impossible to source if you ask for mounts to fit a Zoli.

Before realising that the key was to find the equivalent Husqvarna-compatible mounts, I had Zoli's own designed and manufactured mounts sent over from Italy. These consisted of a one-piece rail and two quad clamping rings, and I was impressed with the quality. Finished in the same blueing as the rifle, they were the perfect complement to mount the Weaver scope. The only drawback – as with any one-piece rail – is the restricted access for top loading.

On the range, the rifle performed admirably. With the light set-trigger adjusted, it was a pleasure to fire, although the non-set option could do with a little work. Shooting 150-grain Hornady ammo, it rattled off groups just over the 1.5in mark at 100 yards with little issue at all. The 165-grain Hornady Performance performed best, tucking three rounds consistently around the 1MOA region. I have no doubt that tuned handloads would pull this in further.

This rifle's design has stood the test of time, emerging from one of the great European gunmakers. Now, in the hands of Zoli, the modern incarnation makes this great rifle available to hunters the world over once again.

With retail prices in the region of £1,665, it goes head to head with

industry standards such as the Sako and the increasingly popular Kimber.

I think to compete in this highly competitive part of the market, Zoli should provide its rifles bedded, and possibly with a magazine – both options that are available as extras. It would also be nice if they came factory screw-cut. Having said that, you will be more than satisfied with this rifle as your staple hunting tool. It will invariably provide decades of trouble-free and excellent service, given the solid heritage. Not to mention, of course, that it now sports the highly respected Zoli name. **BP**

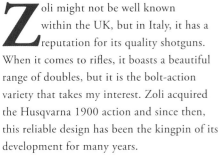

**Z**oli might not be well known within the UK, but in Italy, it has a reputation for its quality shotguns. When it comes to rifles, it boasts a beautiful range of doubles, but it is the bolt-action variety that takes my interest. Zoli acquired the Husqvarna 1900 action and since then, this reliable design has been the kingpin of its development for many years.

The AZ 1900 range of bolt-actioned rifles from Zoli is available in several different models, but it is the custom 'Alpen' edition

that lands on my doorstep from UK distributors Edgar Brothers. As I open the gun case, the quality of the stock and the beautiful embellishments on the action give the impression of a high-quality investment. One of the most important considerations when reviewing a rifle is to understand where the model lies within the plethora of rifles that are available to hunters. The price will be the first clue. A quick email informs me the Alpen has an RRP of £2,395, so it is aimed at the mid to high-end market, competing for

shelf space with established European brands such as Sauer, Blaser and Mauser. The clients for these mid to high-end rifles expect high quality as a prerequisite, mixed with some individuality, and the Alpen certainly seems to offer the latter.

As mentioned, the attractive stock appears to be made from high-quality walnut, with a traditional Mittel European-style Bavarian cheekpiece. It shoulders beautifully, aided by carefully cut chequering around the pistol grip and forend. The base of the pistol grip

and the very front of the curled forend have a darker wood, exquisitely cut in, enhancing the quality of the build. I have a soft spot for the Bavarian-styled European rifles, as they are designed to be shot standing – whether freehand for running game or off sticks – and this is no exception. The Zoli logo stands proud at the base of the pistol grip, finishing off the furniture nicely.

The AZ 1900 action, of Scandinavian breeding, is made from polished stainless steel but embellished with clear engravings

of popular European animals, such as wild boar, mouflon and chamois. The action does resemble a Mauser at a quick glance, and enjoys a very smooth travel, made from one piece of high-quality steel. Removing the stock exposes an integral recoil lug, with no evidence of any form of bedding within the stock. The top of the receiver is drilled to take either Weaver-styled bases or the one-piece Zoli bridge mounts, some of which are detachable.

The highly polished, jewelled bolt shaft uses a twin lugged locking system to the front, sharing a similar ejector and extraction system to the Remington's. It glides beautifully on the guide rails and locks the round into the breach gracefully.

The bolt handle knob is very smooth, although maybe not the easiest to grab hold of, and to the rear, the metal shroud shows off the head of a mouflon – a rather classy touch. To remove, slide the

safety to the rear, squeeze the trigger and out she pops.

I love the barrel. Finished off in a very deep blued finish, it oozes quality. It is profiled in a 23" light sporting profile with a slightly recessed crown, but it is not threaded.

The 'DSS' trigger system comes as standard across the range, with an 'ISS' set-trigger factory-set to 4lb and 0.5lb, respectively. The standard pull has little, if any, creep, and is crisp to pull. I would reduce the pull weight just a little if this was my gun, but it does feel fine. To use the set trigger, push the blade forward after loading, and normal trigger will return if safety is applied. The safety is a two-position design to the right of the action, but to the front of the catch, there is a smaller lever that allows the bolt to be opened with safety applied. The levers do look a little cheap, but they are very quiet and easy to operate, which is much more important.

The one-piece trigger guard and base plate are made from an alloy compound with a red deer stag engraved on to the base of the guard. This is both sturdy and well made. It is a drop plate design holding four rounds in .243 and loads efficiently from the top of the action.

Edgar Brothers also supplied a Bushnell Elite 6500 2.5-16x50mm scope, weaver mounts and rings. At the range, the Remington 95g Accutip achieved a fair 1.25" grouping. Out of interest, I dug out a variety of factory ammo from my store. The 100g Lapua grouped 0.6", 70g Sako at 0.5", and the 58G Norma at 0.5". Not too shabby at all. In fact, I think this is very impressive but it does prove the point that all rifles require a little tuning to find the best performer. I found the trigger a little heavy, but I did not feel any creep, so it is just a case of getting used to it. The rifle feels lighter than the stated 3.3kg (7.25lb) with the recoil being quite noticeable, especially the muzzle lift, when shooting from prone. Off sticks or shooting freehand, the Alpen felt very comfortable and I found the pistol grip and styled forend ergonomically suited my hands very well.

Post-harvest is always a good time to test rifles on foxes, and the Alpen did not disappoint with a kill at 125 yards. Loading, cycling and ejection of the rounds was effortless, proven by my being able to fire four rounds on my running boar target within 50 yards of travel. No problem there. I found the Bushnell Elite very clear in the spotlight, and during the zeroing procedure, it tracked well with no jumps between

adjustments. I was very impressed with its light-gathering ability and crisp sight picture.

The Zoli Alpen was a delight to shoot and has the look of a far more expensive rifle. If I was out hunting with colleagues, I would be the first to show off the beautiful engraving and the high-quality woodwork, but will it take on the other European makers of high-end rifles? Visually: yes. Quality of action and barrel: definitely yes. Accuracy: oh yes,

though the trigger needs a little attention. The Bavarian range of rifles has an RRP of £1,500 to £2,395, so our Italian friends are also fighting against the established Sako brand in the UK.

Zoli is an established name in Italy, so if you are looking for something a little different, made by a prestigious high-class gunmaker, the Alpen could have your name on it. **TP**

**ZOLI .243**

*Models tested:* Bavarian; Alpen
*Price range:* £1,500-£2,395
*Contact:* Edgar Brothers  01625 613177
**www.edgarbrothers.com**

# BAIKAL MP221 ARTEMIDA

**B**aikal produces a comprehensive range of products including shotguns, rifles and airguns. Its shotgun range covers all types – single-barrel, side-by-side, over-and-under, pump and semi-auto. Baikal also produces good single-shot, over-and-under and side-by-side rifles, plus combination guns. All Baikal products are robust, and offer exceptional value for money.

The world's largest manufacturer of sporting arms produces Baikal in Russia; its shotguns and rifles are made from top-grade steel using state-of-the-art machinery and production techniques. With the exception of the budget models, rifles and shotguns are stocked in beech or walnut.

The MP221 Artemida is a unique combination of an 'express' style side-by-side gun featuring a basic appearance, but in classic lines, with an innovative barrel concept that incorporates a unit which provides for close and stable patterning of mean impact point by self regulation. If brand or cartridge load is changed, the mean impact point of each barrel can be zeroed to a common centre via a ribless joint of barrel unit, and the loose fit of the right barrel in the sleeve. This is easily done by moving the jack-type horizontal adjuster.

The gun is a cheap and cheerful chance to own a double rifle that effortlessly maintains a genuinely elegant appearance even though, retailing at £650, it would be well within budget for many British boar hunters that sporadically partake in boar driving weekends on the continent. Indeed, more and more Brits are adding an annual boar *battue* to their calendars, and for the shotgunner who is a non-stalker, or rarely uses a bolt-action rifle, there could not be a better option than Baikal's best.

The stock and forend are made from basic beech – there is also a walnut option – and finished with a rubbed oil finish. Chequering on the pistol grip and forend panels is well cut, even, and surprisingly smooth, making for a comfortable grip. Unfortunately, the stock is a little short, a fault I remember from my old Baikal shotgun from yesteryear. However, this can easily be remedied with the addition of a butt extension sleeve or, for the purist, an extra piece of wood can be shaped and fitted professionally to extend the length of pull. The stock is finished with a black recoil pad.

It features a traditional push-forward shotgun-style safety catch that locks both sears and triggers when engaged. Both triggers on my test rifle were an even three pounds.

Adequate iron sights come fitted, with the rear sight sitting to the forefront of the long scope rail. I have never been a fan of

fitting scopes to doubles but apparently, this particular scope rail on the rifle is being replaced on newer models with a picatinny rail mount. After some initial head scratching, I managed to regulate the rifle using the unique regulating screw provided between the barrels to 'tune' them to shoot to the same point at a desired range with the chosen ammunition/bullet weight.

The rifle I had on test was chambered for .30-06 Springfield and, using Norma 180-grain Dual Core ammo, I achieved a 4in three-shot grouping at 60 yards from the bench, which is beyond adequate for driven boar using the iron sights.

The rifle pointed well and was fast-handling due to its low weight of 3.3kg. It did, however, kick like an enraged donkey,

but this was mainly because the rifle was a little short in the stock. This problem is easily solved with a rubber stock extension sleeve.

As the gun is a non-ejector, I was worried about empty cases sticking in the chamber when the rifle became hot in a rapid fire situation. These fears proved unfounded when I fired off 20 rounds and encountered no problems replacing the empty shell cases. Let's face it, 20 successive shots on a driven boar hunt would be one hell of a good day. Though the top lever was a bit stiff, stiffness isn't uncommon with new rifles, and it could not be considered a fault in any way.

I took the test rifle to Germany on the last boar hunt of the season, but unfortunately I didn't get the chance of a shot because of the excessive snow. I am certainly going to put this rifle through its paces next season. It is a shame that the MP221 Artemida side-by-side is a non-ejector as I believe many more hunters would give this rifle serious consideration if it were. That said, the rifle is a workhorse that will stand the test of time and, with its low retail price tag, it ought to be in most shooters' cabinet if they enjoy a weekend's driven boar shooting across the pond.

The rifle breaks down as per a shotgun for transport and storage and, as with all Baikal products, it is extremely well-made and very strong. There is an over-and-under option – the IZH 94 Express – which uses the buttstock, trigger mechanism and up-rated action from the IZH-27EM ejector shotgun fitted with high-quality 600mm (23.5in) hammer-forged barrels. The furniture is walnut and is available in .223 Rem, .308 Win, .30-06 Springfield and 9.3x74.

The side-by-side model reviewed here is offered in .308 Win, .30-06 Springfield and .45-70 calibres. **PC**

**BAIKAL MP221**

*Model reviewed:* MP221 Artemida side-by-side

*Price range:* £650

*Contact:* York Guns 01904 487180 www.yorkguns.com

# BERGARA BX11

When I think of Spanish-made guns, my mind immediately jumps to AYA shotguns. I have had one for years, and my bargain £80 buy is still my rough gun of choice to this day. Although this may be something of a workhorse, there are some fine-looking guns to have come out of Spain, although they are still better known for shotguns than rifles. Asked to name a Spanish rifle, I bet that the best most people could come up with is Cometa air rifles.

In fact, there is a big name rifle maker that calls Spain home, and it has been making barrels for some big industry hitters for some time. Bergara is certainly a name known among gunsmiths and custom rifle enthusiasts – many fit Bergara barrels to their rifles. Not only do they shoot well, but they are also exceptional value for money. Their story is one that may surprise many.

Anyone from a competition shooting background, or who has contemplated getting their hunting rifle re-barrelled, will more than likely have come across Shilen barrels at some point. Generally accepted to be one of the finest barrels on the market, the company originally traded under the name Shilen Rifles, started by Ed Shilen in 1967. With these rifles, he went on to set not just one or two, but 13 world records, resulting in his induction into the benchrest hall of fame.

In 1992, the focus of the business changed and Ed channelled his expertise into producing the most accurate barrels on the planet. Arguably, he achieved this with many of the top benchrest shooters in the world gracing their rifles with Shilen hardware. This in itself has very little to do with Bergara, other than the fact that Ed Shilen himself now consults for the Spanish barrel and rifle maker. Not a bad person to have on board

in the pursuit of producing accurate rifles. Indeed, the purpose of Ed consulting for Bergara was to bring high-quality, accurate barrels to the wider market at prices more akin to mass production. It certainly seems to be doing that.

In an interview about the collaboration, Ed explained that over the period of a year, he worked closely with the engineers at Bergara. Their aim was to come up with solutions to the problem of producing high-quality barrels while maintaining production rates that would make them cost-effective. He ended by saying: "From what I have seen of what they are turning out right now, they (Bergara) are a very fine production barrel."

With this is mind, you would expect the Bergara rifle I had on loan to shoot pretty well. As the first journalist to test the rifle on UK soil, I was eager to see just what I had. So we will do this review a little bit back-to-

front, and I will tell you now that if nothing else, this rifle could shoot. My best group with 70-grain Federals clustered ½in, and running the value-for-money 105-grain Geco ammo printed a group just under ¾in. It wasn't just me that could shoot it either, as a few friends as well as my girlfriend achieved similar results. This rifle was brand new, with no break-in, and it even delivered that within six shots.

I couldn't help but smile at the results, and immediately decided I would have to take the rifle hunting. A few days later, with friend and *Sporting Rifle* writer Nick Latus visiting, we managed to bag two early-season cull bucks. The Bergara had now officially had its UK christening.

Anyway, back to the nuts and bolts of it. The first thing to note is that this is a switch-barrel, which allows you to shoot anything from .243 Win to .375 H&H with a barrel change and replacement of the bolt head. Barrel replacement is achieved in a similar way to the Sauer 202, only with two hex-head screws instead of three. Forestock removal is considerably easier, though, with a catch on the bottom much like a shotgun. Providing easy access to remove the barrel, the mechanism is maybe not quite as secure as I would like, allowing sideways movement of the forestock.

The barrel itself is secured in place by a contracting collar and location grooves corresponding to the hex-head screws on the action. A locating lug ensures the barrel sits correctly after each replacement, while the bolt lugs locate inside the barrel to ensure that head spacing is maintained. It's not the fastest switch-barrel in the world, nor is it a new idea, but it does work. Shooting single shots between barrel removals, I still achieved groupings under an inch with three shots. I repeated this enough times to feel confident in the results.

The groups may not have been quite as tight as three straight shots, but I am sure

most of that had to do with my changing shooting positions.

Now, if you fancy alternating your rifle with calibres that are not in the same family group, you will need to change not only the barrel but the bolt head as well. On the Bergara, it's a pretty simple affair, flicking up two recessed legs on the bolt shaft before slipping the six lugged head off and replacing it with an alternative size. Securing the new head is a reverse of the procedure, making sure to fit the small sprung leg back through its locating hole.

The bolt itself is substantial, and for the smaller calibres is considerably oversized. But this is pretty standard for switch barrels, as the action has to accommodate such a wide range of case lengths. It's something you just have to put up with in most rifles if you want multi-barrel functionality. Bolt cycling is pretty

smooth, with feeding and ejection functioning as they should. A generous proportioned synthetic bolt knob will ensure you have a firm grip of proceedings, while the two-position Remington-style safety is positioned to the right of the bolt shroud. It's a little on the noisy side, but some firm pressure will aid a more covert operation. The only real criticism I would have is that the bolt shroud is synthetic, and as I have said about Tikka rifles, it's not particularly desirable.

Removing the rear section of the stock allowed me to examine the receiver, which above the stock, boasted some aesthetically pleasing lines. This told an interesting story.

Although I had assumed it was a machined receiver, it was evident that it had actually been formed through a casting process, which is cheaper and easier than machining a solid piece of steel. Bergara

joins American gunmaker Ruger in its decision to use this process.

The magazine is a straight stack design, and seems to work just fine, although it lacks a solidly constructed feel about it. Replacing the mag into the rifle does expose an unusual peculiarity, in that unlike most rifle makers, Bergara hasn't fitted a magazine well sleeve. As a result of this, the magazine fits straight into the wooden stock. This makes insertion a bit sticky at times.

Finally, we get to the trigger, which initially I didn't think was that great. However, after a bit of adjusting, it turned out to be quite satisfactory. I wasn't a big fan

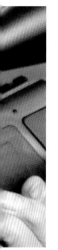

The name 'Bergara' is well known in the custom rifle world for high-quality barrels. Hailing from the Basque region of Spain, the company supplies gun manufacturers all over the world. Heading up the team since the late 60s is Ed Shilen of Shilen Barrels, with a reputation for producing some of the most accurate barrels out there, aided by high-quality steel and superb engineering. Recently, Bergara decided to diversify into the assembling of 'semi' custom rifles, and over the past 12 months, a new generation of switch-barrel design emerged.

Bergara's offering is more than capable of competing with fellow switch-barrel models from Blaser, Mauser, Sauer and Merkel, and has a lower price tag to boot. So when I received a phone call from UK importer RUAG asking if I wanted to test one, the answer was a resounding yes.

The Bergara BX11 multi-calibre rifle is available in either a standard American Walnut or, as supplied, a Synthetic stock in a wide range of calibres from .243 to .375 H&H. The one on test was the popular .308.

Once shouldered, the rifle feels much lighter than the stated 3kg, well balanced with a firm grip. The 'palisander' inserts of the pistol grip and forend give it the 'soft touch', as clearly stated in the promotional literature. When tapped, the stock does feel hollow, maybe not reflecting a rifle of this quality. As for the forend, it has a shotgun-type release mechanism to facilitate the removing of the barrel, resulting in a loose-fitting affair. There is a pressure pad to the front that rests against the barrel, giving it more rigidity for the fitting of a bipod. To the rear, the synthetic model comes with a meaty pre-tightened recoil pad and inserts for length of pull adjustment. Overall, the stock might have had the feel of a budget build, but it nevertheless worked well in terms of grip and comfortable ergonomics.

The receiver was supplied with a picatinny rail, allowing easy fitting of a variety of scope mounts and night vision optics. The bolt is long, which is common for most switchable systems, with two easily removable heads to accommodate all the different calibres. The six lugs engage directly into the barrel, resulting in a tight 60-degree throw. To remove, simply prise the two levers located just behind the head outwards, and pull off. The bolt is reasonably smooth, aided by a decent-sized bolt handle and knob, with safety being a simple two-position device located to the right of the action.

The steel magazine holds four rounds and sits a little proud of the underbelly of the stock. It was not the easiest to insert or remove, but I put that down to it being a new rifle. Feeding and extraction worked

of the thin trigger blade, but that certainly didn't seem to affect the shooting.

Taking a look at the overall rifle, it does look quite good. You wouldn't describe the woodwork as stunning – it seems to be a lightweight, soft grade, but it is comfortable, and the chequering alternative is firm to grip. The metal is finished in matt black, although I am unsure exactly what method was used, as it seemed softer than other finishes I have come across. What this rifle offers is some convincing pedigree when it comes to barrels, and evidently Bergara can put a rifle together in a way that makes it shoot. Bergara is very much unknown in the UK rifle market, but I am sure we will be seeing more and more of it. As far as switch-barrels go, they are priced competitively, coming in around £1,500 for the synthetic model. Replacement barrels won't break the bank either, in the region of £300. Worth checking out next time you're in the gun shop. **BP**

well, and loading was easy. The trigger is fully adjustable from two to three pounds, but is not the most crisp I have tested.

The heart and soul of the rifle is the 24in lightweight barrel made from AIS14140 carbon steel finished in matt black. To change barrels, simply remove the forend and loosen the two hex-head screws clamping the barrel to the lower part of the action [06/05]. With a firm tug, the barrel slides straight out of the action. To replace, carefully align a locating lug, and reverse the process. For a multi-barrelled design, it is straightforward and relatively quick to implement.

The BX11 was put through its paces on the range, shooting by day and by night. For accuracy, I fitted a Kahles 3-12x56 using 170-grain Geco soft-pointed ammunition, also supplied by RUAG.

At 100 yards, a more than acceptable group of 1in was achieved. This was narrowed to 0.75in with lighter ammunition. I removed and replaced the barrel on three occasions, and the point of impact moved by about 1in. Again, this could be down to the rifle having to bed in from new. At night, I used a Pulsar Digisight N750 – courtesy of Thomas Jacks – that yielded three foxes at distances from 60 to 150 yards. I took two off sticks, and the other off a bipod. I found

the recoil was less noticeable than many .308s. The .308 is not the most suitable calibre for foxes, but it really allowed me to test the Bergara in the field.

Attaching a bipod to the forend was not the firmest fit I have witnessed, but this is designed as a lightweight, all-round rifle, not the sort a bipod user typically goes for. As previously mentioned, the trigger was a little too spongy for my tastes – I had a bit of trouble anticipating the breaking point.

The BX11 is certainly an accurate rifle, and so it should be, considering its provenance. If you want a competitive, switchable system that performs, the Bergara BX11 is worth serious consideration – not least because most other models retail at over £2,500. Extra barrels won't break the bank either – they're cheaper than other manufacturers' at about £300. All in all, the Bergara would be a worthy addition to many gun cabinets. For those who enjoy a spot of African or European hunting and could do with two calibres, it's a must. ⊞

---

**BERGARA BX11**

**Model reviewed:** BX11 multi-calibre

**Price range:** From £1,500

**Contact:** RUAG  01579 362319
**www.ruag.co.uk**

---

# BLASER R8

For those not familiar with the Blaser concept: Blaser uses a straight-pull bolt action when the case is being recycled, which gives it a faster cycling time than a traditional turn bolt movement. This is very useful in situations such as shooting driven boar, and that's one of the reasons why the older R93 model was apparently the best-selling rifle in Europe for many years. Blaser also offers quickly interchangeable barrels in a wide variety of calibres.

Although I have only shot the Blaser R93 on a couple of occasions, I have heard that the top-loading magazine was fiddly and not to everybody's taste. The new R8 has addressed this issue, at the same time tweaking the bolt and trigger system.

Let's start with the bolt. Being a straight-pull system, it only requires the bolt handle to be pulled backwards. My early attempts to lift the bolt made me feel a little clumsy, but I quickly mastered it. The bolt assembly slides into the back of the barrel, helped by two long guides that slide along the stock to the lower side of the barrel.

Once the action has picked up the round and driven forward to chamber, a circle of locking tabs expands symmetrically into the rear of the barrel, locking the bolt. This system has the advantage of reducing the length of the action and barrel assembly by 3.5in, making it much easier to use in confined conditions such as woodland stalking.

To cock the mechanism, there is a large lever assembly on the rear of the bolt that also acts as a safety catch, cocker and de-cocker. When you apply forward pressure to this lever, it will come out of safety and cock the mechanism. To de-cock, press directly down and it will slide back into safety. While it seems a little strange, it is a very safe system. If you want to slide the bolt backwards to remove the round with the safety on, just push it down and the bolt will slide back. I discussed this with my local gun shop as I found it very stiff to push forward, but they have had no complaints about it or on the older R93s.

Now we come to the most interesting innovation: the magazine. As I already mentioned, the old R93 could only be loaded

from the top. The R8 sports an entirely new design: a detachable magazine that incorporates the trigger assembly. Some might be worried about losing this, rendering the gun completely useless, but it is nevertheless a clever yet simple design. As soon as the magazine is released, the bolt de-cocks. It is easily removed by squeezing a spring clip on either side – pull it out, then reload it in the normal way.

The .308 model holds four rounds; as for the construction, the trigger guard and base plate are made of aluminium, but the rest is made of high-impact plastic. If you prefer a top loader, slide a catch to lock the magazine into the stock and insert the rounds in the normal manner. This also eliminates the worry of dropping the magazine. In my test, I found the magazine to be compact and sturdy, but it did have to be forced into the stock – possibly due to the gun being brand new.

As for the trigger, there are no springs – instead, there is a desmodromic mechanism that moves a plunger in the stock, allowing the cocking mechanism to do its bit. This didn't seem to affect the trigger, though – it released at a consistent two pounds, and felt superbly crisp and light.

> ❝ AFTER THIS TEST, I CAN SEE WHY SO MANY BLASER RIFLES HAVE BEEN SOLD. THEY PROVIDE FANTASTIC ACCURACY– YOU SHOULD BE GUARANTEED A 'RIFLE FOR LIFE'

The 17mm barrel is attached to the stock by two captive nuts, which can be removed within seconds by means of a supplied hex key. Heavier barrels are also available. I'm told the R8 barrels are much easier and faster to break down than R93 barrels, but surprisingly, the R8 and R93 barrels are not interchangeable.

With a barrel length of 23in, the R8 will retain its compact design even with a moderator fitted. There is also plenty of gap between the forend of the stock and the barrel, which allows a fully floating barrel. It is also screw-cut for a moderator.

This model is available from .222 all the way to .500 Nitro. To change the calibre, all you need is a new barrel (along with magazine insert), and possibly another bolt head depending on the calibre selected.

The stiff, high-quality synthetic stock comes with studs fitted to the rear and the very front. If a bipod is required, there is a position for an extra stud already machined – a small yet very useful addition. The anti-slip inlays fitted to the pistol grip and under the forend enable a perfect hold in all weather conditions. The comfort and feel of the stock left me with no doubt that it is a quality chassis.

The inspection was complete – time to head to the range. Once I had zeroed at 150 yards, I achieved a group of 1.5in using some home-loaded 150-grain soft nose bullets running at 2,750fps. This was without any bipod or rear restraint – I just laid the forend on a shooting bag. The group tightened up a little after a few more shots, and I have no doubt that with more use and a little experimenting with different ammunition, this rifle can shoot even better.

Now it was time for the long-range test. I achieved groups of approximately 5-7in at 500 yards using cheaper ammunition, without a bipod and with a light wind blowing. Multiple shots also did not seem to affect the accuracy. Considering that this is a lightweight hunting

rifle, less than 1 MOA is very respectable with popular ammunition.

A short time later, I travelled up to Scotland to help control the red hind population on the Ledgowan estate, near Achnasheen in Ross-shire. As ever, I checked the zero again before we departed to the hills, and achieved a ¾in group at 1in high at 130 yards with the forend lying on a small grass mound. No issues with accuracy there, then.

After a few days' stalking, I was able to shoot some hinds using 150-grain soft nose ammunition. This proved effective in quickly dispatching the animals. The weight of the rifle (8.5lb including scope) was a real bonus, especially in the wet and windy conditions. The quicker cycling of the rounds was helpful when a follow-up shot was required. As it was a relatively short gun and in .308, the muzzle lift was quite apparent just after each shot, but I found the better manoeuvrability to be more than worth it. The conditions were very wet and cold and I struggled a little with the safety or cocking lever, as well as the loading of the magazine. With more time, I expect that these niggles would soon go.

The trigger was an absolute delight and I can see why this is so popular in Europe when used for both woodland stalking and driven boar. My colleagues Matt and Darren, both experienced riflemen, had a great time with the rifle as well, and the only negative point they raised was value for money. The retail price of approximately £2,750 (plus £390 for mounts) might put some off, but the R8 is nonetheless attractive to the specialised group of sportsmen who buy into the name and reputation of Blaser.

After this test, I can see why so many Blaser rifles have been sold. They provide fantastic accuracy – you should be guaranteed a 'rifle for life', bearing in mind you can add extra calibres to the same chassis. It is a divisive rifle – you will either fall in love with it or put it straight back into the gun rack. No prizes for guessing what side of that division I am on – when I next go boar shooting, I know what rifle I'll be taking. **TP**

A t my local stalking patch in East Yorkshire, a colleague often calls for my assistance when his time is limited and fraying activity by roebucks is giving the farmer some serious cause for concern. During the last season, three of us had hit the roe population hard on this particular farm due to significant damage to restocked hardwoods and commercial willow.

I had been vigilant since the does went out and the buck season started, but I had not seen any bucks across the 500 acres or so of arable and woodland habitat that the ground covered. However, a weekend in April brought some sunshine, and it was an excuse to take the rifle and Rommel – my newly acquired Bavarian bloodhound – for a walk in the woods.

Furthermore, it would give me a chance to try out the Blaser R8 in the field. I had already put a few shots through the rifle on the range, and was impressed with its accuracy and speed of reload with the already legendary Blaser straight-pull action. The model I was using was definitely a workhorse in its one-piece green synthetic stock 'professional' version, but it was nevertheless a thoroughbred, and soon proved its credentials on its maiden outing.

This is a rifle with fine lines; I was immediately impressed with the practical aspects of the overall construction. The anti-slip inlays on the forend and pistol grip of this straight-combed stock gave confidence in mounting, and even with the heavyish scope, the set-up was perfectly balanced and extremely pointable as the rifle came to the shoulder.

One of the more remarkable features of the R8 is its drop magazine/trigger system. The trigger guard, blade housing and the base of the four-round (in .30-06) magazine box are combined in a single unit. Pressing two easily accessed but unobtrusive catches on either side of the unit will dump the mag and de-cock the gun.

The movement is crisp and efficient, and I really like this system despite the regular whines heard about making it easier to lose the whole unit. I don't think it is any easier to lose this unit than it would be to lose the standard drop magazine seen on other rifles. Admittedly, if you lose the unit, you lose your trigger system too, but in reality you shouldn't

rcally be losing bits of your gun. The trigger was a real joy to use in practice, and the release was consistent at two pounds.

To fire, push the de-cocker situated on the top of the tang forward until the slide stops, exposing a red square indicating fire mode. Every time you fire and re-work the bolt, the action is automatically re-cocked. To make safe, push the catch in and forward at the same time.

The straight-pull system is designed for speedy reloading – not always necessary to British stalkers, but a distinct advantage to driven boar hunters on the continent. That said, rapid reloading may well be the key to putting an animal in the larder if the initial shot does not quite fly true.

The day dawned warm but mousy – that is, to those who do not understand Yorkshire vernacular, with heat haze or hanging mist. I hadn't much confidence in finding a buck as we had hit the population hard the previous season, but I was still happy to be out with rifle and hound. However, severe fraying on the corner of a willow stand restored hope

– a buck had obviously recently filled the vacant territory.

With renewed interest, I scanned the ground more carefully and worked into the wind along the boundary marked by an ancient hawthorn hedge. Then things began to happen fast. Occupied though I was spying through the Leica Duovids, Rommel soon caught my attention with an agitated half woof. Following the hound's gaze, I immediately saw a fox heading straight towards us. Not one to pass on a sitter, I mounted the rifle in the 'v' of the shooting sticks, and drew a bead on Charlie's chest. He realised his mistake and turned to avoid us, but the 180-grain polycarbonate tipped bullet was on its way and dealt the predator an instantaneous death.

Miraculously, a roebuck then stood up almost next to the fallen fox, and the rapid reload of the R8 came into play. I followed up the fox shot with a perfectly placed shoulder shot on the six point buck, which burst forward through the hawthorn in a final rush of adrenalin.

I cast off the hound, and squeezed through the thorns to find Rommel happily chewing at the exit wound on the now dead beast. It was one of the shortest but most enjoyable stalks I have ever experienced. Sometimes you just have to take what nature offers. **NL**

| **BLASER R8** |
| --- |
| *Model tested:* Synthetic Professional |
| *Price range:* From £2,750 |
| *Contact:* Blaser Sporting  0207 6222116 **www.blaser-sporting.com** |

# BROWNING A-BOLT

My very first rifle was a little .22 Browning SA automatic, similar to the one used in fairgrounds in those far-off days. I must have put thousands of rounds through it, and it served me well for years. Since then, I have owned both rifles and shotguns by Browning, and have found them to be unfailingly reliable and accurate. My own preference for a foxing rifle is normally .223, and this particular model is supplied in just two calibres: .223 and .243. The test rifle was the latter, and having used a .243 in the past, I know what a good all-round calibre it is.

As I have said many times, my preference is for wood-stocked rifles, but recently I have been taken by some of the synthetic models now available. Opening the case, the Browning A-Bolt Composite Stalker UK model really looked good; the overall dark grey and charcoal finish of the stock and the black barrel was set off nicely by the polished, non-rotating bolt housing, the gold trigger and the usual Browning logo etched in gold on the trigger guard.

Taking a more detailed look, the composite stock is excellent – it really handles well. The chequering is really 'grippy', which would be excellent in wet weather. There is no cheekpiece that would make it ambidextrous, but there is a palm swell on the right of the pistol grip. To finish off the stock, there is a black rubber recoil pad. Studs are fitted for the attachment of sling swivels.

The barrel follows the current trend for shorter rather than longer and is free-floated. The A-Bolt has a 22in, tapered, sporter-type barrel, threaded 14x1mm for a moderator. I think this barrel length is an excellent compromise and allows for easy handling when used in heavy woodland or within the confines of a vehicle.

The A-Bolt action is already well known, getting its name from the way the locking lugs are arranged; the bolt face is deeply recessed and is fitted with a spring-loaded claw extractor. This system has proved highly reliable for some considerable time.

The bolt, as already mentioned, has an outer casing that remains stationary when the bolt is operated. The plain, flattened and comfortable bolt handle has a low lift, keeping it well clear of the objective lens of the fitted scope.

I found the magazine rather intriguing. It took me a while to work out that what appears to be a floor plate design in fact houses a detachable four-shot magazine (five in .223) and can be released from its housing when the magazine is dropped by pressing the release button on the trigger guard. To add to this, Browning has thoughtfully provided a spare magazine.

AS ONE WOULD EXPECT FROM A TOP-CLASS RIFLE TOPPED WITH A FANTASTIC SCOPE, ACCURACY WAS VERY GOOD, PRODUCING SUB-ONE INCH GROUPS FROM THE WORD GO

The adjustable trigger was set at just under four pounds and released really crisply with no discernible creep. Finally, the safety situated at the end of the receiver is substantial, has a cocking indicator, and comes easily to the thumb.

The rifle was fitted with a Zeiss Duralyt 3-12x50 scope with an illuminated reticle. I have tested another of the Duralyt range before and found them to be really good value for money; this was the larger model and the one that is proving to be the most popular in the range. The illuminated reticle was a crosshair with a dot controlled by two buttons on the ocular bell; only the dot was illuminated in use and could be varied in intensity.

The optics were excellent as you would expect from this manufacturer. At about £850 for the illuminated model, you get a class unit with a name to be proud of. For foxing, which is my main occupation, the low light capabilities of this scope became apparent early on when the recent hot spell broke and heavy cloud cover appeared. Late evening work became much easier thanks to a scope that could cope easily until the light really failed.

The turrets were on the small side and I had to remind myself that the adjustment was 1cm at 100 metres, not my more usual quarter inch at 100 yards. In use, adjustments could be made easily and the zero position

can be set by lifting the turret against a spring. Simple but effective.

Finally, for the accuracy test, I used Winchester 95-grain ballistic Silvertips. This is somewhat weightier ammo than I normally use for foxes, but as they say, dead is dead and for test purposes this was what I was supplied with. With their characteristic nickel-plated brass cases, black Lubalox coated heads topped off with a grey polymer ballistic tip, they certainly looked the part. With a muzzle velocity of 3,100fps, they certainly weren't going to hang around. Zeroing turned out to be easy; it has been some time since I used an unmoderated rifle and although the A-Bolt is supplied threaded for a mod, my 14x1 didn't fit, so it was back to the old days. I have to say it was rather pleasant using a rifle as nature intended.

Recoil was totally manageable, and as one would expect from a top-class rifle topped with a fantastic scope, accuracy was very good, producing sub-one inch groups from the word go.

I would say Browning has produced a very good rifle that I am sure would give any buyer pleasure of both ownership and practical function. Unfortunately, although I did my best to find an obliging Charlie to try out the 95-grain Silvertips on, there were no volunteers. The rifle needed to be back, so reluctantly I had to abandon the search for a fox, and said goodbye to a rifle that was a pleasure to use. **MP**

### BROWNING A-BOLT

**Model tested:** Composite Stalker
**Price range:** From £550
**Contact:** Browning 01235 514550
**www.browning.eu**

# BROWNING X-BOLT

One of the most successful rifles I have owned was a Browning A-Bolt. It was reliable and superbly accurate, especially when shooting lighter ammunition. My local gamekeeper still uses it. I was hoping the newer Browning model, the X-Bolt, would be able to rekindle fond memories.

I started warming to the rifle as soon as I plucked it from the packaging. The Dura-touch Amour coated stock fitted my hands beautifully. It is slender at the forend, it is lean and it has

no raised cheekpiece, but its simplicity seems right. It has an all-over soft, rubbery feel, with the pistol grip and forend feeling a bit more grippy. There is also a high-quality soft recoil pad at the rear – suitable for the larger calibres available. Once removed, it sounded slightly hollow when tapped, but on further inspection, I found the forend has a star-shaped web to give more rigidity and save a little weight. The front and rear of the action were synthetically bedded, telling me this could be an accurate

rifle. I suppose the words that describe it best are 'ergonomic' and 'practical' – a good start for sure.

The bolt is similar to that on the A-Bolt, with a three-lugged front locking ring with a very efficient extractor aided by a plunger ejector. The short lift bolt handle leans back at a slight angle, with the knob made up of an oval flat shape. To the rear, a small cocking indicator informs the shooter if the action is cocked. Another new feature is the unusual square button, allowing the bolt to be cycled when the safety is on.

The typically angular stainless steel receiver is another reminder of the A-Bolt. The bolt release catch is to the left, but another change is the Weaver-type bases ('X-lock' system), each secured by four screws to guarantee a solid fix. Weaver and other makes of ring can be fitted with ease. The safety catch sits at the rear of the action – simply move the thumb without the need to change the grip.

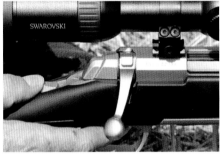

The adjustable 'feather' trigger has little creep and is set to a crisp 4lb. The aluminium silver trigger guard and matching surround to the magazine may or may not be to everybody's taste. The heavy plastic magazine is based on a rotary design that carries four rounds, with the release catch located to the front. It is a tight, flush fit owing to a simple spring tensioner, and very easy to remove and refit.

The 22in stainless steel, non-reflective barrel is a fully fluted, light sporting grade and comes threaded to allow the fitting of a sound moderator. It is fully floating from the front of the receiver, again being stainless. Overall, the X-Bolt Stainless Fluted Stalker looks functional, and weighing in at under 7lb, it gave me high hopes that it would perform in the field.

Fitted to the rifle was a Swarovski 3-20x50mm with a 30mm tube – a great optic for deer stalking and general fox control. I also tried the Nightforce 5.5-22x50 NXS for night-time foxing. Up to the shoulder, the rifle feels light and very pointable, especially without a moderator fitted.

For the test, I used a variety of ammunition, from 55-grain ballistic tips to 100-grain soft

points. Loading the magazine was a doddle – it feels solid and clips back into the stock very firmly. Moving the thumb to push the safety catch forward, the bolt gently moves the round into the breech with a beautiful smoothness. With the safety back on, I could open the bolt by pushing the button at its base.

I understand Browning boasts 1MOA (1in at 100 yards) for the X bolt. My first round was the 55-grain Winchester Silvertip, firing at 3,900fps with a devastating group of under half an inch. With a twist rate of 1 in 10, the rifle may appear to favour the heavier ammunition, but the 95-grain Winchester Silvertip ammo gave me a much larger 1.5in group. At 200 yards – my preferred zero for foxing – the lighter bullets stayed within a one-inch group.

The trigger, while heavier than I would like, was firm and very crisp with very little movement through its travel. These tests were done with the use of a front bipod to simulate most fox shooting, but I did find the forend was touching the barrel. While this was slightly disappointing bearing in mind there was no moderator fitted, it did not seem to affect the point of impact or accuracy on this test.

The stock was a joy to use, helped by the narrow pistol grip and forend, making me feel at one with the rifle. Bearing in mind the lack of moderator, the recoil was a little snappy, even with the lighter bullets. It was a very easy gun to use, with the safety catch and bolt release button found easily by the thumb on the trigger hand. The lightweight fluted barrel, despite warming up after 15 shots, did not have a huge effect on the accuracy, telling me that it not only looks like a varminter but can also compete with the heavier barrels.

I fitted the Nightforce scope along with an old T8 Moderator, and I also took the liberty of trying to reduce the trigger pressure to around the 3lb mark. While this made a difference, I found it hard to anticipate when the firing pin would release. The break point seemed to vary, making it rather tricky, especially when I had a fox looking unintentionally down the barrel. On one shot, the delay allowed the fox to move a few inches, resulting in a still fatal shoulder shot as opposed to a mid-chest point of impact.

The Browning X-Bolt retails for £888, which, in my opinion, is brilliant value for money considering the accuracy and fluted barrel. I can see many gamekeepers taking a shine to it, as the stainless steel will require little maintenance and the stock is extremely durable. **TP**

### BROWNING X-BOLT

**Model tested:** Stainless Fluted .243

**Price range:** £888

**Contact:** Browning  01235 514550
**www.browning.eu**

# CHAPUIS ARMES UGEX

The French Chapuis Armes company was founded in the 1920s by Jean Chapuis, the father of current owner René. The company's success and subsequent growth saw a move to a new factory facility in Saint-Bonnet-Le-Château, just outside of Saint Etienne at the end of the 1980s. These premises enabled Chapuis to manufacture all the parts needed to produce its firearms itself, eliminating the use of outside contracting. In-house manufacturing meant exceptional quality control could be adhered to before final assembly by the company's master gunsmiths.

UK importer York Guns kindly lent me a Chapuis Ugex double rifle from the Progress Series 3 range in .30-06 Springfield. It arrived in a nice motor case equipped with double combination locks. When I took it out, what first impressed me was the highly figured AAA-grade walnut stock.

This woodwork comes from hand-selected, centuries-old trees where after rough planking, the rifle makers pay great attention to colour and contrast before the initial machine shaping. Once this procedure is finished, the company's professional stock makers carry out the important final shaping, sanding and chequering by hand, taking care to ensure the stock and forend complement each other perfectly.

The scalloped and sculptured all-steel action is engraved with chisel-chased floral borders complemented by images of a roebuck to one side, a wild boar on the other and a red stag underneath the action. This superb engraving and flawless woodwork results in a very aesthetically pleasing double rifle.

The 600mm cold hammer-forged barrels come with a quarter rib, on which a luminescent rear sight and a height-adjustable front sight have been seated. These had been regulated on the factory's in-house range for use with 180-grain Federal ammunition, but more of that later. Also on the top of the glass-like finished but blued barrels is a facility to mount a pair of bases for a telescopic sight. Placing the barrels into the action and fitting the forend, I appreciated the attention to detail and tolerances that the craftsmen work to, as everything mated together perfectly.

Shouldering the rifle for the first time, I was impressed with how well it fitted me. My eye was drawn down the rib, lining up the sights perfectly. With an all-in weight of 3.2kg (7.04lb in old money), mounting this gun was an effortless process – it truly felt as if it had been custom-made to my dimensions.

York Guns had also supplied a quantity of 180-grain Sellier and Bellot ammunition, so it was going to be interesting to see if I could replicate the groups on the two targets included in the rifle case (to prove it could shoot 1½in or less at 50 metres).

As I would be testing the rifle's accuracy and not my skills at shooting freehand, I made comfortable on the zeroing bench after setting a target up at a measured 50 metres. Slipping two rounds into the breech, I closed the action and applied the safety, all in one smooth motion. So far, so good. Mounting the rifle, I adjusted the sandbags until the target centre was comfortably covered. Slipping off the safety and squeezing away the front trigger opened business.

I have to admit I didn't know what to expect regarding the recoil from this rifle. However, I can say that this little double was a revelation, apart from the obvious muzzle flip. Recoil was very low for such a punchy calibre. Drawing a bead once more on the target, I squeezed away the rear trigger and sent a second round downrange.

As I broke the action, the powerful twin ejectors crisply sent the two spent cases over my shoulder. Inspecting them confirmed everything was as it should be, and I walked down to the target. I was impressed with a two-shot group of around 1¾in. Over the next half an hour I found that this initial grouping was no fluke as I constantly shot similar groups – good enough for the boar hunt I was joining the following week.

When I arrived at the Bavarian hunting ground seven days later, there was a definite chill in the air. Temperatures had dropped overnight, and we were told there was a possibility of snow later in the day. Unperturbed, the hunters were split up and shown to their respected stands by our German hosts. There were around 60 hunters, and expectations were high – hopefully I was going to get a shot at a fleeing pig. Unshipping the Chapuis, I dunked two rounds into the breech and made ready for action.

The hunt would be around four hours' duration, but two hours in, all remained quiet. Light snow began falling through the

forest canopy, but apart from the occasional roe deer, hoofed game was noticeable by its absence. Then I heard hounds speaking and seemingly approaching my sector. Judging by the numerous rifle reports I could hear, pigs were now on the move. A movement on the right caught my attention. Dropping my flask cup, I rose to my feet just as a biggish keiler burst out of the frosted briars, running full tilt some 40 metres out. Shouldering the rifle, I swung through and pulled the trigger. The rifle report masked the sound of the 180-grain soft-point hitting flesh and bone as the bullet struck home, The pig dropped in a spectacular display of animal gymnastics, no doubt because of its forward motion.

Breaking the rifle saw the spent shells ejected positively, and I quickly replaced them with live ones in anticipation of some more action. Sadly, that was the only chance I had that day, but it had been a wonderful opportunity to test the Chapuis in the field. I was certainly impressed with this well-made and affordable double. Its sheer 'pointability' was a revelation; it handled extremely well,

and it looks as pretty as an English equivalent 10 times its monetary value. Plus it had secured me an 85kg keiler. What more can I say – it definitely does what it was built for. For any driven boar enthusiast who has ever flirted with the idea of buying a double, this rifle is well worth the investment. **NL**

**CHAPUIS UGEX**

*Model tested:* Chapuis Armes Ugex Double .30-06

*Price range:* £4,350

*Contact:* York Guns  01904 487180
**www.yorkguns.com**

# CZ 527

Many years ago I, along with quite a few others, thought the CZ rifles, although quite accurate, were a bit, shall we say, agricultural. This is certainly not the case today. A shooting friend of mine purchased a CZ rimfire recently, and I was impressed with the out-of-the-box build, accuracy and finish.

While the company is best known for its rimfire rifles, more and more serious fox shooters are turning to the CZ centrefires on offer – there are an increasing number of very enthusiastic owners.

One of the biggest attractions of CZ rifles has to be the price. They are inexpensive – so first-time shooters and old hands alike can get their hands on an accurate, well-finished rifle that won't break the bank.

One of the latest offerings is the CZ 527 Varmint. The 527 is a variant of the classic bolt-action, the Mauser 98. Tailored for calibres such as .204, .222, and .223, its small size matches the choice of cartridge and keeps overall weight to a minimum. While I have to say that my preference for an out and out foxing round would be .223, the .204 Ruger seems to be the calibre of choice at the moment.

The Varmint model has a heavier barrel, which has become the norm for this type of rifle. The action is small, very small – everything has been scaled down and the bolt is no exception. The locking lugs, however, have been left pretty well as normal to ensure safe and secure bolt closure. In common with most Mauser designs, the external extractor is non-rotating and acts in

conjunction with the bolt-stop positioned ejector spur, to eject used cases positively. The bolt cocks on opening and the rear bolt shroud is used as the cocking piece. The bolt handle is straight and rather short, but the comfortable small ball operating end ensures a smooth and trouble-free cycling action. Although the bolt is inclined to be a little on the tight side from new, after 50 rounds or so it eases off to give the normal smooth operation one has become accustomed to in this type of action.

Integral dovetails are machined onto the top of the receiver, probably still the simplest and best system of scope mounting.

The single-column feed magazine is detachable, which to my mind is the best system – although its capacity is five shots, which should be enough for pretty well every eventuality, it is always useful to be able to swiftly refill, should the need arise. Because the action is so small the magazine does seem to protrude rather a lot, but this is not a problem and certainly to my eye anyway, does not detract from the overall appearance of the rifle. In fact, I am inclined to prefer a magazine that can be gripped easily rather than waiting for it to drop out of its housing. Another thing I like is that the magazine is made of steel, preferable to a polymer construction every time.

The trigger is adjustable and has a set trigger fitted as standard. The initial factory setting, as is common on many foreign rifles, is heavy at 5½lb, though this can be lightened. The trigger action has some creep, though it does break cleanly enough. The rolling catch safety is fool-proof; pushing it forward or back exposes a red dot – and it is simple to operate by the thumb without breaking the firing grip hold.

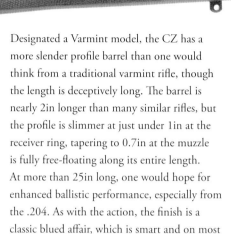

Designated a Varmint model, the CZ has a more slender profile barrel than one would think from a traditional varmint rifle, though the length is deceptively long. The barrel is nearly 2in longer than many similar rifles, but the profile is slimmer at just under 1in at the receiver ring, tapering to 0.7in at the muzzle is fully free-floating along its entire length. At more than 25in long, one would hope for enhanced ballistic performance, especially from the .204. As with the action, the finish is a classic blued affair, which is smart and on most CZ rifles tends to be hard-wearing.

The stock is walnut and as the quality of CZ guns has steadily improved, so has the woodwork. As well as walnut, there is a choice of Kevlar and laminate depending on the model chosen. The slim stock has a straight comb, a slim black rubber recoil pad and is finished without a cheekpiece. The rounded forend and the pistol grip are finished with what appear to be hand-cut chequering. In the 527 range, CZ have produced a very nice, sensibly priced rifle that will fit the bill for very many shooters.

If you are looking for the .204 calibre offering, then the choice of ammunition is rather limited, with only Remington and Hornady available at present, though Winchester should also come on stream soon.

Factory ammunition dictates that only 32-grain and 40-grain projectiles are available, which is fine, as the CZ 527 barrel twist is 1:12,

allowing near-perfect bullet stability for such bullet weights. On a more practical note, using the 32-grain bullet and zeroing the rifle at 100 yards, you should still be in the kill-zone of a fox right out to almost 300 yards – that's more than enough for me and most others too.

CZ have been with us for a very long time, and looking at their latest products it is pretty well certain they will be with us for a long time to come. You can spend a considerable sum on new rifles today, and in general you get what you pay for. The CZ 527, at somewhere around £700, represents extremely good value for your

money; it shoots well, handles well and, as is normally the case with CZ, is trouble free. One tiny gripe is that they do not come threaded for a moderator, but I have to say I really like these rifles, and any of the smaller calibres would be an excellent choice for fox control. **MP**

| **CZ 527** |
| --- |
| **Models tested:** Varmint walnut; American synthetic |
| **Price range:** £700 |
| **Contact:** Edgar Brothers 01625 613177 **www.edgarbrothers.com** |

# HEYM 88-B

I distinctly remember the first double rifle I ever had the pleasure of handling. I had been in Africa for two months when I travelled north to the edge of Kruger Park to catch up with a friend for a few days. Staying at a farm deep in the bush, the owner turned out to have been quite the hunter in his day, and one afternoon I had the privilege of looking around his trophy and gunrooms.

When I stepped into the lodge for the first time, my jaw nearly hit the floor. The room spanned a length and height that would swallow your average two-bed house, adorned from front to back with heads of every species you could think of. At the far end, a shoulder mounted elephant looked down on us, with frozen scenes of fighting lions and leopard grappling game either side in glorious full mounts. I had never seen anything like it, and this was before I had even reached the gunroom. I had seen bedrooms smaller than this walk-in gunroom, with every space on the wall filled with rifles and pistols. I had rarely seen anything so beautiful; I was in heaven. As I was informed later, this was only half the collection. But it was not just fanciful hoarding – every one had a story. I must have stood in that room for more than an hour hearing the back-stories to just a handful.

It was here that my fingers first curled over the heavyset barrels of a double rifle. Chambered in .416 Rigby, this old girl was a stunning combination of elegant lines and strong, precision construction. Even with nothing in the chamber, the rifle made me feel like I could tackle the world. Some years later, when carrying one in the veld for the first time, this feeling was compounded, with the robust twin barrels providing a calming and comforting effect.

Although having used double rifles before, I haven't been around them enough to claim any great knowledge, so this review will be much more general than my usual bolt-action ponderings. The original double rifles were designed with a single ethos in mind. When a hunter's life was on the line, a double would provide the greatest level of reliability for two single shots. That should be enough to, at the very least, bring any animal to the ground, which would allow a further two rounds to be loaded if necessary. Doubles, in essence, are very simple, and not dissimilar to a shotgun, with two firing pins, two tubes, a locking mechanism and a trigger. Assuming the ammunition is up to the task, there is very little to go wrong and prevent a shot from going off. This is of particular importance when a wounded buffalo is heading full steam in your direction. Modern moves have begun, in my opinion, to over-complicate double rifles, with magazines to reload another two rounds being the latest development.

One of the biggest barriers to double rifles has always been price. These are not mass-

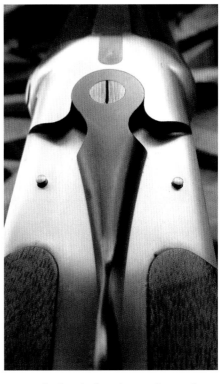

produced items. They are hand crafted, hand fitted, tested and regulated. Of course demand is relatively small, and apart from the odd one seeing use for driven game in Europe, they are almost exclusively seen used in Africa.

Heym has a long tradition of building rifles, in particular drillings and double rifles. Established in Suhl, Germany, in 1865 by Friedrich Wilhelm Heym, the company remained under family management for many generations. It soon earned a solid reputation for producing excellent sporting rifles, with production only broken by the two world wars. After 1945, the factory was re-established in Bavaria, producing the first post-war firearms around 1952. Relocation occurred once again in 1996, when the factory moved to a state-of-the-art facility in Gleichamberg.

The flagship 88B-Safari has seen use for many years. With rifle weight varying dependant on the chosen calibre, easy handling is maintained by ensuring the balance remains 'between the hands'. This rifle sees 24in Krupp steel hammer-

forged barrels as standard, with the precision fitting, beautifully engineered action boasting a triple lock up with double lugs and greener cross bolt. Cocking indicators on the tang at the rear of each barrel confirm the rifle is loaded and, in turn, once it has been fired. Double triggers operate in two stages, allowing the shooter to take up a firm pressure first before unleashing hell with a final squeeze. Ejectors are fitted as standard, quickly and energetically dispensing of spent cartridges ready for the next two should the need arise. There are a number of options available as well, including sights, grip caps, ejector/extractor switch and custom engraving to name just a few. In this way, you can take the standard rifle and truly make it yours, with a fitted stock boasting fine European walnut as standard, with an option to upgrade as well.

Enjoying the success of its Safari model, Heym realised there was a need for a working double rifle, omitting the more unnecessary aspects such as walnut and hand engraving. In response to a client request, Heym built the 88-B Professional

Hunter, for those looking for a working tool over aesthetic embellishment. Sticking with a proven formula, it stripped down its Safari model to provide everything apart from the superfluous engraving. The end result is a very understated, well-made double that is offered to the market at a much more affordable level.

Many may disagree with me, but I would rather hunt with a bolt action Mauser 98 than a double in the big calibres. Having said that, I have always dreamed of adding a double to my collection – if only to use as a back-up rifle when I have the opportunity to join my PH friends on

dangerous game hunts. The Heym PH is exactly the kind of rifle I was looking for.

The particular rifle I had on test was chambered in .470 NE, a true dangerous game calibre, and widely used across Africa. Coming in at 10.5lb, it is a solid weight in the hand that would take most UK stalkers by surprise. For such a calibre, however, it is just right, helping to absorb some of the recoil from the massive .470 NE case. It was not so heavy that you would be wishing you had left it at home after a long day, but I suspect it would still take a bit of training to get comfortable with lugging such a rifle around over an entire safari.

Although this rifle wasn't fitted to me, it came up very nicely, and shooting it was fairly comfortable. For my frame, making use of the front trigger did cause my middle to press against the trigger guard, and this was a mistake made only once. A fitted rifle should resolve this issue.

Rather unusually for a double rifle, these have been regulated with Hornady ammo. For those who are unfamiliar with doubles, one of the biggest challenges is to get both the right and left barrel shooting at the same point of impact. This process is called regulation, and all double rifles should come with a note informing you of what make and weight of ammunition it has been regulated for. I was unable to source the Hornady ammo used for regulation, but fortunately Kynoch came to my rescue, and very generously gave me 10 rounds to test. At 50 yards, even with the unregulated ammo, I managed to put two shots together at the same point of impact twice in a row. You can't ask for much more than that with a big bore double.

For a time, the double rifle seemed to be going the same way as the dinosaur. Much is owed to Heym for its resurgence, being one of the first to push the new doubles into markets in America and offering rifles at much more affordable prices due to modern machining techniques. The 88-B PH offers everything you could possibly need from a double. It is a functional, reliable, no-frills rifle and I hope to one day be able to carry one in pursuit of dangerous game. **BP**

---

### HEYM 88-B

**Model tested:** 88-B PH in .416

**Price range:** Around £10,000

**Contact:** Garlands 01827 383300
**www.garlands.uk.com**

# HEYM SR21

When I got a call from Garlands asking if I would like to test the Heym SR21 in 7x57, my reflex answer was "yes". A rifle I had long had my eye on, it was also in one of my favourite calibres. I was excited and had high expectations. I recalled looking obsessively at a Heym at the Scottish Game Fair some years before, when I had just acquired my FAC. It was a bit pricey for me back then, but remained fixed in my memory as a rifle I wouldn't mind having in the cabinet. I was eager to see if my relatively uninformed opinion would stand true today under closer inspection.

As many manufacturers did in this era, Heym produced Mauser-type sporting rifles for some time, including refurbishing wartime actions. It then began utilising FN-Mauser actions in its rifles before moving on to produce its own SR-20 action. This came about largely as a result of having a contract with Mauser cancelled, leaving the company with a large quantity of unused components. The management at Heym decided to create the SR20 after making a few changes to the design. Along with the evolution of bolt-action rifles, the company is also very well known for

producing excellent double and combination rifles. Today's SR21 has seen more alterations again, and Heym has also added a straight-pull model to its line-up in the SR30.

When I freed the rifle from its box, my initial reaction was one of delight. It was the best looking rifle I had tested in over a year, and it felt satisfyingly familiar in the hand. The slender stock lines were sexy, and the dark wood had a feel of old-fashioned quality. On top of that, it was chambered in one of my all-time favourite stalking calibres. I was already wondering if I would allow the rifle to leave once I was finished.

The metal finish was nice, but not exceptional. It lacked the deep, highly polished bluing found on high-end rifles, and the more modern move towards matt bead-blasted metal finishes. Don't let that make you think the finish was inferior though – far from it. The receiver is round in design, though boasts a nice milled-out face on the top and side, continuing the soft lines of the stock. With a strong closed action, cartridges are ejected from a port on the side, although it is quite generous in dimensions. Unlike rifles such as the Tikka, it is possible to fit your pinky inside

to check if a cartridge is still in the chamber. Drilled and tapped, it will accept most bases.

The bolt release is found on the left-hand side, very much in the same fashion as a Sako. When we get to the recoil lug, the same bugbear that I have mentioned time and again rears its head. Although not immediately obvious with the rifle assembled, the recoil system is a jammed washer design like a Remington. At the risk of repeating myself, this is a design that has worked well, but an integral lug would be better, preferable and stronger. The reason I never noticed before taking the rifle to pieces is that Heym has gone to quite a lot of trouble to join the barrel, recoil washer and action almost seamlessly

> ## THE SR21'S MAG WAS A SOLID, WEIGHTY, SINGLE-STACK DESIGN MADE ENTIRELY FROM METAL. IT WAS ONE OF THE NICEST MODERN MAGS I HAD SEEN IN A LONG TIME

above the stock. Only when looking at the bottom and sides does it become obvious.

Turning our attention to the bolt, the first thing that is a bit unusual is the wooden bolt knob. Matching the stock, it really does look nice, but from a practical point of view it's a poor judgement call from Heym. The bolt handle is the only part of a rifle that protrudes, and inevitably over time it will get bashed. My concern is that this rather elegant handle will get cracked at some point, leaving a rifle that is quite easily fixable but rather awkward to use in the interim. The thick bolt shaft has five flutes and a running groove on the bottom. This helps to facilitate slick cycling by carrying oil and providing dirt and grit a place to escape. It's a solid unit with three locking lugs and the tried-and-tested plunger ejector and sprung extractor that are standard on most rifles these days.

As for the back, you will see that the safety is an integral part of the bolt, much like on a CZ rimfire but in a more refined way. The sliding safety is a joy to use, and I have no complaints there. One interesting aspect is a small plunger on the bolt shroud, which depresses as it meets the receiver on the forward stroke. As far as

I can see, it doesn't serve any major purpose other than to provide rearward tension as the bolt cams down. The only criticism I really have of the bolt comes from what is essentially the cocking piece. Protruding from the shroud, the circular metal is finished with a rather sharp edge. It would have required very little extra work in the machining process to finish this with a generous chamfer and I was marginally disappointed by this.

However this was not quite as frustrating as what I found next. Having separated the metal work from the stock, it was immediately obvious that Heym had gone to the trouble of bedding the action with resin and aluminium pillars – thumbs up. However, closer inspection revealed an incredibly sloppy job. I was more than a little miffed. Like many off-the-shelf manufacturers, this wasn't a full bedding job, but saw resin applied only around the recoil lug area. This in itself is fine, but I couldn't understand why they would go to the effort of bedding the rifle without taking the extra half an hour to make the job a good one. Instead, it looks like they simply squelched in some resin, screwed in the action and left it be – not exactly a confidence-builder.

Looking at the trigger, we also have to bring in the magazine unit. Here, Heym has designed a single unit that separates from the action when the action screws are loosened. Whereas most rifles will part company from the stock with the trigger still attached to

the action, in this case the trigger unit comes away as an integral part of the magazine assembly. I was both surprised and impressed by this. It was a very well thought-out and solidly constructed unit – even the action screws were captive.

The trigger was satisfying to use, with a clean, sensible break. Although externally adjustable, there isn't much scope for altering the trigger pressure, however this wasn't an issue as I was quite content with the factory

setting. There is a 'set' option that is excellent for range work and, unlike every other set trigger I have used, this one actually broke at a sensible weight. I am used to set triggers unleashing their wrath at little more than an anorexic fly's fart. This felt usable in the field.

The magazine put a smile on my face. Unlike the current move to include plastic components wherever possible, the SR21's mag was a solid, weighty, single-stack design made entirely from metal. It was one of the nicest modern mags I had seen in a long time.

When it came to the range, there were no astounding revelations. It shot as I expected, returning reasonable groups across a spectrum of bullet weights. The 160-grain bullets returned the best groups at just inside an inch, whereas the Hornady 139-grain ammo returned about 1.25in. I ran a couple of other bullet weights through the rifle as well, with most returning usable hunting groups. The only exception was the 123-grain RWS, which scattered across the target like a shotgun pattern.

Already owning a 7x57 rifle that will happily cluster three rounds all day, it is definitely one of those calibres where a huge amount of benefit is gained from reloading. The small amount of development I did on the Heym showed this.

The Heym SR21 is a fine rifle. It is most definitely a looker, and for the most part is well constructed. As with almost any rifle, there are a few aspects I have taken exception too, but I had to be hard on a rifle I expected so much from. Heym is certainly worth a look, and the SR21 is undoubtedly a serious contender for anyone looking for a mid-range hunting rifle. **BP**

**HEYM SR21**

*Model tested:* SR21 Standard

*Price range:* £1,915

*Contact:* Garlands 01827 383300
**www.garlands.uk.com**

# HOWA 1500

It wasn't so many years ago when Howa was a non-existent brand among the British hunting public. Behind the scenes, however, rifle manufacturers were well aware of a company that was making rifles for some big brand names. Indeed, today's Weatherby Vanguard comes off the Howa factory floor, branded and shipped under a different name.

When we first began seeing Howa advertised in UK hunting magazines, prices seemed to dictate yet another cheap entry-level rifle. There wasn't anything staggering about their appearance, but nothing suggested corners had been cut in offering such a competitive rifle to the market. The marketing spiel boasted 1.5in groups and a variety of calibres, stock options and barrel profiles, along with an adjustable trigger and three-position safety. Despite this, hunters were guarded about a manufacturer they knew nothing about, and as far as they could tell, had little in the way of a history in making rifles. However, as the story behind

Howa began to filter through, people started to take a harder look at this understated rifle.

Price alone was enough for the Howa 1500 to begin walking out of gun shop doors, but it soon started to build a following and reputation on merit. For those who knew their history, it was hardly a surprise. Howa as a company was established in 1907, then under a different name, manufacturing everything from electronics to heavy plant equipment. In the 1940s, it secured contracts with the Japanese armaments industry, and this started the ball rolling in the production of firearms.

Although initially its focus was on military firearms, a deal with Sako allowed Howa to produce a copy of its soon-to-be-legendary L61 and L579 series, better known as the Finnbear and Forrester. Although hard to confirm, it is thought that the contract hadn't allowed for an exact copy of Sako's rifle, which indeed is what Howa had done with its Golden Bear model. Contract and

patent infringements then forced Howa to stop producing the rifle, and today they are very hard to come by. Today's model 1500 has changed somewhat from the Golden Bear of the 1960s, but it is still based on the great old Sako action, albeit with some design alterations.

The first diversion comes if we start with the barrel. Surprisingly made by Howa, they are formed using the button-rifling manufacturing process. This is the same method as a number of big names such as Walther and Shilen. Sako, on the other hand, has always fitted its rifles with cold hammer-forged barrels. Sako's process tends to create stronger and harder-wearing barrels, although the process is not necessarily better.

In terms of finish, close inspection of the crown offered little to raise an eyebrow about. In fact, it was really quite good, with a slight recess on the muzzle. My own Howa featured last year in a series on bedding a rifle, and I had taken it to a gunsmith for re-crowning. Not because I thought

there was a problem, in actual fact I hadn't even fired the rifle at this point. I just wanted to be sure everything was spot on. However, when it came to it, the gunsmith suggested I test the rifle out first before getting tools involved. As far as he could see, there wasn't anything to complain about.

From that point on, I began to pay much more attention to crown inspection, taking a long look at every rifle that came through, and the Howas were certainly cleaner and sharper on the crown than most other comparable rifles on offer. In terms of barrel profiles, Howa offers a standard Sporter or a heavy varmint barrel. The American listings show a lightweight version, which among others comes chambered in 7-08 Rem, but they are hard to find and all but impossible to get in the UK.

The modern-day model 1500 trigger unit wasn't inherited from Sako, and there is a considerable difference here. Sako triggers have always been excellent, and they are one of the best factory units on the market. The Howa trigger is not terrible by any stretch, but it's not great. The original trigger was a single-stage unit, which could be brought down with a bit of adjusting to break quite nicely, but lacked the breathtaking crispness of a really good trigger.

There were two choices: either send the unit away to be tuned by the likes of Roedale Precision, or fit an after-market trigger. Easy and cheap enough to do, this brought the rifle back in line with the best on the market. Howa has now upgraded its triggers to a two-stage unit, which has also flowed through to the new Vanguard Mk2, which it brands for Weatherby. I can see where Howa tried to refine it, but unfortunately I think it actually took a step back. I am informed they are a bit harder to tune now, and further to that, the first stage is anything but smooth, and almost feels a bit gritty. I am not saying the current offering is bad – it could just be better.

The receiver is a strong, solid unit with similar lines to the old Sakos, although the metal finish was most definitely a higher quality when the Finns were in control. There is nothing too fancy here, with the top machined, drilled and tapped, and a flat bottom supported by a substantial integral recoil lug. This is where the strength lies, and the tapered lug makes for a very easy bedding process.

The bolt has changed a little, with the old Sako guide rail being removed in favour of a guide groove found on the right hand locking lug. It's hard to say if this is better or worse, although the

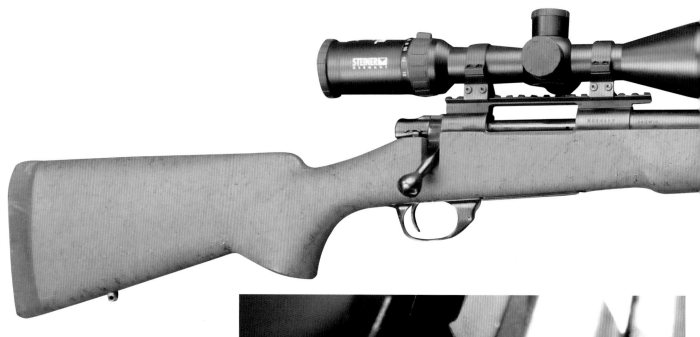

test rifle was a bit sticky on the forward stoke. This was down to the running groove catching in the rail, but I have never come across this before. My own Howa is spot on, and of the many I have fired there has never been an issue.

Turning to the bolt head, there have been a few alterations. The extractor is similar, with a sprung claw clipping over the case head, but I would say Howa has the edge here. The extractor is a much longer and more substantial design than even the modern Sakos. The ejector is completely different. Sako has always fitted its rifles with a fixed ejector running through a slot in the bolt face. Howa has adopted the ever-popular spring plunger approach, the same as you will find in a Tikka or Remington.

Like the old Sakos, the bolt has simple twin locking lugs and a recessed face. The rear of the bolt is similar too, with an open shroud

showing the cocking piece. Today's Sakos have improved this with an enclosed shroud, and it would be nice to see Howa do the same at some point.

With the metalwork out of the way, we get to the stocks. Here I have to applaud Howa for acknowledging what the market wanted and updating its product to accommodate popular demand. The original Hogue overmould stock was not great. The rubberised outer felt very

secure in the hand, and certainly provided ample grip in slippery conditions, but did tend to pick up fluff and grime quite easily. More importantly than that, though, the forestock was flexible and could easily be made to touch the barrel in every direction. The wooden stock offerings were fine but nothing special, and this probably hampered the initial launch in the UK.

As time passed, many people realising the great potential of the model 1500. Howa

replaced the triggers and fitted the barrelled actions to after-market stocks. Bell and Carlson became a popular choice, with its easy-to-fit drop in aluminium block. With these small changes, the rifle was upgraded to fulfil its potential. Taking note of areas for improvement, Howa began offering its rifles as separate barrelled actions as well as with Bell and Carlson stocks. In a different league to the Hogue, the shooting public have responded. There are still improvements to be made though, as Bell and Carlson dropped the ball on a few finishing touches – in particular the action fit in the recoil lug area, which is not as good as I would have liked.

When it comes to how the rifle shoots, the results can be exceptional. Pillar and resin bedding their barrelled action, along with a trigger upgrade and my own Howa will drop five shots from handloads at 100 yards inside a five-pence piece.

Off the shelf, they are shooters as well, easily shooting sub MOA. Two friends with .243s have been testing some 105-grain Geco ammo, and have had some great results, while the 70-grain Federal Noslers will group under three inches at 300 yards.

The Howa 1500 is quite a rifle for the money and possibly the best-value buy around today. It's hard to think of a reason not to get one. **BP**

**HOWA 1500**

***Models:*** Wide selection available through the Howa 'dream it, build it' package – contact the distributor for details

***Price range:*** From £528.99

***Contact:*** Highland Outdoors
0845 099 0252
**www.highlandoutdoors.co.uk**

# KIMBER MONTANA

Whereas a year or two back, the name Kimber would have drawn blank expressions from most hunters, the brand's reputation has grown in the UK and it is now a top contender. I have reviewed the Classic and SVT before, so will not dwell for too long on aspects that have already been discussed. However, the Montana model is certainly worthy of separate mention, as it is currently the lightest production rifle in the world. I have to admit this statement is slightly misleading, as a new rifle – the Mountain Ascent – will soon claim the title. It is unlikely Kimber will be too concerned, though, as the new champion also comes from its innovative factory floor. I look forward to seeing the results.

As a result of the company's minimal tolerance ethos, the Kimber 84M range is light anyway. When it came to speccing out the Montana, the remit was even stricter. There was to be no aspect of design left unscrutinised. This was a weight-stripping exercise, but it still had to maintain the accuracy, shootability and reliability inherent in Kimber's other rifles. To build the ultimate mountain rifle, it had to not only be light, but also operate faultlessly in the most challenging of environments.

The starting point was the stock. It is unsurprising that a rifle such as this sports a synthetic stock – it is, after all, the best

combination of strength, weight and durability. However, this is no injection-moulded sheath or aftermarket copy. When Kimber drew up plans to build the world's lightest rifle, it began the stock design from day one. In its search for the ultimate lightweight all-weather material, it landed on a Kevlar-infused composite.

Handling the naked stock, it is hard to believe that something that weighs so little can have any strength at all. I was half-expecting a mild draft to float it out of my hand. Any doubts to its long-term durability are soon dispelled, though, after viewing the 'Kimber Rifle Torture' clip on Youtube. To prove the credentials of this Kevlar-based stock, an American magazine hurled a barrage of shotgun ammunition at it before test-firing the rifle. Some minor tweaks were required with a hammer and screwdriver, but it loaded, fired and ejected the case, with no cracking on the stock.

It is an impressive spectacle to watch. I can't imagine a hunting situation where you would need your rifle to withstand a point-blank pounding with SSG, but it does give you confidence. I have no doubt the stock will still be serviceable after any slip or fall that you can survive yourself.

The ingenuity doesn't stop there. Like most of Kimber's rifles, the Montana is bedded with a free-floating barrel, but removing the action doesn't reveal what one may expect. There is no obvious bedding resin, and the aluminium pillars are non-existent.

This may initially seem surprising, but a closer inspection unveils the simplicity of the design. The pillars are moulded into the stock itself, while the bedding is formed during the moulding process. Although I could not confirm this, it seems each stock is constructed around an exact replica jig of the action and barrel. The result is an understated graphite-grey stock, finished with a rough, grippy exterior. It is incredibly comfortable in the hand, and shoulders with effortless pointability.

Despite being bland aesthetically, the stock's functionality cannot be faulted, and the only aspect I would want to see altered is the free space between the barrel and channel. There isn't much room to play with, and I prefer to see a healthy gap to deal with the rough and tumble of serious hunting. Although it is perfectly even and free-floating from an inch beyond the action, an extra millimetre all around would be of benefit.

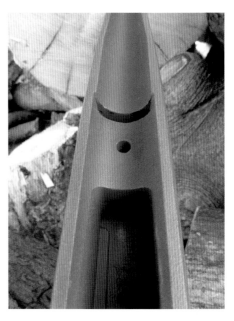

Unusually, the Montana doesn't come with a detachable magazine or even a floorplate. The blind magazine is loaded from the top, and unloaded by semi-chambering and extracting each round. This may seem an inconvenient method, but it does mean more unnecessary weight is shed. This just leaves a neat stainless trigger guard – a decision I have to applaud Kimber for, as it could have justifiably made this synthetic instead.

Most people will be familiar with the action, and if not, a quick scan back at my previous reviews on Kimber's rifles will shed some light on the intricacies. Essentially, the Montana will be the same, using a refined and slimmed-down Mauser-type controlled feed and Remington-style recoil lug. The main difference with the Montana is the super-sleek, weight-minimising barrel profile, and completely stainless metalwork.

I knew Kimber could build accurate rifles, but I was intrigued to see how 5½lb of .308 Win would perform on the range. To minimise any error on my behalf, GMK kindly loaned me a 6-18x40 Leupold VX-II to undertake the tests. For a moderator, I made use of the newly launched Hardy Gen III from Riflecraft (also the distributor for Kimber in the UK).

Most people, including me, would expect some exaggerated muzzle flip and a bit of recoil punishment given the lack of weight. Remarkably, I could detect almost no difference between shooting the Montana and the walnut-stocked Classic. In fact, if I had to draw a preference, I would say the Montana was nicer to shoot.

Removing the moderator to negate any differences confirmed the rifle's sympathetic handling upon firing. Although I cannot be sure, I can only assume that this is primarily a result of the stock material and recoil pad. It certainly

seems that the Kevlar/carbon fibre-based stock absorbs a substantial amount of the recoil. I am in the dark as to how the Kevlar fibres are bonded in the stock, but its use in bulletproof vests distributes the impact force across a wide area through the woven fibres. Similar effects within the stock may explain the results.

The Hardy Gen III moderator also deserves a mention as it is one of the most effective sound suppressors I have ever used. In terms of noise reduction, it is on par with any of the other top market contenders, with reduced report of 22-30dB depending on calibre. However, the recoil reduction is perhaps the Hardy's most impressive quality.

The corrosion-resistant, ultra-light over-fit mod boasts a smartly designed dispersion cone at the front. Combined with the internal workings, this can reduce recoil by as much as 60 per cent. Although I was unable to effectively measure this, it was quite apparent after firing a number of moderators side by side that the Hardy Gen III was the leader of the pack.

Interestingly, I fired the rifle at night on a few occasions, and the lateral dispersion of gases from the cone were obvious. There was very little in the way of forward-projecting gas expulsion, acting much in the same way as a muzzle break.

When you consider that the unit only weighs 360 grams and increases overall rifle length by 100mm, there doesn't seem to be any compromise for this performance (a Jet-Z is 550 grams and adds 150mm).

Establishing the impressive on-paper credentials of the rifle is one thing, but it would mean nothing if it didn't shoot well. Without hesitation, I can categorically confirm that this rifle is a shooter. On paper, my first three-shot

group clustered the 168-grain Hornady A-Max ammo into 0.6in.

Running through some other brands and weights didn't quite replicate this, but at worst the groups opened to 1.1in with the 150-grain Hornady Customs. The Montana certainly preferred the heavier bullets, which makes sense given that the rifle is built around this bullet weight.

Normally, at this point, I would take some longer shots and call it a day, but I was enjoying the rifle so much I couldn't help but burn a couple more boxes.

Trying to simulate some real hill shooting, I pinned up a deer silhouette, pocketed seven rounds and started walking. At 150 yards I lay down, rested on my roe sack and took my first shot. Bang on the money.

The distance went up to 175 yards. Again, the rifle delivered the goods. I repeated the process in steps out to 250 yards, where I took two shots. I finished with five shots touching and two that were just outside the group – impressive shooting from a 5lb 2oz rifle. Even with the scope and Hardy Gen III moderator, the set-up only just tipped the scales over 6lb. A Sako Finnlight, by comparison, weighs in at 6lb 3oz for the bare rifle.

My biggest problem with the Kimber Montana is that now I want one. I think a cheeky little .257 Roberts may just suit this nicely. **BP**

**KIMBER MONTANA**

*Model tested:* Kimber 84M Montana in .308 Win

*Price range:* £1,830

*Contact:* Riflecraft 01379 853745
**www.riflecraft.co.uk**

# KRIEGHOFF BIG FIVE

**M**ost UK riflemen would never get the chance or have the need to use a double rifle. More intriguing is that the intended quarry for this calibre would be more than capable of dispatching the person behind the butt if things did not go to plan. So why is the double rifle format so popular in Europe and abroad?

Around the 1900s, the double-barrelled rifle was apparently much cheaper than its early bolt-action equivalents. More importantly, there was less to go wrong in extreme conditions such as in Africa and India, where it was essential when dealing with dangerous game. They lost their appeal – no thanks to the two world wars, which accelerated the development of the multi-shot bolt action – but there has been a renewed interest in this classic design over the past 30 years.

They are safe, the action is easy to open but, most importantly, they are quick and uncomplicated to reload, not forgetting the simplicity of cleaning and ability to be taken apart for easy transportation. In the field, they are generally shorter than a normal bolt-action

rifle, as the bolt action is not required, making them more pointable, but it is the ability to fire the second shot quickly that really drives the popularity of this design.

Enough of the history – I welcome you to the Krieghoff Big Five rifle in the uncompromising .470 Nitro Express calibre. The Classic Big Five is available in many larger calibres from the .375 H&H to the .500NE but, interestingly, a pair of 20-gauge barrels can be fitted if you want to test your skills with flying game.

As it's a .470NE, you would have imagined this would be a large and heavy monster, but as I lifted it out of its case, I realised it wasn't. While it has the feel of a solid but beautiful piece of German engineering, the boxlock design gives the impression of a slender shotgun, and when raised to the shoulder, it feels compact for a 10lb rifle.

The stock, made from the finest European walnut wood, oozes undeniable quality thanks to its deep and beautifully coloured grain, with delightful chequering on the wide pistol grip and forend. The design of this stock is

critical for these heavy calibres, as it has a low-straight comb with a curved cheekpiece, all of which is designed to help with the greater recoil from standing.

Moving forward, the 'combi-cocking' lever dominates the top tang. This cocking lever allows the rifle to be carried when fully loaded, without the fear of an accidental discharge. As the 'Big Five' is raised to the shoulder, the thumb pushes this lever forward ready for firing, but does not automatically decock the firing mechanism when the action is broken for reloading. Some may say this is unsafe, but this is designed for dangerous game where reloading and subsequent shots must be executed in the fastest possible time. So you break the barrel, reload, raise it the shoulder and fire without the need to cock the action again. Simple and effective.

The action itself has reinforced walls for extra strength with high-quality 'small Arabesque' engraving to the sides. On to the two triggers: the front activates the right barrel and the rear the left, both set at 3½ to 4lb, aided by virtually horizontal firing pin placement for fast lock time. Most doubles have much heavier trigger pulls, but the patented Krieghoff Universal Trigger System prevents both barrels from being fired at the same time owing to heavy recoil – always a worry when lighter triggers are used. Interestingly, the front trigger is hinged to protect the trigger finger when shooting the

## YOU WOULD HAVE IMAGINED THIS WOULD BE A LARGE AND HEAVY MONSTER, BUT AS I LIFTED IT OUT OF ITS CASE, I REALISED IT WASN'T. IT FEELS COMPACT FOR A 10LB RIFLE

rear trigger, as the recoil will push the rifle backwards, driving the front blade into the back of that finger.

As with any double-barrelled rifle, the 'regulation' – making sure that both barrels shoot the same point of impact – can be tricky to set up. On the .375 H&H or smaller calibre rifles, this is adjustable at the muzzle, but fixed at the factory for the larger calibres. Most doubles are set to a 50-yard zero and guarantee an accuracy of 2in at this distance using their factory-recommended ammunition. The 23.5in barrels on this model come with fixed front moon sights and an open 'V' to the rear on the raised central rib. As an extra option, I would recommend the folding express rear sights to help shooting at a variety of distances. When breaking the action by using the top lever, the opening is very short, designed for very quick extraction – but this model does not come with extractors as standard. I spoke to Alan Rhone, who informed me that this is not

always essential, as all one does is roll the rifle over to allow both spent cases to fall out, and then reload. Also, many hunters feel ejectors are another thing to go wrong – in other words, keep it simple.

Out came the huge Kynoch .470 Nitro Express rounds in solid and soft point, kindly supplied by Kynamco. My immediate thought was for my poor old shoulder, as these rounds have a 500-grain bullet, being pushed out at 2,150fps, not forgetting the 5,000ft/lb of energy. I put on an extra layer to give my lean

frame a chance of being able to shoot more rifles in the future for this magazine.

With the use of sticks, the time of reckoning could not be put off any longer. I must admit I snatched the trigger on my first shot, but one can describe the recoil as a large but firm push, as opposed to an almighty kick as experienced with shooting, for instance, a .338 Lap Mag. Well, maybe it was a bit of both.

At 70 yards, I achieved a 3in group and with practice, I am sure I could improve, but eight shots was all that I could put up with without the need to rest my aching shoulder, let alone my starting to flinch in anticipation of the recoil. Krieghoff takes pride in the design of the stock, combined with the larger pistol grip, and folding front trigger blade, as all these features allow the rifle to handle the immense recoil very effectively. It seemed a little strange that the rifle had no ejectors, but as soon as it was tilted over, out slid the spent cases. I can understand why they are so popular in the close bush thanks to the short barrels, making it very pointable and easy to shoulder very quickly.

This is the first time I have tested a double rifle in .470 NE and I was pleased to have the opportunity, but I learned one important fact. You cannot expect to pick one up quickly and wander off into the bushveld thinking you will easily kill your quarry. Despite the immense power and simplicity of these rifles, lots of practice is essential. It does not matter if you have open or closed optical sights – to make an accurate shot, you need a technique that is somewhat different to the normal bolt-action rifle. It does not stop there – reloading under pressure, understanding the bullet drop over

very short and longer distances, are important factors if you have a large angry beast running towards you.

These are specialised rifles that appeal to a small portion of hunters, but if you find the opportunity to pick one up, study the engineering and embellishments, and you will see why they have that special attraction. A sincere thanks to Kynamco for supplying the rather expensive ammunition for calibres such as this. **TP**

---

**KRIEGHOFF BIG FIVE**

*Model tested:* Classic Big Five Double .470 NE

*Price range:* From £6,000

*Contact:* Alan Rhone  01978 660001
**www.alanrhone.com**

---

# LYNX 94

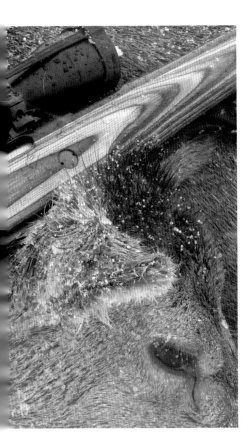

The Lynx is manufactured by Pirkan ASE, based in Finland. Specialising in handcrafted rifles, the company works with the Finnish Defence Forces Technical Research Centre to test weapons and projectiles. Pirkan ASE is renowned for developing high-quality sporting and competition rifles since 1979.

The Lynx 94 was designed by Torsti Laaksonen, a Finnish master gunsmith, and is a patented straight-pull bolt-action rifle. This makes it ideal for driven game and most hunting applications. It is the recently launched Light Hunter model, built with a high-quality laminated stock, that I am reviewing, as well as testing its reputation for quality and accuracy.

As the action is the most interesting and unique aspect of this rifle, I feel this is the best place to start the review. It is a tubular design with a closed, small ejection port. Fitted with an integral 17mm dovetail, the action allows for fitting the popular Tikka Optilock mounts or the more expensive but easily removable Ziegler ZP claw mount system.

The most impressive aspect of this straight-pull system is the smoothness of cycling the rounds. It may have yards of travel, but displays quality engineering and has been case-hardened to survive the harshest conditions you might find yourself in. To lock the bolt, a sliding crossbar located towards the rear of the action is used. This is similar in principle to the Browning T-Bolt system.

Other straight-pulls, such as the Blaser R8, rely on an expanding radial locking system that locks the front of the bolt head. And the Merkel Helix, for example, uses a multi-lugged head that twists into the rear of the barrel assembly, reducing the

need for a strong, and therefore heavier, action. It may be one of the smoothest actions to use, but simply grabbing the large cylindrical bolt knob in the normal fashion will result in your fingers being trapped between the knob, action and stock. As with all unusual rifles, there is a knack that can quickly be mastered within a few shots: simply use the tips of the thumb and next two fingers (or push forwards using the palm). It requires more of a delicate grip as opposed to the normal grab and slide.

To release the bolt, pull down the odd-looking lever, located to the front of the trigger. It does look a little strange, but the more I examine the Lynx, the more I see that it has been designed by engineers who maybe have sacrificed looks for practicality.

Overall, the action and bolt assembly, while highly engineered, are in some ways simplistic and very mechanical to operate. This is not a criticism, but more of an observation, that will either attract or put off a prospective buyer.

What a great trigger! It is fully adjustable from 0.5 to 1.2kg (1.1 to 2.5lb). Despite breaking at 2.2lb, it feels much less. Whatever those engineers have done, it is superb, offering the slightest of creep and a crisp breaking point. The trigger blade can also be adjusted before and after, with the two-position safety catch located on the left-hand side of the action. While this lever looks a little crude, it is easy to operate in very cold conditions when wearing gloves.

The steel box magazine holds three rounds and is robust and easy to fill. To release it, simply pull down the lever that sits just in front of the trigger guard. Once again, everything is designed around the wearing of gloves, so the lever is large, stiff and easy to drop out using one finger.

The 585mm (23in) medium-grade barrel is made by Lothar Walther and, being the Light Hunter, is without front and rear open sights. As with the rest of the metal work, it is of a high quality, blued finish and supplied with a 15x1mm thread for a sound moderator.

Probably the most striking aspect of this rifle is the laminated wooden stock in a variety of brown, silver and ebony colours. The last Lynx rifle on test was the solid Hunter, furnished with a high quality walnut stock in a thumping 9.3x62 calibre. The new Light Hunter is much lighter, by about 1.2lb. It feels sleek and very comfortable, thanks to the narrow forend and pistol grip. Both areas receive a coarse chequering pattern, which makes them both rough and very nice to grip.

As it comes up to the shoulder, it is comfortable thanks to the medium-height

cheekpiece but feels a little more quirky than most rifles – no thanks to that chunky, vertical bolt handle protruding from the right-hand side of the action. But how does it perform?

For this review, Alan Rhone kindly sent me the Light Hunter in .308, complete with a Zeiss Diavari 2.5-10x50 and 66 reticle using the easily detachable Ziegler ZP claw mount system. To release the scope, push back the outer bases on the front mount, lift the front of the scope and out it comes. I used the same rifle in the .30-06 calibre to demonstrate straight-pull rifles with Byron Pace for *The Shooting Show*, so my observations are based on using both of these rifles.

Using Lapua 150SP ammunition, kindly supplied by Viking Arms, I zeroed the .308 Light Hunter at 150 yards and achieved a 1.5-1.75in

group. I have no doubt this could be reduced after further use, but more than acceptable for its intended game. I found it a little snappy, though this is not unusual for the .308 calibre. Despite removing and refitting the scope, it retained zero within one click thanks to the quality of the Ziegler ZP claw mounts.

The Lynx in .308 was off to be tested in the highlands of Scotland, culling hinds on the Kinlockewe Estate, Achnasheen. This was done under the careful eye of experienced stalkers Ronnie and Kenny Ross. As we arrived in the evening, the temperature started to drop to -10 degrees. This made the last 15 miles very treacherous because of black ice on the roads. The rest of the week was spent stalking through a mixture of thick snow up on the tops of the hills. The temperature ranged from an unforgiving -10 up to zero degrees during the day.

With a Harris six to nine-inch bipod fitted, the Lynx claimed several red hinds, calves and sika throughout the week. I found the magazine easy to fill, and it cycled effortlessly despite the cold temperatures and driving snow. The trigger was set to the ideal resistance, allowing me to easily feel the breaking point while wearing gloves.

Very quickly, I mastered the Lynx straight-pull system. I can see it being ideal for moving targets, such as running boar, as it is so quick to cycle a second round. It somehow felt lighter than the quoted 7.9lb (3.6kg) and, despite many layers of clothing and a variety of warm headgear, it was comfortable to shoot. On many occasions, it was dropped and dragged through the snow (sorry Alan Rhone) but it is designed for these harshest of conditions, so no problems arose.

The Lynx Light Hunter is available in calibres from .22-250 to the feisty .375 Ruger. With an SRP of £3,495, it is a specialist buy for someone who wants something a little different. Each rifle is guaranteed for accuracy, depending on the ammunition used. While the action is beautifully smooth, it has a mechanical feel. It may not be to the tastes of some, but others will love it. I cannot question the quality and functionality of the rifle, although it is in the same price range as the Blaser and Merkel straight-pulls, so it has stiff, very well known competition. But it certainly is a contender. **TP**

## LYNX 94

| | |
|---|---|
| **Model tested:** | 94 Light Hunter in .308 |
| **Price range:** | £3,495 |
| **Contact:** | Alan Rhone  01978 660001 |
| | **www.alanrhone.com** |

# MARLIN X7

**M**arlin is probably best known for its underlever actions and rimfires in the USA, rather than for hunting rifles. I have been told they are good value for money, and more importantly, that their accuracy is 'just darn good'! With an RRP of £715, the X7 is an entry-level model, maybe for the first-time buyer of a centrefire – but does it punch above its weight?

The Marlin X7 range of rifles come in short and long actions, chambered in calibres from .22-250 to .30-06. For the review, I had the X7Y Short action model in .243, but it is also available in 7mm-08 and .308 Win. It is fitted with a lightweight synthetic stock as standard – when tapped lightly, it sounded hollow and 'plasticy'. My first impressions were that this was a budget build. When raised to the shoulder, the raised cheekpiece fits well, as does the narrow,

chequered pistol grip. To the rear, the 'Soft-tech' recoil pad is comfortable, and I imagine it would be forgiving when shooting the larger calibres.

The action itself is bedded on steel pillars within the stock, to reinforce the mounting area, resulting in a very solid fitment, secured by two hex-headed screws. This should improve accuracy for what seems a fairly light rifle, weighing in at 6¾lb. The forend is designed to touch the barrel in two places. This may change the point of impact when a bipod is fitted or affect accuracy when the barrel heats up. (In the USA, bipods are not used by most hunters other than long-range varminters.) QD mounts are also fitted in the normal places.

The rear of the bolt is fully enclosed with a cocking indicator, and is fully fluted along the length of its body. Thanks to this fluted bolt, it cycles smoothly with the bolt head being pinned

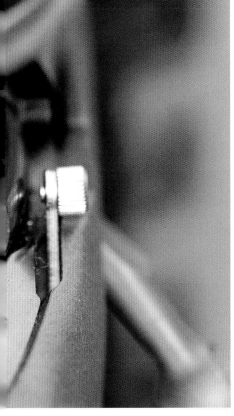

to the body, allowing the round to self-centre for enhanced accuracy. There is a two-position safety catch mounted to the right that when applied, locks the trigger, but allows the bolt to be cycled. To release the bolt, simply press a lever down, located to the left of the bolt, and out she slides. On top of the action, a Picatinny-style rail or bridge is a standard fitment, allowing a wide variety of Weaver-style mounts to be used.

The lightweight, tapered 22in sporting barrel boasts a button rifling process for the rifling and is threaded with a recessed crown. With a twist rate of 1 in 10in, it maybe favours the heavier bullets, but that is common for many .243s. Similar to some of the Savage rifles, there is a locking collar next to the action to guarantee the exact head spacing measurements during manufacture.

The 'Pro-Fire' Trigger is easily adjustable from 2½lb with this rifle set to just over 3lb from the factory. With a hint of creep, it is very crisp and I had no need to adjust it to a lighter pull, as it felt just right for everyday hunting. Similar to the Savage I reviewed in the past, the Pro-Fire trigger has a central safety blade that has to be pressed first before the main blade moves. This forward safety blade system allows the trigger to be adjusted to below 3lb without the worry of falling foul of the American laws. Also, it prevents the rifle firing if it is dropped heavily.

The X7 does not support a detachable magazine or floor plate. With a 'blind magazine', it is a pure top-loader, so there is plenty of room to press a maximum of four rounds in from the top. To unload, every round has to be individually extracted by cycling the bolt. Overall, it has the feel of a budget rifle, no thanks to the hollow stock, but it is light, well balanced and fitted with what seems to be a quality trigger. So does it perform in the field? The Marlin X7 came with a Weaver Super Slam 3-9x56 and Millet Angle-Loc mounts, all supplied by Edgar Brothers. As it came threaded, I fitted my Reflex T8 moderator, and for ammunition I used Hornady Superformance

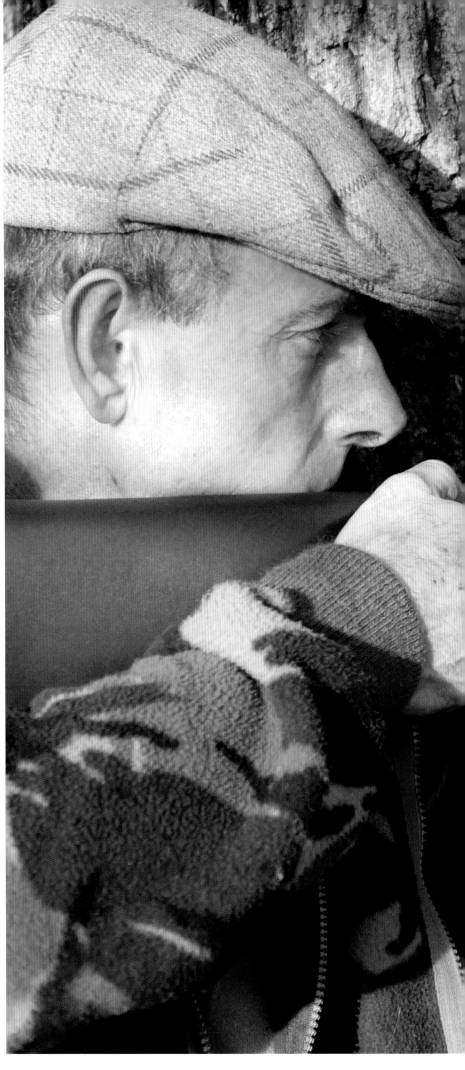

95-grain SSTs flying out at a feisty 3,180fps. Before using a collimator, I made sure the windage adjustment on the scope was in the middle of its travel. I then adjusted it to the central line of the collimator by adjusting the base screws on the Millet Angle-Loc scope mounts. This can be a useful option for those times when, for some reason, the scope will not line up properly. I see this rifle being used for everyday fox and deer control, so I set the zero at 150 yards – just right for close woodland stalking, and, with lighter bullets, foxes out to 250 yards.

Within four shots, the zero was achieved and the X7 recorded a 1.5in group at 150 yards, which is respectable considering it was shot off my shortened high seat with the rifle resting

on my hand. I found it comfortable to shoot thanks to the slim pistol grip and grippable, chequered forend.

Out to 250 yards, now using a bipod, the Pro-Fire trigger was a delight to use, but I found that the grouping increased to 3.5in with the 95-grain ammunition. I then tried, at the same distance, some home-loaded Nosler 55-grain ballistic-tipped rounds (MV 3,825fps) and they surprisingly achieved a group of less than two inches.

I mentioned that the stock forend is designed to touch the barrel in two places. Adding a bipod can alter the point of aim owing to increased pressure on the barrel from the forend, but it did not seem to change it by more than an inch at 250 yards. The cycling of ammunition was smooth, and there were no faults with the feeding from the blind magazine.

To sum up, the Marlin X7 has the feel of a budget rifle, largely because of the low-cost stock, but once lifted to the shoulder, it certainly performs a lot better than one. I see this attracting the first-time owner of a centrefire, or the gamekeeper who wants a totally reliable, lightweight workhorse.

With an RRP of £715, consistently shooting well below 1MOA, what else do you really need out of a gun? In the USA, it retails for $434 with a scope thrown in, so it is seen as one of the more inexpensive centrefire rifles available. The more I shot the X7, the more it demonstrated its ability to shoot well. Does it punch above its weight? It certainly does. **TP**

**MARLIN X7**

*Model tested:* Marlin X7Y short action in .243 Win

*Price range:* From £715

*Contact:* Remington UK  01206 795333
**www.sportsmk.co.uk**

# MAUSER MO3

The well-known MO3 range from Mauser is based on a modular concept, allowing a wide range of stocks and barrels to be fitted with different levels of quality and design.

The Mauser Alpine and Stutzen are classic examples of Mauser's high-quality workmanship, aimed at the client who enjoys hunting with beautiful rifles. When I mentioned to Robert of UK Mauser importer Open Season that I would love to try the Stutzen, he had one specially delivered to me within two weeks, despite this design not being popular in the UK (unlike the rest of Europe).

The modular concept starts with the manual cocking safety system. This is a wonderful design that combines a safety catch and cocking lever. Push the bolt assembly forward and lock it into the breech. To shoot, push the lever on the rear of the bolt to the right, and to return to safety, press a small knob located below the lever to let it spring back to the left, at the same time de-cocking it. With safety off, one can cycle and shoot a round without having to go through this procedure each time, which is very useful. When de-cocked, the stainless steel bolt handle cannot be moved.

This action is exceptionally well put together, beautifully smooth and highly engineered. Some may say it is too complicated. As the MO3 can

interchange with most calibres, the bolt travels nearly five inches to accommodate the longer cases, and for the smaller calibres it does feel excessive. The bolt is locked into the action with three double lugs, and the head is easily interchangeable by overextending the cocking lever to the left.

The 2.5lb trigger is crisp with no creep, and a delight to use in all disciplines. These models have the luxury of a set trigger, activated by pushing the trigger blade forward. When de-cocked, the set trigger automatically returns to normal. The steel magazine, once again, is of the size to accept a wide variety of calibres. The open receiver design enables easy loading and with a capacity of four rounds, it can be removed by pressing a large button located to the front. This can also be locked by twisting the release button.

So how do these models differ? Both subtle 'hog back' stocks are made from grade five fine-grained Turkish walnut, and share the same beautifully crafted 'double fold' Bavarian cheekpiece with elegant pistol grips and slight chequering. The ebony pistol grip caps and forends are beautifully made, with the Alpine sporting a 23in barrel, the Stutzen a 19in. The Stutzen's 'split' forend is attached to the barrel, allowing the rest of the barrel to be fully floated, maintaining accuracy in all conditions. Most

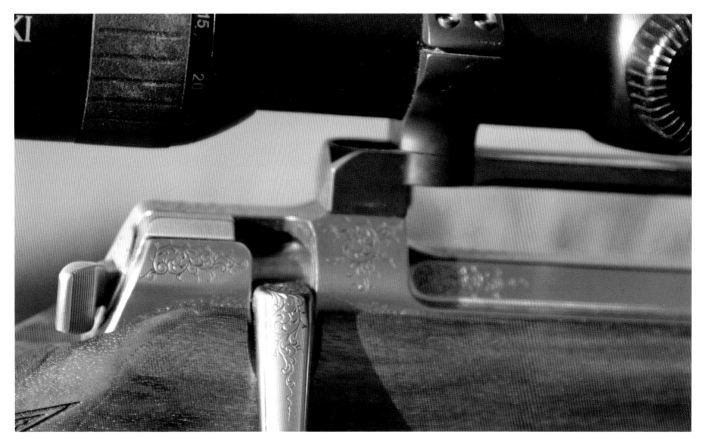

Stutzens have accuracy issues when they become a little damp, or when the barrel becomes warm, because the wood is directly secured to the barrel. This clever design avoids these issues. If you wish to change the look of the rifle, remove the barrel and replace it with another to make it into an Alpine. Simple. This particular model also has the detailed engraving, finished off to a high level of detail.

For the review, I was lucky enough to receive a Swarovski Z6i 5-30x50 P with 4A illuminated reticle. Unique to Mauser, a QD saddle mount

is needed (at an extra cost of £405) to fit any optics to the rifle. It is located to the front and rear of the receiver and can be easily removed by pushing forward the locating levers to release the levers backwards. Once again, it is beautifully engineered, which is essential to retain zero when removed or refitted.

So how do they shoot? As with all the MO3s, accuracy is not an issue, constantly achieving around a one-inch group at 100 yards (1MOA), which for an all-round hunting rifle in .308 is perfectly adequate. With 2.5lb triggers, each

rifle is skilfully balanced, but they feel different to shoot. The longer-barrelled Alpine gave less recoil and muzzle flip, with the Stutzen being quite lively thanks to the 19in barrel. I love the classic Stutzen design. It feels compact, very pointable, ideally suited to close woodland stalking or mountainous terrain.

I was able to take the Alpine to the Forest Estate in Dumfries and Galloway to undertake a spot of wild goat stalking. Despite the weather being against me for most of the trip, my keen eyed stalker John managed to move me into a herd of 15 animals. This culminated in a billy from about 125 yards, which dropped instantly with a well-aimed shot to the vital organs. Imagine his face when he asked me the price of becoming the proud owner of a MO3 Alpine.

Both these rifles are at the top end of most people's budgets, with prices starting at £4,000 for the Alpine and £4,500 for Stutzen (with the engraving another £1,750). I have a soft spot for the MO3 range – especially with the Stutzen, my heart sank watching the courier's van take it away up the farm drive. What more can I say? **TP**

### MAUSER M03

**Models tested:** Alpine and Stutzen

**Price range:** Alpine from £3,969, Stutzen from £4,500

**Contact:** Blaser Sporting 0207 6222116
**www.blaser-sporting.com**

# MERKEL 161

Merkel, based in the city of Suhl, Germany, has been making high-quality sporting guns since the 17th century. The company has a worldwide reputation for its unique engravings, along with a training school for engravers and a gun-making 'technical school'.

When a friend mentioned to me that he owned one – and, more importantly, that it was an unusual model with unique engravings in a feisty 9.3x74R – I knew it was time for me to start pleading. He had only fired it a few times, but he eventually succumbed to my request with the agreement that I was to guard it with my life. He would clearly be enduring some sleepless nights worrying about the safety of his prized possession.

The Merkel 161 is the sister model to the 141 boxlock, but with a side-lock design. These models are made for medium to big game hunting, especially driven boar. The double barrel concept is popular as it allows a very quick second shot. To accommodate larger African game, Merkel has a much heavier safari range of rifles with more robust calibres to suit.

As soon as I lifted the gun from the cabinet, its elegance and quality became apparent. The 161 is built as a slim version of Merkel's double rifle range. Based on a 28-gauge shotgun

chassis, it weighs in at a lean 6.7lb (3kg), making it ideal for quick, responsive shooting. The short, 'tin soldered' 22in (55cm) barrels have open sights as standard, together with highly engineered bases for swing-off Merkel mounts. This gun had been set to a 100-yard zero – adjustments to this can be made using a hex-headed key fitted into the regulating ports between the muzzles. The barrels are produced

in 6.5x57R, 7x57R, 7x65R, .30-06, .30R Blaser, 8x57 IRS and 9.3x74R. There is also a sling mount to aid portability.

The side-lock Anson and Deeley action comes with a double trigger in the 161. The front trigger can also be pushed forward to act as a set trigger. Most models have injectors, but for an unknown reason this one did not have them fitted. There is also a cocking indicator, and the safety automatically comes on after breaking the barrel – very similar to many shotguns.

The side-lock panels are normally presented in an Arabesque style. On this custom rifle, you can see the detail of typical Germanic beer-drinking scenes, mixed with hunting dogs and woodland backdrops. If you look carefully, you can see the tiny mouse on the floorboards, being stalked by the cat, close to the traditional Bavarian walled timepiece. Merkel states in its

promotional literature that 'ultimate freedom of expression is offered,' and that's certainly no lie.

The optional 'luxury' finely grained walnut wood is a work of art and a pleasure to handle, with a beautifully designed pistol grip and a cheekpiece that oozes elegance. Once again, a wide variety of options are available, from Scottish and fish scale surface finishes to the hand-polished traditional English finish.

So what is it like to shoot? For this review, I used RWS ammo that kicks out a 258-grain bullet at 2,640fps, so I was anticipating a fair amount of recoil. With the zero set at 100 yards by Merkel, it will drop 1.5in at 150 yards and 5in at 200 yards. Fitted to the rifle was a Swarovski PV1 1.5-6x42 with an illuminated round reticle with central dot, designed for running boar. To remove the scope, turn a section of the rear mount to release it, swing the

assembly to the right until it is 90 degrees to the barrel and lift it off.

With a one-metre round steel target set at 100 yards, my first shot was some 15in high thanks to me snatching the firm trigger in anticipation of an impending recoil. Despite it being a short rifle, the muzzle lift was very controllable, and while the recoil was highly noticeable, I managed to achieve a 5-6in group at this distance.

As with most double rifles, there is an acquired technique to shooting the 161 reasonably accurately. With practice, I am sure I could do much better. Having said that, these types of rifle are not built for supreme accuracy, so anything around 3-4in at this distance would be acceptable. Meanwhile, the Swarovski optics were up to their usual high level of quality, and I could see how the reticle would be easy to use on running game. Using the open field sight, I found most targets a breeze to aim at, mostly thanks to the well-designed foresight.

The Merkel 161, being short and extremely pointable, was an absolute pleasure to use. With a starting cost of £11,000 for the standard model, you're bound to expect the highest quality workmanship, and this rifle is a most beautiful example. I can see myself using it on a wild game hunt, whether in Europe or Africa, when suddenly a wild pig is spooked and scampers some 50 yards to my right. In one movement, the gun comes up to the shoulder, and the trigger is immediately squeezed off with fatal effect. All I need to do now is use it on the real thing. I can hardly wait. Any offers? **TP**

**MERKEL 161**

**Model tested:** 161 Double in 9.3x74R

**Price range:** From £11,000

**Comments:** Viking Arms 01423 780810 www.vikingarms.com

# MERKEL RX HELIX

The RX Helix manifesto states: "Hunting has moved on in the 21st century. It has become faster, more versatile and more exciting. This demands better gun ergonomics: ideal combination of responsiveness, speed and accuracy." It continues: "The hunt doesn't begin on the hunting grounds nowadays, but starts instead with the preparation for the journey to the hunt." All sounds great, and UK importer Viking Arms's claim that it is the fastest straight pull on the market had got me excited. But has Merkel really developed the best hunting gun for the 21st century?

Merkel is a well-known German manufacturer of luxury hunting rifles and shotguns, based in Suhl. The R in RX Helix refers to 'Repetierer', which is German for a bolt-action rifle, and the X has a double meaning: the Roman numeral stands for the launch year 2010 and is also from the Latin alphabet representing the word 'Helix'. Helix refers to the way the bolt locks into the breech.

For this test, Viking Arms sent the Helix in .308 with a beautiful grade six walnut stock and an eye-catching wood finish, but it is the action and barrel that really sets the rifle apart. The Helix is a straight pull design, but the bolt is within a 'closed system housing'. When the bolt is pulled right back, it does not extend behind the action, which means it does not hinder the shooter, especially when cycling rounds very quickly. As the bolt handle is positioned directly above the trigger guard, the trigger hand moves instantly to the bolt after a shot.

But how can the bolt knob travel such a short distance when the action is able to deal with both short and long rounds? This is where it gets smart: For every inch the bolt knob moves, the bolt face travels two inches. Merkel informs me: "The linear motion of the bolt handle is transmitted to the bolt head with a ratio of 1:2. It travels along a helical path as part of a special design, and moves gently and quietly into and out of the locking position." This results in the quiet and fast cycling of rounds.

I had to slowly cycle the bolt several times to accept that this is a clever piece of engineering. I only hope it doesn't prove too complicated or expensive to repair after several years of use in the field.

With regard to safety, the Helix uses a manual cocking system, with a cocking lever located behind the action, simply located for the use of the thumb. Forward position puts the firing system under tension to fire; depress to return to safety. A Picatinny rail is integral to the action, allowing the fitting of Weaver-style mounts, accommodating most styles of optic.

Moving to the front of the bolt, the supreme German engineering once again shines. As the bolt is thrust forward, the bolt head rotates as it stops in the breach, locking all six lugs. This is about as safe at it gets, as some other makes of older straight pulls had apparent issues with bolts flying backwards after firing. As for the firing mechanism, without going into infinite detail of the whole linkage-driven hammer system, it apparently cannot be fired until the breech is fully locked, making it totally failsafe.

Many rifles are now designed to be easily portable, as well as being fully switchable, meaning the barrel and bolt head can be easily changed for another calibre. The Helix is no exception. To remove the 22in sporting weight barrel, press a button located to the underside of the wooden forend, slide forward and put away. Pull a lever downwards, situated to the left-hand side of the barrel, slide the barrel forward, and out she pops. It takes less than

six seconds to remove and refit the barrel assembly. If the bolt is left in the forward position, the bolt head is locked and stays within the barrel when extracted. It is as easy as that.

As for dimensions, the rifle weighs in at 6¾lb (2.6kg) before optics and is 40in (110cm) long, making it a light and compact design – ideal for deer stalking or driven boar shooting. So far, so good – but I was beginning to worry that the accuracy might have been compromised by this new concept of straight pull bolt design mixed with the quick take down facility.

For this review, Zeiss kindly sent me the Duralyt 3-12x50 with an illuminated reticle. For ammunition, I used a variety of hunting rounds from 150 to 165 grains. I also used adjustable Millet Angle-Loc scope mounts, supplied by Edgar Brothers.

With the possible exception of the smaller calibres it is available in, the RX Helix is designed for both European and African shooting such as running wild boar, deer stalking and medium to large plains game species. So it is engineered to be shot standing freehand, off sticks or resting on anything from a rucksack to the side of a tree trunk.

Up to the shoulder, the straight-cut stock immediately told me that the Helix is perfect for quick target acquisition. The model sent for this review was finished in grade six wood, which looks and feels fabulous. Moving forward, the chequered pistol grip and palm swell make me feel at one with the rifle. The robust cocking lever is also perfectly positioned for the thumb. To de-cock, I found the small release button, located at the top, a little fiddly to press down, especially when wearing gloves, but I don't think this will be an issue with a little more practice.

The trigger, set at about 2.5lb, was a delight to use. After firing, lift or twist the trigger hand upwards, and you'll instantly find the bolt handle. As with all straight pulls, unless you have used them for a long time, it does take time to train your mind to 'pull' and not 'twist' the bolt, but once I accepted that I do not need to pull the bolt back as far as most similar actions, I could squeeze off multiple shots in no time.

The expected levels of recoil and muzzle lift – this is a .308, after all – were the only factors that slowed me down taking another instant shot, owing to the slight change of sight picture when firing. As for accuracy, at 100 yards, the Helix shot all weights of bullet to 0.75-1in accuracy, which is more than adequate for its intended application. Point of impact did not change after barrel changes. When I was filming a piece for The Shooting Show, despite shooting a volley of at least 20 shots in quick succession, it grouped a maximum of 1.5in at 100 yards, demonstrating the quality of the barrel.

Bearing in mind that the Helix starts at around £3,000, with the model on review retailing for £4,250, what is my honest opinion? When I first laid my hands on it, despite the obvious quality of the wood, I was not convinced about the feel of the quality of the action, as I always associated Merkel with top-end, high-quality guns. But my doubts didn't last long. It has a quicker action than the Blaser R8 equivalent, and is easier to take down. The Helix's main selling point is the shooter's improved stability when taking multiple shots thanks to the short pull action, which is, in my opinion, superior to that of the hugely popular Blaser. A quicker and easier switchable system is a selling point, but this is normally undertaken before the hunt starts, so speed is not indispensable.

After shooting 200 rounds at animal targets out to 200 yards and simulated running boar at 80 yards, I appreciated the thought that had gone into the design and ergonomics. The grippable forend allows good hold of the rifle when cycling and the open field sights are one of the best I have used for a long time. The sturdy magazine was no problem to use and can be loaded from the top if required.

I have the pleasure of handling a wide variety of rifles in my line of work, and the acid test of a rifle is whether or not I miss it after returning it. That certainly applies with the new Helix – I would love to use it for a variety of my hunting. That said, with extra barrels (including bolt head) at £910 and magazines an extra £120, this would be a specialist buy.

As soon as I am lucky enough to point something long and noisy at a running boar, I know what my first choice of rifle will be. If you need an easily portable rifle with switchable barrels and you hunt running game, the Merkel Helix is, in my opinion, the market leader. **TP**

created a rifle that offers the slickest barrel change on the market.

The first step simply involves removing the forestock. Keeping things as fuss-free as possible, this is achieved by depressing a button under the stock, at which point the whole thing slides off the metalwork. After that, it is a straightforward case of rotating the now exposed lever at 90 degrees to the rifle, then pulling the barrel gently from the action.

To insert a new barrel in an alternative calibre, this process is reversed. Of course, changing between calibre families will also require the bolt head to be swapped. This too is completed quickly and easily. As long as you ensure the bolt is in the forward position when the barrel is removed, the bolt head will be conveniently held in the chamber ready to be twisted out and replaced. I doubt if this could have been made any easier, and any

other rifle manufacturers that try to compete with Merkel will be hard-pressed to create a better process.

Moving on to the rest of the rifle, the synthetic stock maintains the standard you would expect from Merkel, offering no points to criticise. Conveniently, Merkel makes the RX Helix receiver with an integral Weaver rail, allowing for an array of mounting options. This is a pleasing move by Merkel, since a number of other German gun manufacturers have opted to corner shooters into using the maker's own mounts. As excellent as the mounts are, they come at a considerable cost.

The trigger in the RX Helix is a crisp affair with an even, light break. My only complaint is that the blade itself is thinner and smoother than I would like. Moving on to the safety, we find a similar cocking lever

system to the Blaser, which is something you either love or hate.

The shootability of the RX Helix is without question superb. It feels natural in the hand and comes to the eye nicely, whether using the iron sights or with the rifle scoped. On the range I did find myself having to go through a few brands and bullet weights to find something the rifle enjoyed firing, but once I settled on 150-grain Hornady loads it returned the industry standard of 1MOA. As always, some more fine tuning and worked up hand-loads would bring this in further.

Wanting to test the consistency of the switch-barrel changes, I repeated accuracy tests with this ammo as standard, first grouping between barrel changes and then grouping with single shots and a barrel change between each. I could detect no difference in the rifle's ability to group having changed the barrel. There did seem to be a marginal point of impact shift, which led to my second test opening the group to around 1.5in given the barrel swap between shots. For the practical purposes this rifle was intended for, this makes little difference.

The RX Helix is one of those rifles that has to be used to be truly appreciated. It provides a modern innovation in design concepts, which have not been challenged for many years, and I will be interested to see what shape Merkel's next development takes. **BP**

**MERKEL RX HELIX**

**Models tested:** Walnut; synthetic (switch-barrel)

**Price range:** From £3,075

**Contact:** Viking Arms 01423 780810
**www.vikingarms.com**

# MERKEL KR1

Merkel has been a well-known name in shotgunning circles for some time, but in recent years the German manufacturer has become famous for producing the world's most affordable classic double rifle – not to mention drillings, and the firm's popular single-shot rifle. Yet in the KR1, Merkel has created a thoroughly modern rifle along classic lines, which has the potential to eclipse the Blaser R93 straight-pull – a rifle that has proved popular on both sides of the North Sea and English Channel.

The Merkel KR1 is different from traditional bolt-actions – in fact, it's different from any bolt-action on the market today. It is actually a turn-bolt action with forward locking lugs, but the resemblance to the classic Mauser action stops there, as the bolt only has a short uplift. The body of the bolt actually acts as a shroud that encases and protects the entire receiver. This is what makes the Merkel system stand out; like the Blaser R93 straight-pull it allows for speedy

bolt manipulation, but still has that added feeling of security on lock-up, as it is still a true turn-bolt – unlike the Blaser. This design also allows for a very short return, and offers better protection from dust and debris than almost any other action available on a modern hunting rifle.

The three-position safety is of the tang shotgun-style; when you place your thumb on the locking lever, it automatically depresses, avoiding the possibility of accidental operation. When set on safe, either cocked or uncocked, the bolt remains securely locked.

The KR1 comes complete with a single set-trigger as standard. The trigger breaks with a predictable single stage pull at 3lb. The set trigger, achieved by pushing it forward, releases at 2lb (on the test rifle, at least). The set trigger is a little too far forward, which could be a problem for some smaller-fingered people; but the trigger guard is large and accepts a gloved digit very easily.

Other standard features include good quality iron sights and a quick detachable one-piece saddle scope mount. The supplied scope mount attaches positively and gives a sense of rigidity in the system; the clamping movement is engaged by rotating two levers forward to lock the mount – an integral pop-out bar indicates when they are tight enough.

The KR1 is a switch-barrel rifle, which is the current vogue for many German rifle makers (Sauer, Blaser, Mauser, and so on); standard

barrels come in 20 or 22in, magnum in 22 or 24in. Barrels chambered to cartridges of like case-head diameter can be swapped by removing the bolt assembly and two hex-head screws, the rear one under the hinged floor plate, the second a couple of inches forward in the bottom metal. To go from standard (.30-06) case-head diameters up to belted magnums, a locking bolt head with the appropriate bolt-face diameter and the proper detachable magazine are required.

After a few attempts, I soon became familiar with the procedure and could change the barrel in a matter of no more than two minutes. The saddle scope mount is mounted on the barrel as there is no receiver in the traditional sense, (again similar to the rifle's closest rival, the Blaser R93) hence the barrel scope mounting system. Therefore with a scope and mount for each barrel one can switch calibres back and forth, even in field conditions, with complete confidence in the rifle maintaining its zero.

The walnut stock on the test rifle was close-grained, good quality and richly coloured, and capped with a thin recoil pad. Merkel have opted for a traditional Germanic look on this modern gun, and it works well – the finished result is extremely pleasing on the eye.

When shouldered, the KR1 pointed very well, the hogs-back stock profile without a cheekpiece had an adequate length of pull that fitted me perfectly. A Bavarian cheekpiece is available on higher grades, and a Monte Carlo cheekpiece comes as standard on the safari version. Chequering adorns both the pistol grip and forend, enabling firm and positive mounting. The rifle handles brilliantly and comes up smoothly with the scope but, at least for me, it also comes up well with the iron sights, which I favour for both driven boar, and up close on dangerous game. The KR1 is a really remarkable hunting rifle that is a clear contender to the

popular Blaser R93 straight-pull alternative. The test rifle that I used was right-handed, but left-hand models (both locking housing and stock) are also available for true southpaws like me.

In the field, the action was extremely slick and very fast; it seemed quieter in operation than the straight-pull action of the Blaser R93 that I recently tested, but does that really matter? I didn't get the chance to shoot a boar with the rifle, but on the running boar target on the range I found the KR1 a real joy to use – I look forward to trying it again next season. It may also have a place for some dangerous game hunting, although the top end calibre is limited to .375 – a little light for elephant and buffalo. However, this fast-handling offering from Merkel would certainly be up to adequacy for both big cat and bear hunting.

The .30-06 test rifle was married to a Kahles 1.5-6x42 Helia scope, and after only initial laser bore sighting it consistently shot 1in three-shot groups at 100 yards using Norma 180-grain Dual Core ammunition. I was impressed with both its handling and accuracy. Personally, I like the set trigger system, and it helped achieve good groups on the range; I can see it would be a real advantage when stalking. But when driven boar shooting, the crisp trigger is perfectly adequate – the set trigger is pretty much impractical during driven game hunting, of course.

Overall this solid, well-balanced rifle with its quick-change barrel facility should suit UK stalkers, European boar hunters and possibly those going on safari. **PC**

---

**MERKEL KR1**

*Model tested:* KR1 switch-barrel (tested in .30-06)

*Price range:* £2,500

*Contact:* Viking Arms  01423 780810
**www.vikingarms.com**

---

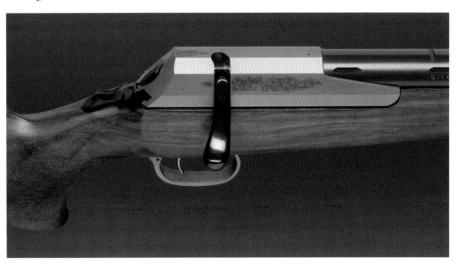

# NOSLER MODEL 48

When anyone mentions the name Nosler, the first thing that springs to mind for most sporting rifle owners is bullet heads, such as the Partition and Ballistic tip, which other ammunition manufacturers also use. These high-performance bullets need a rifle of similar quality, so Nosler decided to make just such a rifle, with a guaranteed accuracy of 1MOA or less when using its ammunition. The Nosler Custom Model 48 rifle comes in three models: the cheaper Trophy Grade, the Varmint and the model on review, the more expensive Custom Sporter in .308.

When I first handled the Nosler Custom Sporter, my initial reaction was to question its RRP of £2,400 as it does not immediately have the look or feel of what many people would call a top-end rifle. Nosler says: "The Model 48 breaks the myth that accurate rifles must be heavy. They all weigh just under eight pounds and deliver guaranteed sub-MOA groups." Most rifles take little time for me to appreciate what they are all about, but this one, I have to be honest, took some time and many shots.

The stock, designed by Nosler, is fully synthetic, using layers of Kevlar and carbon, resulting in a rigid and light (1½lb) chassis. The black, speckled grey-coloured finish is textured for superior grip obviously designed for tough, arduous conditions.

The rear of the butt is high, reasonably straight combed (the drop is ¾in), and sports a cheekpiece and a superb recoil pad, offering increased levels of comfort for the heavier calibres. Once removed, the action is only bedded to the front, and has quite a small recoil lug, which I found surprising. However, Nosler tells me this is its preferred technique, allowing the rest of the action to be fully independent of the stock.

The external metalwork is protected using Cerakote, which is a ceramic film that guards the rifle from the harshest of hunting conditions. Most of the internal surfaces have a coat of Micro Slick, which helps reduce friction and wear, including the internal parts of the bolt. The top of the

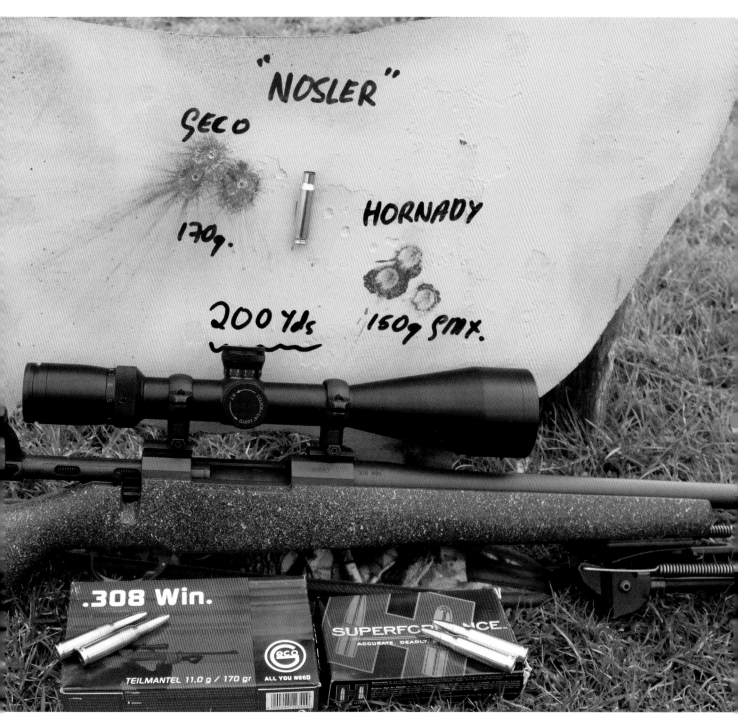

rounded receiver is pre-tapped, ready to take a wide variety of Weaver-style blocks.

The bolt has six shallow flutes with two locking lugs, and it cycles smoothly throughout its travel. There is a series of vent holes in its body, useful in the event of primer failure, making much of the firing spring mechanism visible. Rounds are ejected using a large claw extractor and plunger ejector system with a one-piece steel handle – easy to grip on cycling. I have been told that the M48 Nosler has a greater percentage of its weight in the action, resulting in a well balanced rifle.

The 24in barrel is built by Pac-Nor, a renowned manufacturer of high-quality tubes. It is fully free-floating, hand-lapped, lightweight and made of stainless steel to the highest standards. With a twist rate of 1 in 12in, it will be suitable for anything from the lighter 140-grain to heavier 175-grain bullets.

Nosler uses its own 'Rifle Basix' fully adjustable trigger assembly set to 2.5lb. The one-piece trigger guard and floor plate are made of a high-quality

alloy, emblazoned with the Nosler logo and finished to a high standard. It is a top loader, so to drop a maximum of three rounds from the magazine, just press the easy-to-use release lever located to the front of the trigger guard. For safety, a three-position catch is located to the right of the action – rear position locks the bolt and trigger, middle position locks the trigger but leaves the bolt free to cycle, and forward is fire.

The more I handled the Nosler Sporter, the more I could see and feel the superior quality of its build and design. Would it perform in testing conditions at both short and long range?

Supplied with the Nosler was the Weaver Super Slam Euro 3-9x56 scope with a 30mm tube. Standard bases were required, so I used Millett standard bases and Millett Angle-Loc adjustable rings. After making use of a collimator, I was ready to venture down to the range. For ammunition, the distributor had supplied some impressive Hornady Superformance 150-grain GMX, belting out at a sizzling 2,940fps, while I also used a box of Geco 170-grain soft-points with an MV of 2,656fps.

For this test, I decided to set the zero at 100 yards. For the sound moderator, Jackson Rifles kindly sent an over-barrelled modular A-TEC Maxim 4, which extended the length by 4½in, weighing a miserly 370 grams.

One must make allowances when first shooting new rifles. They rarely shoot to their full potential for the first 25-50 rounds. I found zero quickly thanks to the easily adjustable Super Slam, and achieved a grouping around 1¼in without too much difficulty. Nosler guarantees ¾MOA accuracy using its own ammunition, which made me sure I could extract an improved performance after further practice. After several shots, the Hornady achieved a group of under 1in and the Geco 1.2in.

As for the Rifle Basix trigger, at 2.5lb it is crisp and feels just right. Despite testing in freezing conditions with a temperature of -2 degrees, I found the bolt very smooth, feeding the Hornady rounds through to the breech with little or no resistance at all. I had problems with the nose of the blunter, soft-pointed Geco 170-grain ammunition being pushed into the front of the

inner magazine box. This is annoying and I hope it is a one-off, but if you shoot heavier bullets, try before you buy.

The Sporter is a light hunting rifle chambered in .308, so despite the addition of the Maxim moderator, the recoil was very apparent. It comes back at you in a firm, controlled manner, but within expectations for a light unit.

The texture of the stock and narrow pistol grip gave me a firm hold on the rifle, especially with gloves. One colleague, who is blessed with hands like shovels, found the trigger too close to the pistol grip, resulting in him either slipping the palm away from the grip or pulling the trigger with the base of the finger. After further investigation, I realised I had a similar problem despite my smaller hands, but found it was fine when using gloves. A raised cheekpiece would be useful, especially when using the larger optics that sit higher than most general purpose riflescopes.

I deviated from the Hornady factory ammunition for a while to see if the accuracy varied a little and found that 165-grain home-loaded Hornady SSTs (2,650fps) gave me a tighter sub-¾in group. Now that was more like it!

Now that I was happy with the first test, I packed the rifle up and called upon experienced stalkers Matt and Chris. WMS in Wales was our next port of call, courtesy of Andrew Venables. As this rifle purports to be a custom-built rifle, I was expecting it to perform well out to distances well beyond those of most responsible hunters. To do this, I decided to upgrade the optics to a NXS Nightforce 8-32x56.

After playing at ranges between 200 and 500 yards with accuracies of about 1MOA in winds of 5-10mph, we picked a 10in disc at 800 yards to really test this custom build. Matt was using high quality 168-grain match-grade ammunition (MV 2,750fps) resulting in consistent hits, showing no less accuracy than the two high-quality military sniper rifles that were also on test. Impressive for a lightweight hunting rifle, and OTT for its designed purpose, but it demonstrates the quality of engineering.

So what is my final conclusion? To be honest, I am undecided. It is a well designed, purpose-built hunting rifle, and I have no doubt it will put up

with the most arduous of conditions – but is it value for money? At £2,400, it is in the high-quality Sauer market and the lower end of the well known European brands such as Mauser and Blaser. The Nosler Custom is able to maintain and guarantee accuracy despite its light weight, but that is not unique in today's market.

Imagine the question being asked when you turn up for a highland stalk or a plains game hunt. 'Good morning Sir, what are shooting with today?' asks the stalker or PH. 'Well actually, I have the Nosler.' Does that work for you? If you want something quirky and different, this could be for you. The more I shot the Nosler, the more I took a shine to it, and I can accept it has something extra to maybe justify the price – but as a local gun shop said to me: "Will customers pay £2,400 for an American rifle, compared to a German equivalent? Some will; many won't." **TP**

I first came across Nosler rifles by mistake. Browsing through a gun trading website for a new rifle, my search for a 7-08 Rem gave up half a dozen results. Of these only two tickled my fancy, and a Nosler Custom 48 was one of them. It seemed to tick all the boxes, apart from the 'price' box, but still I liked what I read. It seemed functionally spot-on, with a simple, robust action that had a satisfying familiarity. I was soon politely asking the distributor if I could have one on test.

If I think of Nosler, I think of bullets. Indeed, I reload their 55-grain ballistic tips in my .22-250. It may seem an odd move for a bullet manufacturer to turn its hand to rifles, but if any company knows about the importance of precision engineering, it's a high-grade bullet maker. Still, it is a completely different set of skills and I was eager to understand the process Nosler had gone through to make its rifles.

Unlike the established gunmakers we are all familiar with, Nosler doesn't make any part of the rifle itself. Instead it outsources all the components, identifying and commissioning where necessary, so each part of the rifle adheres to its exacting specifications. These are then assembled in the Nosler factory. This is even more effective than producing everything in house, as the best companies can be called upon to work in their specialised fields. What Nosler essentially does is create a custom rifle with the best components available and offer it to its customers as a completed package.

As we all know, a good barrel is an essential part of an accurate rifle, and Nosler has been careful with its selection process. Button rifled, hand lapped and relieved, Pac-Nor has a good reputation and helps Nosler provide a ¾in-at-100-yards group guarantee using its own branded ammo. Screw-cut as an option, it is fitted with a standard sporter profile. Like the rest of the metal work it has been finished with Cerekote, with the internal moving parts coated with a Micro Slick dry lubricant.

Cerekote is an excellent weather-resistant, hardwearing ceramic-based finish. This provides the action with a self-lubricating property, as the tiny ceramic particles polish against one another. Riflecraft is currently the official UK dealer for Cerekote, offering it as an extra on Kimber rifles as well as for anyone looking to customise their own rifle. Barrelled actions can be coated in a choice of colours for £160, with whole rifles coming in about £270. Having seen the process myself, I immediately got two of my rifles done, and the rest will soon be following. A similar effect to the Micro Slick lubrication can be achieved with Tuf-Glide from Sentry Solutions. Available from www.forestandhill. co.uk, this specialised oil dries to leave a dry lubrication and is excellent on working parts such as bolts and triggers.

The Model 48 Custom is fitted with a commissioned synthetic stock from Bell and Carlson. Manufactured with hand-laid Kevlar and carbon fibre, this provides strength and

durability in a lightweight platform. The whole series is finished in the same mottled grey colour and what Nosler brands as its 'C2 treatment'. This basically renders the stock chemical and weather-resistant, while providing a textured, grippable surface.

As you would expect, the barrel is free-floating, with the action glass bedded on stainless steel pillars. The bottom metal is also bedded. Although better than most of the factory bedding jobs I've seen, for a rifle that is almost in a semi-custom league I expected a bit more refinement and attention to detail when it came to finishing the internals of the stock. The rifle is also fitted with a recoil reducer inside the butt. I can't say I really noticed any tangible difference, although in .308 Win and unmoderated I was happy enough to shoot it all day.

Now we turn to the heart of the rifle, which is of course the action. The Model 48 action is a solidly constructed and well thought-out design that has stood the test of time. It shares certain characteristics with the old Sako Forrester, and more recently the Howa 1500 action. In fact, apart from some alterations to the aesthetic machining on top of the action, there is little

difference at all. The bolt also remains largely the same, with twin locking lugs, a long sprung claw extractor and a plunger ejector. The bolt shroud has been re-designed, and instead of the simple spaced circular ports on the Howa's shaft, the Nosler has flutes and oval gas vents. The bolt knob has also been altered, with a knurling band aiding grip, while the underneath of the receiver is practically identical.

There is of course nothing wrong with taking the Howa action as the blueprint. It is based on a strong Sako design and is currently one of the best designs on the market, especially if we look at value for money. The idea of taking a proven design to use as a basis for building a rifle is also nothing new. Many of the semi-custom rifles around the world are based on Remington 700 actions, with refined and precision after-market copies of these actions being used for fully customised rifles. On a recent trip to Africa I was surprised to find that many of my hunting colleagues had opted to use Howa 1500 actions for their custom commissions, as opposed to the default Remy choice seen in the UK. Lastly we get to the trigger and bottom metal. Again Nosler has outsourced here, obtaining

its specification trigger from Rifle Basix, a respected aftermarket trigger manufacturer based in the States. Breaking at a crisp 2lb, you're unlikely to have any complaints in this department. Fitted in the same place as a Howa, the three-position safety is also identical. The floor plate is fitted nicely, coated with the same weather-resistant finish as the rest of the rifle, and is bedded into the stock. Some hunters may prefer a magazine, and this is available as an extra.

This particular model comes with a ¾MOA guarantee, which is one of the

tightest-grouping factory rifle guarantees on the market. Of course, the caveat to this is that Nosler expects hunters to use its own 'prescribed' ammunition to achieve it. Unfortunately I couldn't get my hands on any loaded Nosler ammo, and had to make do with what I had in the cupboard. Shooting a variety of Federal, Winchester, Hornady and Geco, I achieved consistent results from 150 grains up to 168 grains, but nothing that showed the rifle performing to its advertised potential. The very limited time I spent working up handloads did show a marked improvement, though, and I have no doubt that Nosler's promise will hold true.

Nosler certainly undertook an ambitious project when it ventured into the world of rifle production. The concept is a solid one: pulling together the best producers of each component to assemble the 'perfect' Nosler rifle. On paper it seems to have all the answers, although at £2,400 the price might put wallet-conscious hunters off. That said, I hear that Nosler has also released a few models with more affordable price tags. They might be just right for UK rifle shooters. **BP**

**NOSLER MODEL 48**

***Model tested:*** Model 48 Custom in .308

***Price range:*** £2,400

***Contact:*** Highland Outdoors
0845 099 0252
**www.highlandoutdoors.co.uk**

# REMINGTON 700

The importer of the Remington brand asked me which rifle I wanted to review. Well, which should I choose? On my wish list were the models that are at the top end of the range, so I asked for either the Sendero chambered in .300 Win Mag or the VSSF. As I unpacked a variety of rifles, scopes and mounts, I immediately saw I had been sent a Remington 700 VSSF II in a sizzling .220 Swift. Immediately, I took pity on any foxes, crows and rabbits around the farm, as long-range varminting is my passion. Indeed, the VSSF stands for Varmint Stainless Steel Fluted.

Most shooters are familiar with the Remington rifle and I will not harp on about the standard features other than the easily recognisable bolt knob and action, as this rifle has most of the bells and whistles generally associated with more expensive custom rifles. This is not a budget build. We have a stock designed and made by a specialist maker, and a great-looking fluted barrel that tells me this should be a very capable varminter.

I like to concentrate on how a rifle feels, shoots and performs when used for the application it is intended, so I will try not to get too bogged down with technical details. If you like detail, go to the Remington website and fill your boots.

As soon as I lifted the VSSF out of the box, the imposing H-S precision varmint styled stock made me want to grab hold of it and quickly lift it to the shoulder. In short, it felt great. The composite stock is reinforced with green aramid polyamide fibres that result in a stiff and hard-wearing chassis, aided by an integral aluminium bedded block system. I would call the stock a chunky functional design – the ambidextrous palm swell is very prominent, as is the wide, target-styled forend. Wrapping my hand around the pistol grip, I immediately felt that perfect fit of the palm and trigger finger. A great start.

Moving on to the ironwork, both the standard length Remington action and fluted barrel are made of high quality 416 stainless steel. The 26in spin-polished barrel is made with six black powder-coated, 20in long flutes, designed to help heat dissipation if not to reduce a little weight. The .220 Swift barrel is hammer forged and comes with a 1-in-14in twist, 0.8in at the muzzle, and is finished off with a shallow target

crown. This rifle also came with a 18mm x 1 thread for a moderator or muzzle brake.

The bolt has a great looking jewelled finish, making it stand out from the more common models. It cycles smoothly, with the ammunition fed from a floor-plated system. The release levers for the bolt and floor plate are located to the front of the trigger assembly, but within the trigger guard. Both are reasonably easy to find and press.

Another surprise was the new X-Mark Pro trigger, which is now fitted as standard across the Remington range. It can easily be adjusted with the aid of a 1/16in hex-headed key, supplied with the rifle. A screw is located within the trigger blade, making adjustment easy from two to five pounds. When dry firing, it seemed to be very crisp with no creep whatsoever, so it felt like a high-quality mechanism.

Other things to note are the two-position safety catch located to the right of the action and the handy twin QD mounts on the forend, one for a bipod and the other for a sling. Both the trigger guard and floor plate are aluminium, with a high-quality finish, far from being just a cheap afterthought.

To sum up the VSSF, the action and barrel are beautifully finished, as is the bolt and floor plate, supported by a high-quality stock and bedding system. It gave me the feeling that it has all the attributes of a highly accurate rifle, ideal for long-range varminting.

Supplied with the rifle was a Weaver Super Slam 3-9x56 scope with a 30mm tube. In

common with most Remingtons, the base mounts had to be screwed into the action first before fitting the rings, all of which are made by Millett. The Millett Angle-Loc rings are able be adjusted sideways, which is useful if you are having problems in centralising the windage of your scope.

As the .220 Swift is a noisy round, I borrowed a MAE T12 Standard moderator from Julian Savory of JMS Arms. For the ammunition, I used Norma 50-grain soft-nose bullets and Hornady 55-grain V-Max Super Varmint, flying out at 4,000 and 3,680fps and supplied by RUAG and Edgar Brothers respectively. Considering they are very flat,

fast-moving projectile bullets, I settle for a 200-yard zero – a 225- to 250-yard zero may suit it even better, but I am used to this set-up with my other rifles.

I adjusted to zero in five rounds, with the Weaver Super Slam tracking logically without any large jumps. With the use of a bipod and no solid rear support, emulating conditions in the field on live game, the Norma achieved a 1.5in grouping and the Hornady a shade smaller at 1.2in with a 200-yard zero. I have no doubt that groups of less than 1in or 0.5MOA could be easily accomplished without the light winds and more secure support to the rear of the stock. In short, it

shoots better than I do – although I suppose that's not that hard.

Since the VSSF is a varmint rifle, it was rude not to take it out to 300 and 400 yards and try it out on my side-facing fox target. This resulted in groups of 2.5in and 3.5in (6in and 15in drop respectively).

As soon as I was confident of the accuracy, and more importantly, I was fully conversant with the trigger, bolt and ammunition feed, it was off to do a bit of night shooting. This resulted in one of the best looking dog foxes I have dispatched for years. After I had spotted a couple of very lamp-shy Charlies, this one just sat on the top of the river bank some 200 yards away, letting me gain a safer position in terms of backdrop without any concern about the noise of our shooting wagon. I picked a spot just above the white blaze his chest to lethal effect from 150 yards. Interestingly enough, the bullet did not exit the animal, demonstrating the fantastic fragmentation of the Hornady 55-grain V-Max bullet.

So how does the Remington VSSF feel? I adjusted the trigger down to 2.7lb, which was as low as I could get it, but despite me being used to very light triggers, the X-Mark Pro was predictable and a delight to use. Recoil was

minimal owing to the rifle's unladen weight of 8.5lb – heavier than many hunting rifles, but this is a varminter. The only niggle, which caused me to be too slow on my first fox, was the Hornady ammunition not loading from the magazine. The Norma soft-nosed bullets were fine, but the pointed ballistic tips seemed to foul before entering the rear of the barrel chamber. I expect this would be the same for all ballistic-tipped ammunition, not just Hornady.

The palm swell and pistol grip gave me total control, and the texture of the finish enhanced the feeling of the rifle. Ok, a 26in barrel is not

the easiest rifle to shoot in confined spaces – but this is a specialised rifle and is not really designed for deer stalking.

With a recommended retail price of £2,030, the VSSF, in my opinion, offers a fantastic alternative to those who feel that accuracy can only be guaranteed with a custom build. It is also available in .204 Ruger, .223 and .22-250 – and I am certainly tempted to buy the .204 for shooting crows out to 300-400 yards. Overall I was very impressed with the quality and performance of VSSF. In my opinion, it ticks all the boxes. **TP**

### REMINGTON 700

*Model tested:* 700 VSSF in .220 Swift

*Price range:* £2,030

*Contact:* Remington UK  01206 795333
**www.sportsmk.co.uk**

# REMINGTON VTR

Despite the vast number of rifles that pass through my cabinet for testing, this was the first time a Remington had made its way to me – mainly because there wasn't much that excited me about doing a review on a Remy. Not because of anything particularly negative about one of the most popular rifles in existence, but because there isn't a lot that hasn't been said already. I have handled plenty over the years, with a number of my good hunting friends furnishing their armouries with the classic model 700. However, when the VTR (Varmint Tactical Rifle) came along I couldn't resist getting my hands on it – it's not every day a rifle comes along that makes me do a double take.

The VTR, like most of Remington's rifles, is based on the famous model 700 action. Launched in 1962, it became the biggest selling rifle of its time. Today the model 700 is the all-time best selling sporting bolt-action in the world. When it was originally conceived, the design concept focused on the rifle being easy to manufacture, which kept prices down. The round action is machined from a single bar stock, while the recoil lug is essentially a jammed washer held between the barrel and action. This allowed for a simple automated machining process, and the ability to mass-produce is one of the reasons for Remington's runaway success.

At the time plenty of rifle enthusiasts laughed at the idea of Remington's 700, tarring it with the 'cheap and nasty' brush. However, there was no denying it was a good-looking rifle and, being so competitively priced, it took the market by storm with its 'three rings of steel' – the recessed bolt face, chamber end of the barrel and front receiver ring all encasing the cartridge head. As well as reliability, the rifle gained a reputation for being accurate out of the box, and soon won over those who had shunned the new model.

The market was tough to crack, especially with favourites such as the Winchester model 70 imbedded in the hunting psyche. Remington had some luck, though, as two years later the much-loved pre-64 model 70 saw an upgrade that did not please gun critics or the market. Undoubtedly this helped the Remy 700's takeover of the American market. It continued to gain popularity, and myriad after-market accessories followed as the number of Remy 700s grew. Today more 'bolt-ons' are available for the model 700 than any other rifle. It also found favour with those wanting to build custom rifles, using the action to build their dream hunting combo.

There is no doubt that the Remy 700 has fans and is a reliable rifle that serves millions of people around the world. But what would I make of the VTR now I had to cast a critical eye over it for a review?

The most striking part of the VTR is its futuristic triangular barrel. According to the Remington literature, the VTR is a "revolutionary system optimised for extended-range precision and mobility". The explanation for the radical barrel profile is down to "years of rigorous research and development focused on reducing weight, enhancing rigidity and promoting rapid heat dissipation". This is a useful design quality, and pertinent for shooting extended strings. It is easy to see that varmint hunters may find it particularly useful, but whether any of this makes a difference in the field is another matter.

The first point to investigate further is the claim of "enhanced rigidity". There is a lot of maths that we could go into, and I am not going to bore you with screeds of formula here, but will try and help you visualise Remington's assertions.

The formula for rigidity can be viewed (to the best of my understanding) as the formula for the moment of inertia, so shorter, fatter barrels will be stiffer. Anything that removes

we have a greater surface area (constrained by weight, as we have already said), but further to that the triangular barrel offers a particularly useful quality when it comes to dispersing heat.

Varmint barrels take a lot longer to heat up than sporter profiles as they consist of more material. Warming up from the bore outwards, the heat takes longer to reach the external surface, and this is dissipated over a larger surface area. The flipside of this is that once a varmint barrel heats up, it takes longer to cool than a sporter. With a triangular barrel, three sides sit very close to the bore, allowing heat to travel quickly to the surface and cool, while also being dissipated over a larger surface area than a sporter profile. A fluted barrel works in a similar way – a triangular barrel is basically a form of fluting. It appears that Remington's claims ring true on paper.

Any tangible benefit is difficult to test in the field because it would involve matching barrel weights perfectly to keep tests fair. I will have to provide a subjective evaluation.

The rifle handles nicely – its stock may be a fairly cheap injection-moulded affair, but

material from a standard barrel shape, such as fluting, will essentially reduce the stiffness of the barrel. So reducing the amount of material to bring a round barrel down to a triangle also reduces stiffness. However, what is important here is producing the stiffest barrel possible for a given barrel weight. You can look at this as triangles inside circles, or circles inside triangles.

The bull barrel has a lot more material, and therefore weight, than the equivalent diameter triangle barrel, and will be stiffer. But looking at it the other way round, a triangular barrel will be stiffer than the sporter barrel that could fit inside its dimensions. Essentially, for a given weight you are able to get a stiffer barrel with greater surface area from a triangular shape than a standard profile. This also takes care of the "promoting rapid heat dissipation" part of Remington's marketing spiel. Here

it's a nice compromise between a varmint and stalking profile. The rigid frame combined with rubberised inserts is pleasing, and functionally I can't complain. Most people are familiar with the model 700 action, and there are no surprises here. I have never liked the 'c-clip' extractor on a Remy, preferring the sturdier sprung claw on a Howa, but it still works.

The bolt cycles as expected – neither particularly slick or noticeably restricted. The push feed and ejection is positive and the lock-up on the twin lugs is nice and snug without having to be forced. Not following recent trends, the safety is just a two-position, found at the right-hand side of the bolt shroud. It is noisy to operate unless you apply reasonable pressure and consciously release it softly.

Machined as a round receiver, the recoil lug is not an integral part of the action – this is my biggest grumble with Remingtons. Essentially, the barrel is threaded longer than the action, allowing a recoil washer to be jammed between the two pieces of steel. This is efficient from a manufacturing perspective, but not the strongest of designs – that said, many very accurate rifles have been built on the 700.

One of the biggest improvements over the years has been Remington's triggers – historically heavy and pretty terrible compared

to European competitors. The new X-Mark Pro trigger, introduced in 2009, is a marked improvement. Adjustable down to 3lb on the spec, it will turn down a little more with an external hex screw. I have to say, I was impressed. Nice and crisp with a wide trigger blade – thumbs up to Remington.

Returning to the barrel, it sits on a pressure band at the end of the stock instead of being

free floating. I am unsure why, but assume Remington found it was required to tune barrel harmonics. I haven't tested the rifle with a fully floated barrel, but noted a small reduction in accuracy shooting from a bipod compared with the sandbag.

Now we get on to how the rifle shoots. Very well is the short answer. I got lucky with bullet selection as it ate up the 50-grain Hornady V-Max on my initial firing. Consistently clustering three shots, there isn't much more to say. It can definitely shoot.

This rifle looks like it's been dragged straight from Gears of War (sorry oldies, younger generation reference). But it's built on an action that has stood the test of time and, although I am not particularly fond of a few aspects, millions of rifle owners tell us that it works and works well. The only thing that will seriously affect its popularity in the UK is an aspect I have omitted until this point: the rifle comes with a built-in muzzle brake. As it should, it whips out some of the recoil, but not to the same extent as a good moderator – and, of course, fitting a moderator is not an option. This is the main hurdle the VTR has to overcome on British soil – but if there's a rifle with the quality to overcome it, it's this. **BP**

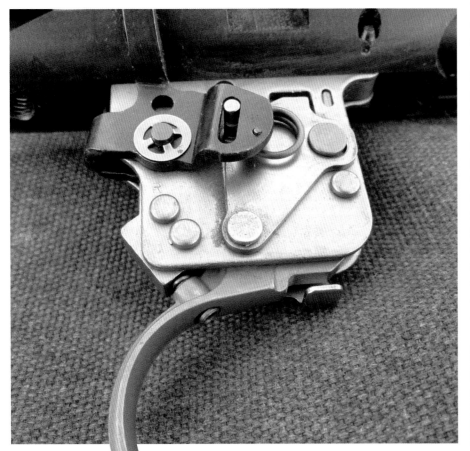

| **REMINGTON VTR** | |
|---|---|
| *Model tested:* | 700 VTR in .243 |
| *Price range:* | Around £1,193 |
| *Contact:* | Remington UK  01206 795333 **www.sportsmk.co.uk** |

# RPA HIGHLAND STALKER

Having owned an RPA rifle for several years, I was pleased to see a long-action model added to their list of sporting rifles. As ever, I will review this rifle based on its practical performance as well as how it copes when faced with live game in the highlands of Scotland.

The Highland Stalker comes in .270, .25-06, .30-06 and 6.5x55 and is specifically built for the hunter who has a preference for a long-action rifle. RPA International is renowned for its highly accurate rifles, and many rifle makers use RPA's proven actions.

The heart of any RPA is the robust Quadlite action, which as its name suggests uses a bolt with four lugs on the front to lock into the action. The whole assembly is very well built, if not over-engineered, but it does guarantee nothing is taken for granted in terms of quality. The bolts slide very smoothly, and when pulled back to eject, the lug grips the case very firmly, ensuring a very positive ejection. The plastic bolt knob and angle of the

handle give the cycling process a firm and positive feel, especially at speed when a quick follow-up shot is required in the field. This model comes with a three-shot magazine as standard, but a five-shot one is also available at extra cost. To release it, squeeze a catch located to the right side of the magazine, and out it drops.

Whenever anyone tries an RPA, the first thing they comment on is invariably the fantastic trigger. Coming from a target stable, RPA rifles use the company's own two-stage trigger with a pull set at one pound as standard. There is a distinctive feel when the trigger reaches the second stage of the pull. If you are used to heavier triggers, be a little careful with this one, especially when wearing gloves – it is easy to 'pull off' too early just as you are acquiring the target. The safety catch, which lies to the right of the action, is quite simply forward to shoot and push to the rear for safety, although it can be a little fiddly on some occasions.

The Highland Stalker has a high quality solid synthetic stock made of reinforced epoxy with Kevlar and glass fibre. This medium-weight stock is very strong compared to many others, and grips well in cold and wet conditions. The stock can also be lengthened by removing the butt pad and inserting some rubber spacers. It also comes with an adjustable cheekpiece, which is very useful when using larger optics, and accommodates both right- and left-handed shooters.

Once again, the emphasis of the rifle is accuracy, so it uses a near fully fluted varmint-style barrel (1-in-10in twist) and comes with a 17mm x 1mm screw thread for a moderator or muzzle brake. My existing RPA has shot over 2,500 rounds; when I inspected it, there were no signs of wear and the muzzle crown was as clean as the day I picked it up, despite using a moderator. It is made of high-quality stainless steel that will not alter the point of impact, even after a session on the range using multiple shots.

For this test, the rifle came with a Zeiss 6-24x56mm Diavari using Weaver mounts

and standard bases, but a Picatinny rail can be easily fitted if required at extra cost. Also, I fitted a 6-12in Harris bipod to the front sling attachment point. The rifle weighs 10.2lb (4.6kg), which makes it a few pounds heavier than most sporting rifles but means it is heavy enough that shooters can fire many rounds without knocking themselves about too much.

I wanted to test this rifle both in the field and at long distances, to see if the Highland Stalker could not only attract the sporting rifleman but also the person who enjoys a little bit of target practice. I also aimed to answer the question: Is the Highland Stalker effective for highland stalking?

At a zero of 150 yards, 150-grain Norma with Nosler Ballistic tips at 2,950fps shot off the bipod achieved a grouping of about one inch and for the long-range test I used some specially made 190-grain Matchking HPBT (2,650fps), which achieved a similar grouping. This would no doubt improve if I spent more time practising supporting the rear of the rifle stock, but most of my shooting in the field is done off the bipod.

My colleagues Matt and Darren immediately took to the Highland Stalker. They both told me it felt just right. The stock allowed a firm grip; along with the raised cheekpiece and the two-stage trigger, this made it a delight to shoot. Being a .30-06, the recoil, while very apparent, was more

than comfortable, no doubt helped by the design and quality of the stock.

After zeroing, it was time to test the long-range ability of the rifle. Using the 190-grain Match ammo, we tested it at ranges from 400 yards to 700 yards in a very light crosswind. As pictured overleaf, the Highland Stalker achieved consistent hits on the smaller crow and frontal fox targets at 400 and 500 yards respectively. At 700 yards, I adjusted 15in of wind and 142in of elevation, and all hits on the disc target were within an 8-9in grouping. Considering that the inconsistent wind was accounting for 3-5in of variation in drift, this is obviously a very well put together and accurate rifle that a multi-skilled rifleman could have also have fun with on the range.

In Scotland, we carried the Highland Stalker in a Country Covers drag bag, and it was immediately apparent that this was not the lightest of rifles for the highlands. It weighed in at 13.5lb (including scope, ammo and bipod but no moderator) – although the drag bag, with its

shoulder straps, made it much more comfortable to carry.

The weather was very wet and cold, and matters were not helped by our stalkers Matt and Tommo, who took great delight in dragging us through various peat hags and burns before finding our quarry. Using the Norma 150-grain ammo, Darren and I had no problems quickly dispatching several hinds, most of which were at distances of 150-250 yards. Despite winds in excess of 30mph, the rifle always held steady, giving all of us confidence when pulling the trigger.

I generally use scopes with target turrets, so adjusting the point of impact becomes second nature to me at longer distances. I wrap some masking tape around the elevation turret and then mark the range adjustments on it that have been tested for the required ammunition. I also note the drop and windage values in inches on the inside of my Butler Creek lens covers for easy access. While anything over 250 yards could be labelled as excessive when shooting large game, most stalkers have a rangefinder, and to be able

to put the reticle on killing zone at 300-400 yards is a blessing if you have a wounded animal that requires another shot to dispatch it quickly on the hills.

I have been an RPA fan for several years, so perhaps I am being a little biased when I sing the praises of this capable rifle. The only downside of the Highland Stalker is perhaps its weight, but having weighed several medium- to heavy-barrelled guns, geared up with high-quality optics, bipods and moderators, I have to say this gun is not excessive. For everyday stalking, the gun is very well balanced and easy to use off bipods or sticks, but you can also have some fun on the range. So perhaps the Highland Stalker is more of an all-rounder than its name makes out.

It is available from many gun dealers at £3,150 plus VAT – so it is in the custom end of the rifle market, but with off-the-shelf guaranteed

accuracy. Don't forget: included within this price is a rifle case, bore guide and Weaver base mounts. From personal experience, my .243 thumbhole Hunter is a darling to shoot, accounting for hundreds of foxes in Sussex, but at the same time, it shoots 75-grain Hornady V-Max bullets out to 1,000 yards with faultless accuracy. Once again this demonstrates the versatility of the brand.

All I have to do now is persuade my shooting colleague Darren to give me back the Highland Stalker or part with some of his hard-earned cash. Enough said. **TP**

### RPA HIGHLAND STALKER

**Model tested:** Highland Stalker hunting rifle in .30-06

**Price range:** From £3,150

**Contact:** Rangemaster Precision Arms 0845 880 3222 www.rangemasterprecisionarms.com

# RUGER SCOUT

The Ruger Gunsite Scout .308 is an interesting-looking rifle, and one that doesn't give away its identity too lightly. The original 'Scout rifle' concept was apparently thought up by the American small arms expert Colonel Jeff Cooper some 30 years ago, being no longer than one metre with a forward-mounted scope, no heavier than 3kg and in the .308 calibre. It was designed for both the military and law enforcement, being able to do anything and go anywhere – but at the same time it can cross over to the hunter, who can acquire beasts up to 500lb. So it is short, light and can be used with a variety of aiming systems. Is this really possible?

The Ruger 'Gunsite' Scout Rifle is modelled on the robust and reliable Ruger M77 action, with the controlled round feed and integral scope mounts. The name 'Gunsite' comes from the name of a shooting school founded by Colonel Cooper; the design and concept was the result of a joint venture between the two parties.

The 16.5in medium contour, matte silver barrel is the most unusual aspect of the rifle, allowing it to be used in tight confines such as law enforcement and working within police vehicles. The muzzle brake and thread have been removed owing to USA export restrictions, which could make an interesting rifle to shoot considering the calibre and shortened barrel design.

An unusual feature of this rifle is its ability to have three different types of aiming system. Firstly, the forward mounted and sturdy Picatinny rail is screwed directly into the barrel. One would think this would interfere with the harmonics, thereby affecting accuracy, but it does allow the mounting of a long eye relief scope or any type of optic to allow shooting with both eyes open for fast target acquisition. Secondly, the regular telescopic sight can be mounted on top of the action using the unique Ruger mounts supplied with the rifle.

Lastly, and first to be tested, were the open sights that consist of a rear-mounted, fully adjustable 'peep' or 'ghost ring' sight, which can be easily removed if a telescopic sight is required. The foresight is a simple post and sits between two slightly rounded protectors to help the shooter as it lines up easily with the peep-hole sight when aimed.

The stock is made from a durable wood laminate in an attractive grey colour with easy to grip chequering around the pistol grip and forend. The recoil pad is very soft, which is useful for what should be a snappy, lightweight .308. Another useful attribute is the stock length, which can be adjusted 1.5in by fitting 0.5in spacers – very useful when wearing a thick winter jacket requiring a short stock, and conversely in the summer wearing thinner clothes when a longer stock would be needed.

The unit comes with a 10-shot magazine as standard. Release is simple – just push forward the exposed lever positioned to the front of the reinforced nylon trigger guard.

So we have a short-barrelled, compact unit with a total length of 38-39.5in, with a hard-wearing stock, weighing in at 7lb. What exactly is the primary function of the Ruger Gunsite Scout? Is it a stalking gun? Is it best suited to quick target acquisition or running game such as boar? Or is it a big

boy's toy that is thrown in with the specialised target rifles and used as a bit of fun with open sights down the range?

Immediate impressions usually give me a good idea of how I should review a rifle. When I lifted it out of the packing box, its short build, large magazine with a long Picatinny rail bolted to the barrel and open sights told me this review was going to include an element of fun.

The first thing I did was lengthen the stock by an inch to accommodate my long arms. When I and several of my colleagues picked it up, our first comments were the same – we all said it felt pleasant and was obviously very pointable. As it was a new rifle, the bolt cycle was stiff and edgy, which was anticipated, and the trigger was very stiff – not surprising with a 6lb pull. The 10-round magazine rattles and is very loose, which I found annoying; I have no doubt a five-round replacement would be better and more suited to stalking, but it spoils the gun.

For the test I used a range of soft-nose ammunition varying from 145 to 168 grains. The first discipline on test was the open sights

out to 100 yards. The rear peep sight easily lines up with the outer, slightly curved pillars of the foresight, leaving the eye to concentrate naturally on the central post.

Shooting with open sights is probably alien to most hunting riflemen as we tend to be accustomed to telescopic sights, but I was surprised how accurate they were once mastered. To start, it was shooting low and 5in to the left, so I loosened off the peep sight adjuster screws, rotated it three times to raise it, and at the same time adjusted it a little to the right.

Once tightened, it shot a 4in group when resting the forend in a tree stump. Not bad considering how hard it is to accurately aim any gun with open hunting sights. At 150 yards, while it was tricky to see the specific aiming point on a frontal fox, I managed four out of five hits on this 8in x 6in steel target.

Once I became accustomed to the open sights, I tested it in all shooting positions: standing, kneeling, resting against tree trunks and branches, even walking up to within 50 yards of targets. I suppose this is classed as playing, shooting many rounds on multiple targets at different ranges, but it was great practice for running boar. The recoil

was not too harsh for a .308, bearing in mind there was no moderator or muzzle brake.

To fit a telescopic sight, first remove the forward Picatinny rail and rear sight, then fit the Ruger scope mounts that come as standard with the rifle. For this test I was supplied a Minox ZA 3 3-9x40 Plex – just right for short- to medium-range stalking. Once zeroed at 100 yards, I managed a group of 1.75in using 150-grain soft nosed ammunition with the rifle attached to a bipod, which I think is respectable.

Out to 175 yards, a 3in group resulted, with a reasonably warm barrel and bearing in mind the rifle twist rate of 1 in 10in. Heavier bullets could well tighten the group. Shooting prone with a bipod and a light gun in this calibre soon becomes uncomfortable, but in all other positions the recoil was entirely manageable.

Finally, the telescopic sight was removed and the front Picatinny rail refitted. Onto it I fitted an Eotech Holographic sight. It was originally designed for the USA military, but it has apparently been found to be one of the best optics for quarry such as driven boar as it has the fastest target recognition of any sight and is designed to be used with both eyes open. This is a completely new concept to me, but the idea is fascinating.

Once turned on, a circle and dot appear through the glass lens with adjustable brightness settings to allow for night and day shooting. Bore sighting and zeroing are very similar to a normal telescopic sight and once set at 100 yards, it was time to see how well this really works.

With the rifle at the shoulder, the red aiming system is easy to see with both eyes open. It is initially quite spooky, but once used like aiming a shotgun, the 1x power optics allowed very quick acquisition of any targets at ranges out to 100-150 yards. I tried it on my simulated running boar with brilliant results from this very clever piece of equipment. It retails at £667, so is much cheaper

than most traditional European scopes and definitely worth looking into.

Two out of the three tests required the quick cycling of rounds to aid target acquisition. The M77 action often snagged, making it tricky to reload rounds. It was not the smoothest of actions despite attempts to clean and lightly lubricate it. I am sure this can be tweaked by polishing the friction surfaces where the action and bolt meet. Maybe this was a one-off, but it impeded the performance and aggravated the shooter.

From previous experiences of the Ruger action, they normally ease after several shots, but this was not the case with the Gunsite Scout, despite shooting over 200 rounds. And with 10 rounds in the magazine, the pressure from this didn't help. Another niggle was that the trigger at 6lb was tough to pull. I understand it cannot be adjusted. Perhaps, at further expense, it would be possible to have a superior aftermarket model fitted. I understand that in the USA most triggers have to be set to more than 3lb, but this trigger encouraged me to 'snap pull' (like a shotgun) when shooting free hand or from the kneeling position, affecting accuracy considerably.

After extensively testing the Ruger Gunsite Scout, I can conclude that it is a multi-discipline rifle that may be slightly biased towards the target market. Many would question the sense of using a 16.5in barrel, giving a small drop in velocity, but with most deer stalking undertaken within 150 yards, manoeuvrability and ease of carrying far outweigh an extra inch of bullet drop.

I am still tempted to add the Scout to my ever-increasing collection of guns, specifically to use it for furthering my skills of open sight shooting and woodland stalking. The superior stock does give it a nice feel, aided by the short barrel. The Minox ZA3 performed well for a £400 budget scope bearing in mind we only used it for short-distance testing. However, it is a shame that a sound moderator or muzzle brake cannot be fitted easily owing to the foresight arrangement.

As an all-rounder, the Scout is exactly that: a reasonable and capable versatile rifle. Is it value for money? The response will be seriously divided but one thing is for sure: You can practise many different disciplines of shooting with one gun, and that surely is a bonus. **TP**

| RUGER SCOUT |
| --- |
| *Model tested:* Ruger Gunsite Scout .308 |
| *Price range:* £1,142 |
| *Contact:* Viking Arms  01423 780810 **www.vikingarms.com** |

# RUGER HAWKEYE

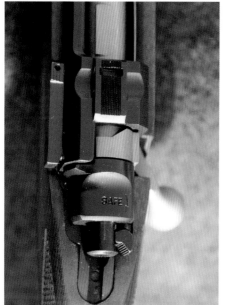

As soon as the Hawkeye was removed from its packaging, I handed it over to my fellow fox shooting colleague and experienced rifleman Darren, to see what his first impressions were – it is always good to have an alternative view. As ever, by the time you add the optics, bipod and moderator, the whole rifle changes in terms of balance and feel, but in the flesh it allows time to focus on the ergonomics and what the gun is really made up of.

"Ok, similar to the Mauser action, so should be very reliable. The stock feels very comfortable," commented Darren, despite having hands like shovels. Not a bad start I thought, so we looked in more detail at the woodwork and enjoyed the quality walnut stock but immediately noticed the forend of the stock bearing against the underside of the barrel. Nothing particularly unusual about this as many sporting guns do not require a fully floating barrel for everyday game shooting, as issues with rising barrel temperature, affecting point of impact, are not a concern. The Hawkeye models all come standard with QD mounts and set of 25mm rings (30mm extra) – the latter must not be ignored as a set of

decent mounts are not cheap. The magazine is a floor plated model, only allowing the shooter to reload through the action and to drop the contents, there is a well-placed release button to the front of the trigger guard.

As we moved onto the action, the three-position safety catch was easy to use – the rear setting applying the safety catch and locking the bolt, middle position applying just the safety but allowing the bolt to be turned and the forward position for firing. Being a new gun, we both thought the action was noisy and a little coarse but by the end of our test, this was not a concern as the cycling of ammunition was positive and crisp, especially at high speed. The 22in barrel comes with no field sights and this particular gun was screw cut, allowing me to drop my T8 Reflex moderator onto it for testing.

For this test, bearing in mind the supplied 25mm mounts, I decided to use my trusty Weaver 3-9x42mm scope that was used for many years for deer control on my .308, perfectly adequate for general purpose shooting. The T8 moderator was then fitted together with a Harris bipod, allowing now to feel the new LC6 trigger (light and crisp).

Both of us enjoyed shooting the gun and once the bipod was detached, it felt well balanced when being shot from all positions as used in the field. Even with the moderator removed, recoil was fine for a light sporting rifle helped by the comfortable stock. One thing to be aware of is that it shoots 2in lower with the bipod attached, probably caused by the increased pressure on the wood against the barrel. I understand the gun is designed for shooting freehand and resting against a soft support, so something to consider if you are used to bipods.

We both warmed to Hawkeye and agreed that the trigger was on the heavy side for a sporting rifle, but it must be mentioned that we are used to high quality and lighter triggers on all of our guns. As stated, the more we used the rifle, the more we liked it. It is lightweight and very pointable – I feel it is a very capable and rugged all-rounder suitable for knocking those foxes over as well as larger animals.

The Ruger brand has a loyal following with many shooters upgrading from the very popular 10/22 model but with a retail price of £1,000, it is not a budget rifle, maybe positioning itself between the cheaper Remington rifles and the more expensive Sauer models – perhaps on a par with Tikka. I know with the right ammunition, it can compete with the best, so what more can you ask for from a rifle? **TP**

Darren found the trigger quite heavy and not as crisp as anticipated, but very quickly he soon adapted to it. I do not believe this can be adjusted, but at a good 4lbs this will have an effect on the accuracy and when shooting the rifle a few days after this test, I was more than comfortable with it.

Once zeroed at an agreed 100 yards, as with many rifles, the accuracy varied enormously depending on the ammunition used. The .243 model comes with a tight 1 in 9in twist barrel, which I would assume should favour

the heavier bullets but in this test, the opposite was found. The 100-grain Winchester grouped at 2.5in, the federal 85-grain and my home loaded 75-grain V Max at 2in, but the Federal 70-grain Nosler ballistic tips at a respectable 1.5in. As already mentioned, the trigger did not help this but anything around 1.5in (1.5 MOA) is more than suitable for deer or fox control, and I have no doubt that a suitable and legal 100-grain combination could be found to achieve this when out on larger deer species.

Over the years I have owned a few American-made firearms, both rifles and shotguns, and I have always come to the same conclusion: American rifles are built to do the job, rather than please the eye of the beholder. Of course, there is nothing wrong with that – in fact, in a way I admire it. Recently Viking Arms was kind enough to lend me one such American rifle, an M77 Ruger Hawkeye in .243 Winchester, for field testing. I was excited to say the least, eager to see how much things had changed since my American rifle-owning days.

The first thing that struck me was the slim shape of the rifle overall – in fact it initially looked more like a .22 rimfire than a centrefire in .243 Win. The woodwork was a well-finished walnut with some graining; the chequering was sharp, well-cut and in the right places.

The classic Mauser action is too well known to describe in detail. It is old-fashioned, admittedly, but extremely reliable. Typical of this design is the amount of 'slop' encountered when the bolt is fully drawn. The full-length Mauser extractor, coupled with the fixed ejector, does the job of removing spent cases very well indeed. The bolt handle, which has been left in the white, has a distinctive look, which I find quite pleasant. The bolt handle, although designed with a cutaway, swings very high when in use – so high, in fact, that it fouled the eyepiece of on one scope I tried. Switching to another scope solved this problem – I'd recommend sticking to scopes with less bulbous eyepieces when using this rifle.

The bolt initially felt rough and it was an effort to get the bolt forward – although this is something you get to some extent with all new rifles, it particularly caught my attention on this model. Closer inspection showed that the bolt raceways had not been polished. After a bit of use and the application of a tiny amount of polishing paste, the bolt freed up quite a bit; I suspect that with a bit more time and effort, this will cease to be a problem entirely.

As mentioned earlier, ejection was very effective. The receiver has been machined from a solid billet, and has integral scope mounts. These are matched with the pair of one-inch rings, supplied by Ruger, which have their own unique locking system that ensures the scope

will not move once mounted. Incidentally, the rings are of different heights, with the higher unit mounted at the rear.

The magazine is the good old internal box type with a floor plate arrangement, loaded from the top through the receiver and supported by a blued metal cage and follower. In .243 calibre, the mag's capacity is four rounds. A hinged floor plate design, which is a bit fiddly but very secure, drops the rounds from the magazine when the catch is operated. The Hawkeye model now has a laser-etched Ruger emblem on the floor plate; while this doesn't make a difference to overall performance, it is a move towards a more attractive overall appearance.

The tapered 22in hammer-forged barrel matches the slim woodwork rather well. I used 80-grain Winchester soft points in the button-rifled barrel, as I hadn't anything heavier to hand. Results would probably have been better using 100-grain fodder, but more on that later. The barrel is stock-bedded rather than free-floating, but that didn't seem to be a problem when shooting the Hawkeye. Stock measurements were standard – I found them ideal.

When zeroing – and also when firing two or three shots in quick succession – the slim barrel heated up quite noticeably. Although this initially worried me, it did not affect accuracy – although I suspect it might begin to if I fired

a longer string of shots. However, this is purely a hunting rifle, so this is more of a theoretical concern – it is unlikely ever to happen out in the field.

Taking the rifle out to zero, I was once again stuck by its lightness. Sadly, most of us now use a moderator. While I appreciate the advantages of them, they add considerable muzzle weight to a light weapon, and to my eyes totally ruin the aesthetics of most hunting rifles. The Ruger came with one of Brügger and Thomet's moderators, nicely finished in matt grey. It weighed in at 635g. I was impressed with its performance, although to my old ears there is not a lot to choose between any of the recognised makes nowadays. This mod – as you would expect of a Swiss-made item – was very nicely presented indeed; it is made in stainless and available in either stainless or black. What is more, it is extremely long-lasting. Brügger and Thomet suggests that an occasional

dunking in solvent is all that is needed by way of maintenance, and Viking Arms tells me it should be good for 10,000 rounds, which would probably see me and most of my rifles out. Although it is not cheap (retailing at £312), in my opinion there are very few better mods on the market.

The scope for this test was one of the Hawke range of optics from Deben. Like the rifle, it is not overpriced but it does the job more than well enough. The Eclipse is a good all round scope, and at under £90 it is good value.

After bore-sighting the Hawkeye, I soon had the first four shots there or thereabouts.

A few rounds and a slight adjustment on the scope later, the little .243 was on the money, printing groups at a fraction under one inch (.977 to be exact). I felt that this could certainly be improved by using 100-grain loads, or even more – with the right load, I would expect the group size to be halved.

The LC (Light and Crisp) designated single-stage trigger consistently tripped at three and a half pounds. This is slightly heavier than I am used to, but perfectly acceptable for a factory rifle. After a dozen or so rounds I soon got used to the trigger, and it proved to be smooth in operation.

How would I sum up the M77 Ruger Hawkeye, and would I buy one for foxing? Well, it certainly isn't a work of art, but it is functional. You couldn't call it sophisticated either – it is more of a downtown man than an uptown girl – but it is a very practical little rifle, built for purpose not pose, which is certainly the correct way round to have the priorities. Extremely light on the shoulder, it would definitely be a joy on an all-night foxing foray or a day-long deer stalking excursion, and retailing at £999 it is comparatively light on the pocket.

I have a strong feeling that this rifle will last forever and take everyday knocks in its stride. If you are looking for a workhorse rifle for foxing, you should seriously consider the Ruger. **MP**

| **RUGER HAWKEYE** |
|---|
| **Model tested:** M77 Hawkeye in .243 |
| **Price range:** Around £1,000 |
| **Contact:** Viking Arms  01423 780810 **www.vikingarms.com** |

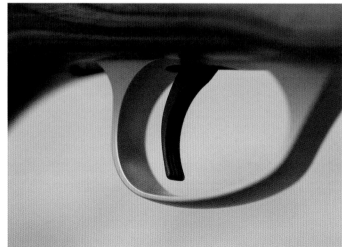

# SAKO 85

The Sako Varmint Laminated Stainless is made with medium- to long-range hunters in mind, as well as maybe target shooters who are looking for proven and consistent accuracy. It did not disappoint.

The action for this model comes in two sizes: extra small (.222, .223) and small (.22-250 to .338 Federal). The rifle on test, being a .222, has the shortest bolt travel, making it feel very neat and compact. What seems a simple construction of the bolt makes it fantastically smooth. Sliding on five raceways, it is quiet and effortless to cycle a round owing to a 'controlled round feed system'. This patented concept helps the round to slide up smoothly from the magazine into the bolt face.

The bolt has three lugs with a single claw-type extractor that relies on the round being pushed out by a small bar when retracted. There are the normal tapered scope rails located on the top of the receiver, facilitating a very firm platform for the Optiock mounts. There is enough space in the receiver to easily load rounds from the top. Most importantly, it is totally reliable and proven.

Moving on to the trigger, it was set to a very manageable three pounds. After a quick adjustment involving the removal of the stock and the use of a hex-headed key, I managed to set it to a crisp two pounds. This model also boasts a set trigger, activated in the traditional way by pushing it forward, with the pressure set at under half a pound.

As anticipated, this whole mechanism is of a very high quality. The two-position safety catch is located to the right of the action, partnered by another small lever located just in front of the safety catch. This allows the bolt to be cycled when the safety is in the 'on' position. This ensures the safe extraction of the round when the firing mechanism is locked in the safety position.

The 'total control latch' is a patented design of the magazine locking mechanism that prevents the accidental dropping of the magazine. To release the magazine, it has to be pushed upwards at the same time as pulling the release latch backwards. Initially it was a little fiddly, but with practice it became much easier to use.

Being stainless steel, fluted and heavy, the 24in barrel looks the part if you enjoy anything from vermin shooting to foxing to long-range shooting. It is fully floating and very well finished. Unusually, the recoil lug on the action locates into a small frame, screwed on to the stock. Without stating the obvious, the fully floating heavy barrel should maintain its accuracy after many shots, aided by a healthy gap between it and the forend. It does make for a heavier gun, but it is very well balanced. It also comes with a 14mm x 1mm thread screw-cut as standard, and a twist rate of one in 14in. For the test I fitted an Ase Utra moderator.

As soon as I took hold of the stock, I could feel its quality. It is made of many layers of wood stuck together using epoxy resin, resulting in a hard-wearing and practical stock that will take a fair amount of abuse. It feels

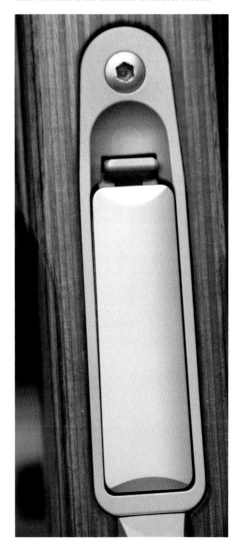

like a wooden stock, but offers a more rigid and stronger platform. The cheekpiece felt perfectly formed, as did the pistol grip. The extra wide, flat-bottomed beavertail forend crosses over to target shooting use and comes with the normal QD stud for easy attachment of a bipod.

With the rifle, distributor GMK kindly included a Leupold 6-20x50 long-range scope with a 30mm tube and the new varmint hunter ballistic reticle. The Optilock mounts were easy to fit, and we were soon set up to zero the rifle at 200 yards. For this test, I used Federal Premium 40-grain Ballistic tip (3,450fps) and Sako 55-grain Gamehead soft points (3,200fps), allowing me to see if the accuracy was affected by using different bullet weights.

The .222 is a lovely calibre to shoot as it offers very little recoil. Both the 40-grain and 55-grain rounds grouped less than 1½in at 200 yards, which was expected but comforting to witness. The trigger reset to 2lb could not be bettered, and as for the set trigger, it required the lightest of touches with no creep whatsoever. The stock fitted very well – a perfectly made pistol grip, with the cheekpiece suiting lower scopes as the mounts supplied for the Leupold scope were too tall.

Owing to the extra-small action, the bolt travel was minimal, making it very quick and easy to reload. When I used a few Winchester 50-grain soft pointed rounds, they would not cycle from the magazine, as they all twisted to the left, jamming against the rear face of the barrel. With exception to these particular rounds,

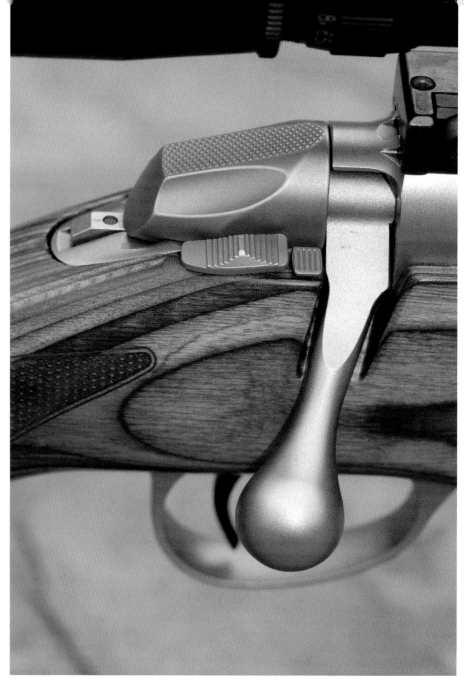

I never experienced any problems with the action whatsoever. The accuracy, thanks to the heavy barrel, was never affected even after I had fired more than 50 rounds in quick succession. Out to 300 yards, both the Federal and the Sako ammunition produced sub-2in groups – a surprising result given the moderate winds blowing from one to two o'clock.

Overall, the Sako Varmint Laminated Stainless looks like a custom rifle but more importantly, performs like one – and with an SRP of £1,725, it is half the price. The smoothness of the action, a very well made barrel and most of all, superb accuracy demonstrate Sako's superior engineering. With a weight of 12lb including scope, bipod and moderator, it is slightly on the heavy side for lugging around the highlands, but this is an all-rounder, perfect for foxing, hunting or playing on the range. Personally, I would prefer to put up with a couple of pounds than to sacrifice accuracy. **TP**

ako has produced many excellent rifles over the years. There are few hunters around the world who will not be familiar with the brand, and the response is usually the same: 'Sako makes some great rifles.' Indeed, even in countries such as South Africa, which holds the Mauser 98 above all others, Sako rifles, both old and new, are beginning to get a foot in the door. They cover a middle ground in the market, providing a rifle well above budget options, yet not in the same price league as a Mauser or Blaser.

Sako started in 1921, originally established to produce rifles for the men and woman of the Civil Guard of Finland. Although its initial focus had been military rifles, the company soon began designing competition and hunting rifles. Having had success with small calibre hunting rifles produced during the Second World War, it also started producing larger bolt-action sporters, launching the now renowned Forrester and Finnbear models. In 1993 development began for a new rifle, based

on the premise it should be the "dream rifle for devoted riflemen". Four years later the Sako 75 was born.

My own experience of Sako came in the early days of my fullbore hunting career. I distinctly remember ogling the Sako catalogue while ordering my first rimfire in the local gunshop, and decided there and then that a Sako was what I wanted. A few years later I parted company with an old Brno .243, which couldn't hit a barn door at 10 yards, and instead a second-hand Sako 75 found its way into our gun cabinet. It wasn't in great nick, but shot well enough, and as far as the rifle design was concerned, I was most certainly a fan. Two years later I had a thirst for a 7x57 to take to Africa, and found a very tidy Sako L691, which found its way north of the border. Since then I have also briefly owned the much-acclaimed forerunner to the L591: the Sako Forrester. All of them great rifles, which, for better and worse, have evolved as time has passed. Now, of course, the model 85 is the flagship Sako rifle, which, as with all the other model updates, has changed yet again.

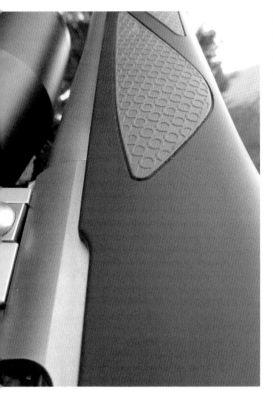

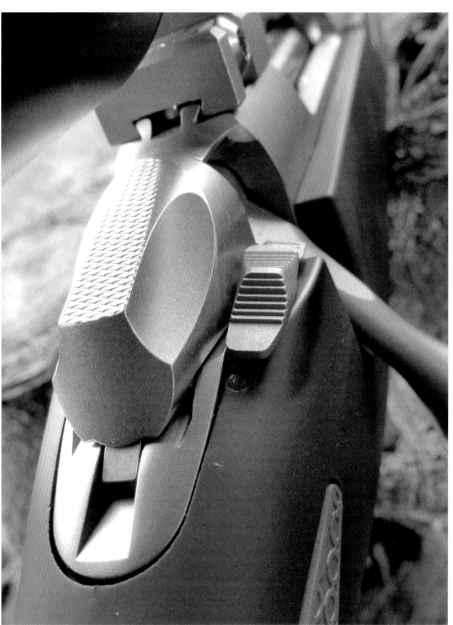

I never had a chance to see the early 85s, although I believe nothing functionally has changed apart from alterations to the synthetic stocks. I had the Finnlight model on test, which is the lightest of the range with a fluted 20in barrel and synthetic stock. Like all other Sako rifles I have picked up, it felt good. I wasn't the biggest fan of the 75's wooden stock shape, much preferring the Finnbear era. However, this synthetic offering felt nice in the shoulder, even if the pull length was a little too long for me. As to be expected from Sako, the synthetic material was rigid and robust, covered with a soft-touch finish and rubberised grips where chequering would traditionally be found. One fault on the 75 equivalent was that the rubber did tend to wear and perish in the hands of professionals who put the rifle to work every day. It seems this has been rectified, with a different material and raised finish. Functionally it was good, and one of my preferred off-the-shelf synthetic stocks.

The barrels haven't changed a great deal over the generations. They are still cold hammer forged and made, as far as I can tell, to the same high standards Sako has always maintained, with close attention to finish and crowning. Having said that, I am aware of a few people who had trouble getting the early Sako 75s to shoot well, but for some bizarre reason this only

**I DISTINCTLY REMEMBER OGLING THE SAKO CATALOGUE WHILE ORDERING MY FIRST RIMFIRE IN THE LOCAL GUNSHOP, AND DECIDING THAT SAKO WAS WHAT I WANTED**

seemed to be with a few rifles chambered for .243 Win. I wasn't able to establish the reason for this, however, when re-barrelled they shot like a dream. Thankfully, this problem hasn't been repeated since.

The trigger is another aspect of the rifle that has altered little over the years despite other major shifts in design. I guess that is a testament to how good the original was. Any tweaks have been minor in terms of functionality and are not worth mentioning.

The Sako trigger is certainly one of the best on an out-the-box firearm.

Once we turn our attention to the receiver and action, we do start to see where design alterations have been made. Shifting from the early and arguably best-loved 'Finnbear' era, the most frustrating and obvious change can be seen with the recoil lug system. Originally we saw a solid, integral, machined lug, much like on today's Howa rifle. This was altered in the 591/691, which saw a machined peg sit

This, like previous designs, was a push feed, lifting each round out the magazine on the forward stroke by simply running it out of the mag shoulder. Here it was effectively in free space until pushed into the chamber, where the extractor claw clipped over the rim edge, and the cartridge head became enclosed.

The Sako 85 takes this a step further, opening up the bolt face on one side to give a semi-controlled feed. It is not fully controlled, as with the classic M98, where the extractor claw has complete purchase on the case during loading and ejection. The new Sako design allows the case to ride up along the face of the bolt, where it is 'guided' forward, before the rim slips under the extractor claw.

It has been suggested that this now makes the Sako 85 suitable for dangerous game. However, I would take such comments with a note of caution. In my mind there is still only one action design worthy of putting your faith in on a dangerous game safari, and that is the classic Mauser 98.

In terms of overall finish, the most notable difference is how the rifles are blued, although obviously my test rifle was a stainless model. The early rifles had very deep, beautifully finished metal work, which would knock current models out the water. Having said that, I am not suggesting that today's rifles are functionally inferior, it is just that the appearance oozed of a higher quality. A high gloss, blued finish is indeed out of fashion now, and for sound reasons.

inside a light alloy lug inside the stock. The 75 was different again, and skipping to the 85 sees a system very similar to the 591/691. It certainly seems to work – although, as I have said before, an integral lug would be far superior, and current trends are merely a way of reducing expense.

The second change is on the bolt itself. Whereas early models locked down with twin lugs and a guide rail, the 75 moved away from this with a stronger tri-lug design. Removing the guide rail also made cycling smoother, and – although I am not completely convinced that three lugs are superior to two – I do like it.

When it came to the range, it was almost a mundane affair. I was expecting no surprises, and true to form the rifle performed well. Shooting the rifle with a handful of ammo brands, the standard 100-yard groups were at worst 1.6in and at best 0.8in (the latter achieved shooting 100-grain Sako Gameheads). Pushing it out to 200 yards and then 300 yards, suitable optics carried the 100-yard results, although the 95-grain Hornady SST ammunition shone through as a better performer, taking groups just on the three-inch mark at 300 yards.

I like Sako rifles and always have. I may not agree with some of the changes that have occurred through the years, but most manufacturers cut costs with design alterations. This, however, detracts nothing from today's rifle, which is a good bit of kit. It would be nice to see some of the aspects of the older designs reincorporated in the next model upgrade. Looking to the past for a few prompts, the next Sako could be the best yet – whenever that may be. **BP**

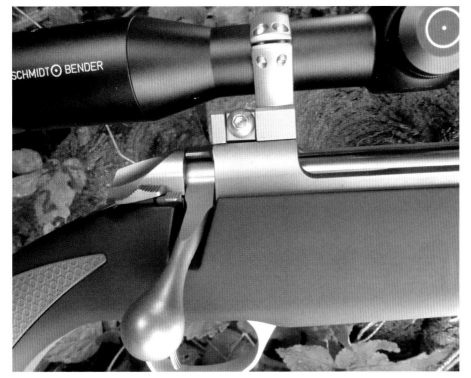

| **SAKO 85** |
| --- |
| **Models tested:** Varmint Laminated Stainless in .222; 85 Finnlight in .243 |
| **Price range:** £1,645-£2,280 |
| **Contact:** GMK 01489 587500 **www.gmk.co.uk** |

# SAKO A7

When I heard that Sako was launching a new rifle, I immediately assumed the 85 would be receiving a facelift – much like when the 75 got an upgrade. However, the A7 presented a totally new range of rifles, designed to fill the gap between the Sako 85 and the cheaper but ever popular Tikka T3 (owned by the same company). I really didn't have any idea of what to expect, but knowing how well Sako and Tikka rifles functioned and shot, I had no doubt that the result would be good.

This could be seen as a brave move from Sako, as the exceptionally well priced Tikka T3 is hard to beat in terms of value for money, even if it has a few undesirable attributes. Obviously the A7 wouldn't quite be to the standard of the 85 given its lower pricing, so it would be interesting to examine which rifle the new incarnation took as inspiration.

The A7 is certainly well balanced, with a slim profile, comfortable in-hand feel and pointable nature. According to the Sako specification, the synthetic stock is made of a glass-fibre

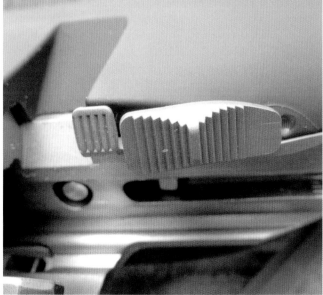

reinforced copolymer polypropylene. It is finished in a soft touch coating, with integrated stippling where the chequering would be found on a wooden stock. It is far superior to the cheap-feeling stock on a Tikka, and similar to the synthetic offering on the 85 – with the exception being the rubberised inserts.

On a purely pedantic point, I didn't like the A7 badge found under the pistol grip, which is made from a soft rubber as opposed to the nice metal plate on the 85. This, however, is neither here nor there. As with Sako's other rifles, length of pull is adjustable via a removable butt plate system and the use of spacers – but these did not come with the rifle.

Slipping the metalwork from the plastic reveals the bones of the rifle. Although not identical, the receiver of the A7 is very close to that of the 85, though the recoil lug arrangement has the same design as the Tikka. This, I have to say, is a bit disappointing as it is one of the biggest criticisms of the Tikka. The bottom of the receiver has been machined out to accept the separate alloy lug, and I just wish a solid recoil lug had been machined here instead. Either that or, for little extra cost, sit the recessed action on an aluminium block. This aside, it is a design that seems to work.

The bolt has been taken from the 75, with three sturdy lugs and classic Sako extractor. The ejector, however, is a spring plunger taken from the T3. The bolt face differs from the upgrade seen on the 85, which now offers a semi-controlled feed by opening up one edge

doesn't appear to be formed from one piece of metal as it has a join just before the bolt shaft. The knob itself has more gentle curves, with a hollow centre filled with a plastic cap – I'm not quite sure why Sako has done this apart from as a weight-saving exercise.

One great feature that the A7 has taken from the 85 is the 'total control latch' design. This requires the magazine to be pressed in before the drop lever can be operated and mag removed. Personally, I prefer a drop plate on a stalking rifle, but this is a simple and clever improvement, adding extra safety against

accidentally dropping your mag. The magazine itself is similar to the Tikka in that it is made almost entirely of plastic with a single stack design. The mag lips have, however, been upgraded with metal inserts, which should provide greater longevity than the Tikka, and it also seems to improve feeding marginally. It does feel slightly more robust, with nicely shaped bottom lines.

You will not be disappointed with the trigger. It is the same unit found in the 85 and, like all the Sako rifles I have fired, is crisp and a joy to use. Unfortunately, the trigger

guard is a plastic composite like the T3, although is the same shape as on the 85.

The safety is a familiar Sako affair, accessible just behind the bolt. This rocker-type safety has worked well for decades and is still my preferred choice. It has been taken from the 75, with the same safety mechanism which allows the bolt to be opened and removed with the safety engaged. In my opinion, the extra tab arrangement that allows this is superior to the more modern move towards three-position safety catches. I want either 'fire' or 'safe' – nice and simple.

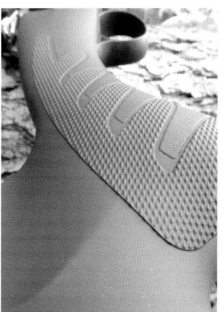

as all of Sako's other rifles. Understandable, as this has proved itself over decades of use.

Unsurprisingly, the rifle shot very well. I would have been shocked if it hadn't, since it combines aspects of two rifles that are well known for producing the goods straight out the box. The .243 Win I tested did find particular favour with the Federal 70-grain Nosler ballistic tips, clover-leafing it with exceptional consistency. Out at 200 yards, I was able to slam home groups averaging 1.7in without any trouble. Pushing the boat out to 350 yards, clay pigeon targets proved little challenge – what more could you possibly want? The 100-grain Sako Gameheads also performed well, if not quite to the same standard. Certainly 100-yard groups around the 1MOA mark were pretty standard.

I did enjoy using the new A7, and looking at the T3, A7 and 85 side-by-side, you can appreciate what extras you are getting for your money. I can't help feeling, though, that the A7 has been restrained by the fact that they couldn't make it quite as good as the 85. At an RRP of £1,445 it does seem quite expensive, but on the shop shelves I imagine you will be able to get it close to the grand mark. I would certainly be happy to spend the extra money to upgrade from the Tikka. It will be interesting to see how the market takes to this rifle. **BP**

---

**SAKO A7**

*Model tested:* A7 Synthetic Stainless in .243 Win

*Price range:* From £1,295

*Contact:* GMK  01489 587500
**www.gmk.co.uk**

---

Interestingly, the A7 does not boast the tapered dovetail that is iconic of all Sako's other rifles. This is a significant departure from tradition. Instead Sako has opted for Weaver-style bases on the rifle.

Mounting a scope only requires the shooter to source Weaver-compatible rings. The only reason I could see for Sako going down this road was to keep overall costs down and further help distinguish this rifle from its 85 models.

When it comes to the barrel, there will be little in the way of surprises. The A7 sports the same cold hammer forged, free-floating barrel

# SAUER 101

To steal an Americanism, every hunter wants a 'tack driver.' These days we strive for rifles that shoot tighter and tighter groups. No longer are we happy with shooting an inch and a half with our lightweight hunting rifle. We as consumers demand neat clustering groups and sub-MOA guarantees.

Rifle makers today certainly do know how to make rifles shoot to a high standard, but that doesn't mean these rifle designs are better than those from 50 years ago. Production streamlining and cost-cutting has led to frustrating sacrifices in design quality. Of course, it does mean rifles arrive on the market at a more affordable level, but sometimes this drive to steal pound coins from production costs leaves rifles in an almost unfinished state. I am always eager to see what steps a manufacturer has taken to introduce a cheaper model to its catalogue.

This is especially true of a rifle maker like Sauer, which has successfully supplied to hunters the world over its famous Sauer 202. This year it launched the little brother to the 202, and its position in the market puts it in the direct firing line of some big contenders. Coming in at £1,350, this mid-range ground has been held by Sako for a long time.

By the time the 101 arrived at my door, I had already watched the YouTube commercials and read the technical details of how the rifle was put together. As I have already said, most rifles these days will shoot sub-MOA given the right

ammo. To be impressed with how a rifle shoots, it really does have to perform. I had already been told that the 101 was not fussy with its lead and copper diet, shooting almost anything at an acceptable level.

After a thorough clean, the 101 was ready for the range. I warmed it up with some 150-grain Federals, which immediately grouped just over an inch. The next three shots tucked under the inch mark at 100 yards. Hornady Custom 168-grain produced almost identical results, with the 165-grain Geco mirroring the results. I wanted to burn a bit more powder to get a good feel for the rifle. This turned me on to the 170-grain Geco ammo that I had in abundance. Ditching the bipod for my roe sack, I slammed a six-shot string down range at the only clean target left. The results were impressive: five shots had cut each other across one ragged hole, with a sixth landing just outside. These results extended out to 300 yards as well, with a group just pushing the 3 inch mark. I wasn't expecting it with my fodder

ammo, but the rifle liked it.

With its accuracy accounted for, the rifle itself is fairly good looking. It had a nice feel to it, though the pistol grip was a little too generously swelled for my hands. The woodwork was nicely finished, although I am not a big fan of the high gloss coat. The metal work was also completed in a satisfying matte blue.

Those familiar with the 202 will notice that the 101 yields a different design, with the characteristic visible chassis absent in the 101. This rifle is not a switch barrel, like its predecessor, but fixed. Sauer opted for a non-threaded, heat shrunk, barrel to receiver fitting. The tell-tale sign of this is where the barrel meets the receiver, showing a visible locating pin that controls depth and rotational correction on fitting. This is an interesting method, following Mannlicher in building rifles without threading the receiver (although the application is different). It is an efficient and cost effective way of producing rifles – though re-barrelling is more time consuming. In theory, however, it may be a superior method of barrel fitting.

Unlike the hammer-forged barrel of the 202, the 101 uses button rifling. Although it may not have the same hardwearing barrel life, it is arguably the superior method when accuracy is concerned. Finished with a generous contour, this adds a bit of weight and stability to the rifle's overall balance.

The 101 does share an important similarity with the 202 in how head spacing is guaranteed. Like the switch barrel, the bolt lugs lock down into the barrel itself. This, however, this is where the likeness ends. The receiver of the 101 is machined as a single tube, milled on top for the classic Sauer lines, with a generously sized side ejection port. In a marketing move, it has also been drilled and tapped to accept standard Remington bases.

The recoil system is interesting and unique in its application, if not entirely original. The 'Ever Rest' bedding system sees the tubular receiver drilled and pegged in two positions. These fit into corresponding holes in a mini bedding block resin-glued into the stock. A central threaded nut, which is not the action screw, then binds the alloy block to the action. In front of the securing point, just over 10mm of the barrel resides on the block. The rest is free floating.

It is the first time I have seen it done quite like this, and ease of production clearly influences it. Fitting the receiver into a bigger alloy lug is not new, though, as the old Sako

L591/691 series had a similar design with a machined peg from the receiver and an un-bedded separate alloy lug. Given how well the 101 shoots, the new bedding system obviously works.

I have one reservation, though I may be proved wrong over time. Where I have previously seen cylindrical recoiling surfaces secured through corresponding holes, in heavier recoiling calibres they invariably become oval. This brings unwanted slack into the system. With the additional tensioning nut underneath its lug, the engineering brains at Sauer may have already addressed this in the 101.

The bolt provides the same slick operation as the 202. Though it has a virtually identical bolt shaft, the 101 has a swept-back handle with synthetic bolt knob. Although the former is more attractive aesthetically, the new design is more functional. The bolt is locked down with six lugs across all calibres – unlike the 202, which sees a three-lug design for the medium calibres. The 101 also sports double-sprung plunger ejectors. These provide firm and positive, almost horizontal, ejection of spent cases. Feeding is smooth, and overall the action is a pleasure to operate.

Looking to the back of the bolt, we can see the new safety design. Opting for a simple two-position version, operation is convenient, easy and fairly quiet to operate. Instead of having a straightforward slide, the fire position requires a small button on the catch to be depressed first. This cleverly ensures the rifle cannot accidentally be made live.

The bolt release on the 101 is multifunctional. When the rifle is

cocked and safe, depressing the round button with your thumb allows ammunition to be ejected while the rifle is still disengaged. In normal operation, the bolt is locked down when on safe, and holding the same button down on drawing back the bolt allows it to be removed from the receiver. Positioned for easy operation, this is an excellent safety feature adopted by a number of manufacturers. I prefer to have it in this form rather than a three-position safety.

Every good rifle needs a good trigger, and Europe is generally reliable in this department. The 101 has a new trigger design, set at a crisp and even 2lb. It impressed me, and was spot on for a stalking trigger. The trigger guard is integrated with the bottom metal in a wrap-around design similar to a Browning X-Bolt. Made from a casting process, it houses the 101's synthetic magazine. Stacking five rounds in standard and four in Magnum calibres, it feels remarkably robust for being made from a polymer. Effortless to fill, it offers smooth feeding and is one of the best synthetic mags I have seen. Ejection is achieved from under the stock via a recessed plastic button. It feels more like something you would pop a CD out with, but it works fine and is unlikely to be inadvertently depressed.

Sauer has taken a gamble moving from its comfortable position in the market into the very competitive middle ground, but it's difficult to draw fault with the result. Simply, I think Sauer has done a fine job. Despite my initial reservations about the 'Ever Rest' bedding system, it has produced an impressively accurate and well thought out rifle. It is comfortable to manoeuvre, with very traditional looks and a tapering fore stock (which increases your ability to grip the rifle firmly into your shoulder).

With low mounts fitted, the scope came up to my eye with little effort. At 6.7lb in standard calibres, it also has a comforting weight. The rest of the market should take a good look at what Sauer now offers. I am trying to think of a reason not to get my credit card out. **BP**

'Old school – new rules' is the slogan Sauer uses to promote its new 101 bolt-action rifle. There seems to be a trend of mid- to high-end rifle manufacturers trying to produce a more competitively-priced model using their high-quality materials and manufacturing processes. It makes sense, but can they really pull it off?

Firstly, what makes the Sauer 101 different to most sporting rifles? I believe it is the clever safety mechanism, the way the barrel is connected, and lastly, the bedding system. I will deal with these new features as I review the whole rifle.

As the 101 lies in the gun case, the dark grade 1 walnut stock is the first thing that strikes you. It oozes quality and refinement around the dark metalwork. To the shoulder, the stock holds my head in the perfect place for a decent-sized optic – it's well balanced and firm. The pistol grip has a double palm swell to accommodate right- and left-handed shooters – though this makes it a wide grip that may not be suitable for some. The chequering here and to the forend is of a high quality, finished off beautifully around its borders. To the rear, the recoil pad is chunky but firm – possibly not that effective when firing the heavier calibres. Overall, it feels comfortable and well presented.

What makes this safety catch different from most? Positioned in the rear bolt shroud, the grippable catch needs to be pushed forward with the thumb to release. To prevent accidental

movement, a button in the middle of the catch must be pressed at the same time. It is more or less silent, smooth in its travel, and effortless to manage. There does seem to be a middle position that will not allow the shot to be taken, so make sure you push it fully forward.

When the safety is applied, the bolt is also locked. To cycle the round without releasing the safety catch, press a neat little button to the right of the bolt lever slot, and back it comes. Maybe it was just the rifle I had on review, but I could also release the bolt by applying a little forward pressure to the safety catch. Most safety

catches lock the trigger mechanism, but this secure bolt design (or Durasafe system) locks the actual firing pin, supposedly making it one of the safest on the market. Most importantly, the wide trigger blade is crisp with no creep, and factory set to 2lb as standard. This one was tested at 1.9-2.1lb.

The bolt itself is a solid design that directly locks into the barrel using six large locking lugs, similar to the Mauser M03 and the Merkel Helix (most rifles' designs lock into the front of their respective actions). The concept ensures better accuracy – the manufacturer guarantees sub-MOA, which is reasonably impressive, but it has to be said, most of today's rifles achieve this.

For ejection of the rounds, a twin plunger ejector ensures a robust 90-degree horizontal throw, aided by a sprung claw on the edge of the bolt face. Overall, bolt travel was smooth, as anticipated, and thanks to the 60-degree bolt throw, combined with a generous ejection port, it cycles rounds quickly and efficiently.

Another unusual feature is the design and fit of the barrel into the receiver. Most barrels are threaded and screw into the receiver, but Sauer uses a friction weld process that involves heating the front of the receiver and pressing the barrel in when it has expanded.

To guarantee the correct head spacing, a lower locator pin on the barrel slots into the front of the receiver, and as the sales material states, it provides a 'tension-free barrel-to-receiver connection'. Once again, this may improve accuracy, but does it mean that any future barrel changes are no longer an option?

The double-stack synthetic magazine is apparently indestructible, and has a capacity of four rounds for the magnum calibres and five for the rest. Some would prefer it to be made of steel or alloy, especially for a premium product such as a Sauer, but there's no denying it is robust and quick to load. To release, press the hidden button to the front of the high-quality, one-piece alloy trigger guard and base plate. It is more or less impossible to release it by mistake. The magazine drops out without any effort, loads quickly and

engages with a positive click, making it one of the most practical designs on the market.

Moving forward, the sporting medium-weight match barrel is available in two lengths – 22in on standard calibres and 24in on magnums – and comes with a 14x1mm thread.

The last notable feature is the 'Ever Rest' bedding system. Instead of using the common recoil lug design, the 101 incorporates two locking pins fixed to the underside of the action. These pins locate into an aluminium block that is bedded into the stock. It looks a neat and tidy design, and is secured tightly by a 9mm hex stud. This stud then accepts the front screw to fix the bottom plate. To remove the metalwork from the stock, release the two lower screws, then use a socket to release the stud. It is nice to the see that the stud directly squeezes the aluminium

bedding block to the action without applying any pressure to the surrounding stock material. Another tick in the enhanced accuracy box.

To summarise, the Sauer 101 unsurprisingly has the feel of a high-quality rifle, incorporating innovative new designs with the unusual barrel fitting process and bedding procedure, not forgetting the superb trigger and safety mechanism. But does it stand above its competitors when tested in the field?

For this review, Swarovski kindly provided me with a Z5 5-25x52P. It is great to notice that I can use mounts that can be fitted many other receivers, such as the Remington 700 series, negating the need to buy bespoke and expensive mounting kits.

After raiding my gun room – helped by the rifle being in the popular .308 calibre – I

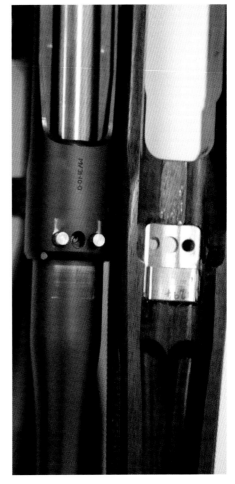

was able to get hold of a variety of factory ammunition to see if the 101 favoured a particular weight or brand. This is not a scientific test, but gives me an indication of its performance under hunting conditions. Using a Harris bipod, the Geco 180-grain, Lapua 150-grain and Hornady TAP 110-grain, achieved 1in, 0.9in and 0.8in groups at 100 yards respectively. This is respectable, but one of the other rifles I took to the range managed to pip it – a 0.7in group with 150-grain Federal Fusion ammunition. Then again, accuracy is not a concern once below the guaranteed 1MOA – most hunters are more than happy with this performance, especially with the heavier calibres above 243. Recoil was feisty, but bearing in mind it is an athletic 6.5lb in weight, this was not a surprise.

The Sauer feels comfortable to shoot, helped by the superb chequering. Perhaps the pistol grip is a little wider than most. The 52mm Swarovski seemed to be in perfect alignment for my shooting thanks to the design of the stock and cheekpiece. Loading, cycling and ejection of the rounds was faultless, backed up by that really outstanding trigger.

I have had the pleasure of using this rifle extensively, evaluating ammunition out to 300 yards in preparation for a week's hind culling in Scotland. For this I used 125-grain Nosler Ballistic Tip heads with 46 grains of Vihtavuori N135, giving me a flat-shooting 3,000fps projectile, with accuracy of under 2in at 200 yards. With a 150-yard zero, the drop is 2in, 4in and 8in at 200, 250 and 300 yards respectively. The Sauer performed well, accounting for several beasts from 80 to 200 yards. I found the safety

a little fiddly, as there is not a huge amount of room below the scope, making it tricky to locate the small integral button, especially when wearing gloves. Despite the cold, wet and windy weather, I could not fault the trigger, and while the recoil was punchy owing to the weight and lack of moderator, it handled beautifully. Despite using the feisty 125-grain Nosler Ballistic tips, carcase damage was minimal.

Is the 101 going to be a popular addition to the gun shops of the UK? It is a premium brand trying to fill the middle market, and most would say that despite an eye-catching RRP of around £1,500, it offers guaranteed high-quality design. I really enjoyed the Sauer 101, not forgetting the XT model with the synthetic soft touch stock that is also available, offering a workmanlike, rugged rifle capable of being used anywhere in the world. In my opinion, I would take a serious look at the XT version, with an RRP of £1,300. **TP**

| **SAUER 101** |
| --- |
| **Models tested:** Sauer 101 in .243 and .308 |
| **Price range:** 101 £1,500; 101 XT £1,300 |
| **Contact:** Garlands  01827 383300 **www.garlands.uk.com** |

# SAVAGE AXIS

aving recently reviewed the Marlin X7, my mind was already on budget guns. Then I heard Ruger had also released an entry-level rifle. The rifle in question is the Savage Axis (called the Edge in the USA), which reports to be one of the most competitively priced rifles on the market. What has been compromised to produce such a competitively priced rifle? The most obvious concern would be accuracy and quality of build – how do these attributes stand up?

While the Axis looks similar to the popular Savage 110 series, I soon discovered that several notable changes had been made. Starting with the blackened action, the top of the receiver is tapped to allow standard Weaver-style block mounts to be fitted. The ejection port is small but long, able to deal with the longer cases up to .30-06, making it strong and stiff.

It sports a detachable magazine constructed of a steel box and plastic base plate, which can hold a total of four rounds in .243 calibre. It is easy to load, but secured by a low-cost plastic tab located to the front. It does work, but I question whether it will remain effective over a long period of time. Having said that, it is simple to load, easy to handle when wearing gloves, and flush with the bottom of the stock.

The bolt shares the same head design as the 110 series, allowing the lugs to slide along both sides of the receiver with the front lugs locking into the front of the action. The belief here is that it allows

for even pressure on the rear of the cartridge, owing to a consistent alignment with the bore, enhancing Savage's claim of superb accuracy. The bolt handle is one piece with no extra grip surface, but looks fine and exceptionally smooth throughout its travel.

The calibre on test was .243, but the long bolt travel will allow it to cope with longer rounds such as the .270 and .30-06. The rear of the firing pin is visible, making it an easy-to-see cocking indicator. To remove it, the trigger and the release lever to the right of the action have to be pressed at the same time. The bolt release lever also doubles up as a cocking indicator. The large, plastic two-position safety button that sits behind the bolt is easy to slide. Push forward to fire, and in the rearmost safety position the bolt can still be cycled.

One of the best attributes with most Savage rifles is the 'AccuTrigger', which can be adjusted down to about 2.5lb, but the Edge has not been blessed with this superior trigger assembly. The smooth trigger blade, set to 5½lb, is a brute to pull and no doubt will be discussed more when on test in the field. The trigger guard is a one-piece design, looks likes it is made of the same material as the stock and is moulded to fit the underside of the chassis.

The matt black synthetic stock gives away the fact that this is aimed at the competitively priced end of the market. It is hollow with QD studs, and the forend will probably touch the barrel if a

heavy moderator and bipod are fitted. The pistol grip is narrow with three moulded recesses to enhance grip and has an effective rubber recoil pad for the larger calibre. Both sides of the forend are angled and textured for a reasonable grasp, especially when gloves are worn.

The .243 Axis is fitted with a 22in sporting weight barrel, and for the UK it is threaded to ½in UNF for sound moderators. With a twist rate of 9.25in, this should suit the heavier ammunition – it will be interesting to see if it can cope with the lighter 55-75 grain bullets. As with all Savage rifles, there is a barrel locking nut between the barrel and receiver to allow superior head spacing settings during the build – another tick in the box for Savage accuracy.

Overall, the Savage is a lightweight sporting rifle weighing 6½lb. It has the feel and look of an entry level rifle, but does this really matter if this rifle shoots well?

Supplied with the Axis was the Weaver Super Slam Euro 3-9x56 scope with a 30mm tube. Similar to most Remingtons, standard bases were required, so I used Millett standard bases and Millett Angle-Loc adjustable. For ammunition, two very different weights are being used: Black Hills 62-grain Varmint Grenade (3,700fps) and Remington Premier Accu-Tip 95-grain (3,120fps), courtesy of Edgar Brothers. JMS Arms also donated a PES Scout moderator, and I used a Harris bipod as I see this rifle being used for both deer and fox shooting.

At a zero of 100 yards, bearing in mind this is a new rifle, the 62-grain Black Hills achieved a 0.75in group and the Remington 95-grain just under 1in. Nothing wrong with the accuracy of the Axis. Interestingly, the lighter ammunition performed better despite the quicker twist rate. Out to 250 yards, 2.5in and 3.25in groups

were obtained repeatably. As mentioned, the narrow pistol grip made for a strong grip and suited the wearing of gloves. When shooting without a bipod, the forend was easy to grip and the recoil pad seemed comfortable. Being made of rubber meant it did not slide easily against my coat, when trying to bring it up to the correct shooting position.

The recoil and muzzle lift, with or without the moderator, were within expectations for such a light rifle, but the trigger lets the Axis down. Having said that, I think we get fussy when it comes to heavier triggers – once you become accustomed to them, they are perfectly adequate. With a pull of 5½lb and noticeable creep, it feels pretty grim, but despite that it still shoots to within 1MOA. If a better trigger was fitted, it would transform the Axis.

The bolt was smooth and extracted effectively. The magazine fed well for both types of ammo.

With or without the bipod, the point of impact was not affected enough to cause any worries, but if a heavier moderator was fitted, this could be an issue. With the lighter PES moderator, the Axis felt balanced and easy to shoot.

In conclusion, the Axis is a functional, lightweight hunter with a fair action. It is very practical, and if scratched when stowed in the Land Rover or tractor, it will not bring tears to the eyes. It also feeds well and cycles well. The trigger is far too heavy, the stock is acceptable but feels inexpensive, the pistol grip may put a few shooters off, as might the plastic magazine catch and trigger guard – but who cares? It shoots darn well. Savage is renowned for manufacturing competitively priced rifles that are accurate, and the Axis is no exception.

If you are on a budget, this is an accurate, entry level model, and what you save on the rifle can be invested into the optics. How often do you hear: 'Spend more money on the glass, not the rifle.' With an RRP of £653, I wouldn't be surprised to see it appearing in many gun shops at the sub-£600 mark, which makes it one of the most competitive centrefire rifles on the market in the UK. **TP**

---

### SAVAGE AXIS

**Model tested:** Axis .243 with 22in barrel

**Price range:** £653

**Contact:** Edgar Brothers  01625 613177
**www.edgarbrothers.com**

# SAVAGE M25 HORNET

For some time now, I have owned and used an Anschütz 17/17 .17 HMR and a Weihrauch HW60J .22 Hornet. When I heard about the new Hornady .17 Hornet, I was intrigued. Where, I wondered, would this calibre fit in, and how would it compare with the two I already have?

The .17 calibre is certainly not new, having been around in one form or another for around 50 years. In 1971 Remington introduced the .17 Remington, an extremely fast cartridge with the ability to shift a 20-grain bullet at over 4,000fps. One of the advantages of these small, high-speed, frangible bullets is that they normally fragment within the quarry and cause very little hide damage. In 2002 Hornady introduced the .17 HMR and, despite some recent issues with ammunition, it has been successful overall. With its 17-grain bullet doing 2,550fps, it is in many ways the ideal vermin round. Hornady's 2005 offering of the .17 Mach 2, which uses the necked down CCI Stinger case, has proved popular with a few shooters. Hornady has now completed its .17 hat-trick by bringing out the .17 Hornet round.

From the box, the rifle's dark grey polymer stock looks businesslike and practical. The forend that houses the free-floating barrel is well-shaped and is comfortable to hold. The

butt is finished with a comfortable butt pad and, apart from the three stippled inserts on the inside of the pistol grip, is unadorned. The four-shot polymer magazine, which has a forward release catch, is well concealed and springs out when the catch is operated. The whole unit is finished in a uniform dark grey and the 22in recessed crowned match grade barrel has a glare-reducing matt finish.

The three-lug bolt has a low lift, and with its polished finish provides a contrast to the overall spartan finish. The well tried M-25 action and its loose-fitting bolt has been well documented over the years; compared with some European makes it does feel a little sloppy but it does work very well, with feed, extraction and ejection well up to scratch. Bolt removal is done by releasing the trigger and simply sliding it out

– perhaps not for the purist but easy to operate.

The rifle is fitted with the Savage AccuTrigger. Conventional two-stage systems can be tricky to get right, to say the least. The AccuTrigger has a spring-loaded front blade that advises when your finger is against the trigger itself. While doing this, the unit also acts as a safety mechanism, preventing the rifle from firing until the AccuTrigger blade is fully depressed. The trigger itself is easily adjustable from 1.5-6lb. For a relatively inexpensive rifle the trigger pull is good – crisp with no discernable creep.

For the test, I fitted an MTC Genesis scope. I really like this scope and always feel it is good value for money. It's thought of primarily as a small bore or air rifle scope, but I have used it for test purposes up to .243 calibre and it really does the job on all of them. It's a well-thought-out piece of kit, and in general use it sometimes makes you wonder why we spend large sums of money on more expensive scopes when something like the Genesis does everything asked of it.

Now to the round itself. It claims to have a muzzle velocity of 3,650fps with the 20-grain

bullet from a 24in barrel. The 22in version I was using didn't quite make that, but it did average around 3,545fps over the chrony, which is still pretty quick.

It also claims to have an effective range of 250 yards, which is about 100 yards better than the .17 HMR and probably 50 yards better than the.22 Hornet. While I have little doubt that this feisty little round is quite capable of these sort of ranges, common sense dictates that unless conditions are pretty much perfect, wind will certainly become a major factor over these distances.

Turning to the .17 HMR, much has been said about the effect wind has on this round. From my own experience, it hasn't been much of a problem when shooting rabbits out to 100 yards – in fact, as I always chest shoot my rabbits with this round, I never make any allowance for wind. Similarly, I like the established .22 Hornet – it is good for many purposes and is more than good enough for foxed out to 200 yards. The downside is its loopy trajectory, which the .17 Hornet certainly doesn't have. The .17 Hornet's trajectory is almost identical to that of a 55-grain round from a .223 and is substantially flatter than both the .17 HMR and the .22 Hornet.

Like the .22 Hornet, the .17 Hornet can be reloaded and I have little doubt that once you have sorted out the best load it won't be difficult to cut your costs. My estimate is that you should be able to load the .17 Hornet for around 40p – less than half the cost of the factory ammo.

So how did the rifle and ammo fare in the field? Firstly, I have to say I have never been the greatest fan of American rifles, preferring the European styling. This is not to say they don't do the job because they certainly do. I always think American rifles are built firstly for purpose and secondly for appearance, and a part of me says this makes perfect sense. The M-25, however, is rather a nice rifle overall and I would have very little difficulty in being tempted.

Next, to try it out in the field. Everything worked well from the start, and it felt 'right' to me. Accuracy was not a problem and after a few rounds to get zero it was doing half to three-quarter-inch groups at 100 yards with monotonous regularity.

I was interested to see what effect it would have on rabbits, suspecting it would be pretty severe. I have to shoot a lot of rabbits, and while many people tell me to head-shoot them, I don't do a lot of this for various reasons – mainly because at night, driving

round, it is more effective and certainly quicker to chest shoot them. I know from experience that the .22 Hornet can be severe on a rabbit carcase, rendering some unusable, whereas the .17 HMR will only occasionally cause any damage.

Eventually, the weather eased enough for me to get out on the sodden land. The rabbits that are left at this time of year are well- trained, and close ranges are not often an option – not a problem with the .17 Hornet though. The first shot in anger dropped a rabbit at a measured 145 yards. Through the scope I could see it never moved. The dog picked it up with some reluctance and on bringing it back I could see why – the tiny round had done a demolition job, and paunching was unnecessary. After shooting several more, it was clear that unless you head-shot them, you should expect substantial carcase damage. Not a problem, of course, unless you need the rabbits for sale.

Over the next week I shot several rabbits and two foxes, both of which dropped at around 175 yards. The result on the foxes varied – one round exited, the other didn't. Internal damage was quite substantial for such a small round.

So what were my conclusions? I thought the rifle was first-class – well-made, and although it might not appeal to the purists, there was absolutely no doubt that together with the .17 Hornet round designed for it, it was an extremely good vermin rifle.

Who would buy one? For the keeper needing a rifle for fox, rabbit and vermin in general it would be perfect. But it would be equally good for the shooter who wanted accuracy and just liked to get out and about after the odd rabbit and long-range crow or magpie.

Did it fit in neatly between the .17 HMR and the .22 Hornet? Not really. Personally, needing a lot of rabbits for sale, I wouldn't take the .17 Hornet after them – not only would carcase damage preclude it, but also

the sheer cost of the ammo would become an issue. Reloading would help but I can't see myself loading the thick end of 75 rounds each week. For my fox control business I would stick to the .223.

My requirements are a bit different to most shooters, though, and if I had lots of money to spare I would really like to add the new Hornet to the collection. When I first saw the rifle and read up on ammo performance, I immediately thought I would get rid of the .17 HMR and the .22 Hornet and get one. After using it I wouldn't, but that doesn't detract from the rifle and ammo in any way whatsoever. I thoroughly enjoyed using it. **MP**

## SAVAGE MODEL 25

**Model tested:** M25 in .17 Hornet

**Price range:** Around £900

**Contact:** Edgar Brothers  01625 613177
**www.edgarbrothers.com**

# STEYR MANNLICHER CLASSIC

**M**y introduction to Mannlicher rifles set the standard for how I would judge all rifles from that moment on. The Mannlicher Schönauer was a legendary piece of engineering with a magnificent history and hunting pedigree. This rifle, in the hands of 'Karamojo' Bell, reputedly accounted for 1,011 elephants during the era of the great ivory trade.

Today's Steyr Mannlicher Classic is touted as a direct descendent of the Schönauer. However, the new model is no modern version of the classic 1903 model. The rifle bolt may look the same, and it still sports the distinctive tool marks on the barrel from the cold hammer forging process, but the quality and impeccable engineering of the 1903 model has the edge on today's rifle. Getting my hands on one of the old rifles from that iconic era is high on my list of desires.

That may be a negative note on which to introduce the Steyr Mannlicher, but don't let this insight into the 'old world' discourage you

from looking at the modern rifle. When stacked up beside comparable offerings in today's market, the current Mannlicher is probably one of the prettiest rifles around. It shoots like a demon, too.

This review will proceed from the inside out, putting the rifle together piece by piece to get a full picture of how it fares. Conducting all reviews in this fashion should provide interesting comparisons in terms of build quality and design when different models and manufacturers are presented side by side.

With this in mind, I reached for the hex-headed keys to remove the stock from the action. My first surprise was not finding a fixing point to the rear of the trigger guard, leaving two bolts to the front. When I removed the well-machined trigger guard assembly, it became clear that a lot of time had been spent fitting it precisely to the stock, including recessing the rear lug slot.

With that, the action could be removed from the stock, exposing the fixing methods

from the inside. I was initially impressed by the aluminium pillar bedding, which is becoming the norm with factory rifles. On closer inspection, however, two issues became apparent. Firstly – and this is relatively minor – the resin used to fix the pillars in place hadn't been completely cleaned off, resulting in an uneven bearing surface for the action to fix down onto. Obviously the pillar bedding aims to achieve improved accuracy over a standard fixing, and I doubt the resin overspill will have made a jot of difference here. It is merely an attention to detail that should have been picked up on.

My second observation was a bit more practical. The rear pillar is bedded in an incredibly thin inlet of the stock, with very little 'meat' to provide strength. If there had been a third rear fixing behind the trigger guard this would have been of little consequence, but as I alluded to earlier, this is not the case. With the leverage of the barrel and action on these stock fixings, any kind of substantial fall with your rifle could land you with a cracked stock.

The stock itself is really quite stunning. The overall shape was incredibly pleasing, with the slim forestock and Schnabel tip drawing your eye down the aesthetically mesmerising barrel. The well-textured and deep chequering was comfortably positioned, and the proportions made the rifle come to the shoulder positively.

At the heart of the action is a chunky bolt with four locking lugs and the classic 'butter knife' bolt handle. In my eyes, it is one of the most beautiful bolts ever to grace a rifle (although the Schönauer's was slightly nicer). The parallel pairs of forward locking lugs

provide an incredibly positive and strong lock-up. Setting it apart from most manufacturers, the Mannlicher's lugs are recessed, protruding only as far as the overall diameter of the bolt itself and allowing the receiver to be machined uniformly along its entire length. The end result is a 70-degree throw and a bolt that glides effortlessly, aided by the corrosion-resistant and polished nickel-plated finish.

The practical application of the rifle has been thought of here too, as ice grooves on the top and bottom of the bolt help ensure faultless operation in freezing conditions. They also act as grime channels to allow smooth reloading even when dust and dirt have found their way into your rifle. Case extraction is carried out by the archetypal plunger and sprung claw, and a user friendly design allows for easy field stripping.

The trigger is at the heart of every accurate rifle, and the Mannlicher doesn't disappoint here. The standard trigger is a little on the heavy side and cannot be adjusted for pull weight, releasing the firing pin with what I would

describe as an adequate break. However, the real treat comes once the set trigger is engaged. With the safety on the first position, you can gently push the trigger forward until it clicks. With that, the trigger is 'set'.

The pressure required to release is externally adjustable with a hex-headed key on the trigger, making the release as light as you could possibly care for. Bear in mind that the 'set' pressure should only be adjusted to the lowest level that can be deemed safe, where no accidental discharge will occur.

The safety is very clever, and positioned where you would normally find a shotgun safety catch. The rotary tang safety operates in three positions. Fully forward is fire, back one click is safe – displaying a white dot – while fully rotated exposes a grey tab, signifying that the bolt has been locked down and the set trigger automatically disengaged. In this position the bolt can be fixed down into a groove in the stock, which locks the firing pin and provides the optimal transport profile. To move back to the 'middle' safe position, the

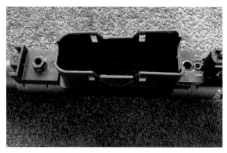

small grey plunger must be depressed, which in turn re-engages the firing pin.

The barrel carries the characteristic and beautiful spirals courtesy of the cold hammer forging process – a method that produces some incredibly hard-wearing barrels. However, there is a theory that barrels produced by this method are not as inherently accurate as the alternatives. For hunting purposes this is merely academic – it will likely only be noticed by benchrest shooters. Indeed, when I had the chance to take it to the range, there was no denying the accuracy of the set-up. Topped with a Zeiss Duralyt scope in 3-12x50 (a truly superb piece of kit for the money) and 100-grain Federals, it got me on zero with three shots. The following three nestled into 0.8in. Not bad for a rifle straight out the box.

The Classic is often described as a 'gentleman's rifle', and I certainly wouldn't disagree. Its beauty and operation speak for itself, but I would stop short of suggesting this particular model was a professional's choice. The issue with the stock fixing mentioned at the start of the article would concern me, especially in the heavier calibres and for serious rough

hunting. I wouldn't want my life to depend on it, anyway. Having said that, most amateur stalkers will never have any issues with it.

The rifle in this review was borrowed from my mate Martin Hodge just after he bought it. Here is an account, in his words, of the first successful hunt with the rifle in the beautiful surroundings of the Cairngorms at the end of the doe season.

"Carrying my new Steyr Mannlicher .243 Win, with a clip of Federal Power Shok 100-grain, we started to climb. And climb. And climb. At the top we glassed several likely does, but a swirling wind carried our scent towards the parting animals. We pressed on across the next ridge, traipsing through patches of snow occupying the hollows among the heather. After an hour and a half we spotted a small group about 400 yards away. Keeping the uneven ground between us and the deer, we stalked carefully towards them, belly slithering the final 50 yards into position.

"At 100 yards I managed to get a nice broadside shot, nestling the fine crosshairs up the inside leg. After a couple of wobbly steps, she fell down in the heather. I was a happy man.

"After a well-tutored DSC gralloch and inspection (I'm doing Level 2), we loaded the roe sack and headed back down the mountain for a well-earned couple of drams. Compared to lowland stalking, hill roe are really hard work and challenging to stalk, but well worth the effort. My new rifle performed faultlessly. Its lightness and manoeuvrability were a joy on the harsh hill. I look forward to the next outing – maybe a trophy next time." **BP**

### STEYR MANNLICHER

**Model tested:** Mannlicher Classic in .243
**Price range:** Around £1,774
**Contact:** Sportsman Gun Centre
01392 354854
**www.sportsmanguncentre.co.uk**

# THOMPSON CENTER ICON

Thompson Center (T/C) is very popular with sport hunters throughout the United States. Indeed, the Contender Carbines made by T/C have become an industry standard across the pond. It was still a surprise to many in the industry, though, when T/C launched a bolt-action rifle named the Icon into an already-crowded marketplace. No doubt the closing of Winchester's New Haven plant encouraged the company.

Paul Mauser developed his 1898 action 110 years ago, and hosts of talented people and arms companies have reworked, refined and augmented that design. That said, T/C has produced a truly new design of centrefire rifle with detachable magazine, combining the best elements of several rifles to make an excellent contemporary stalking rifle.

The handsome walnut stock has clean, classic lines, a relatively open grip and 20-lpi borderless chequering. For a rifle in this price bracket the walnut is surprisingly high quality. Apparently T/C has 600 walnut blanks in stock from its old days in the wood trade, which would suggest that if this rifle takes your fancy, you shouldn't hesitate to buy one – there may be a price hike when this walnut is exhausted.

At present the calibre choice is not that varied: .22-250, .243, .308. and the new .30 T/C are currently available. However, the Icon Classic long action version offers .270 Win, .30-06 Sprg, .300 Win Mag and 7mm Rem Mag. What other calibres are needed for foxing or stalking?

The rifle's well-figured and red hued walnut stock had a smooth oiled finish. Generous panels on grip and forend feature neatly cut chequering. Equally, the Icon Weather Shield medium action comes with composite stock and stainless barrel, with a choice of black or Realtree camo finish.

A black rubber pad caps the butt. There is no forend tip, grip cap or palm-swell. The comb is straight, with a pull length of 14in. Overall the stock has clean, classic lines, giving it an agreeable conservative look. A relatively open grip and forend welcomed my hands; it shouldered well and pointed effortlessly.

A one-piece, CNC-machined receiver action sits in a single-piece aluminium bedding block via three integral recoil lugs, giving strong solid bedding. T/C's own 24in, medium-contour barrel is button-rifled and came screw-cut for a moderator in ½in UNF.

The Icon comes with integral Weaver-style bases built into the bridge of the receiver. There are, of course, many rings on the UK market that fit this type of mounting system.

The full-diameter bolt has three front-locking lugs and a sleek, sloping rear shroud – reminds me of a Sauer – which slides smoothly in the action rails. With each Icon, T/C supplies a polymer 'donut' for disassembling the bolt. It sounds awkward but it's actually a quick process. The spoon-style bolt handle, part of the bolt assembly's primary parts, is easily removed – as it is not integral and can be exchanged for an optional round-knob, knurled or butter knife version.

The Icon's bolt stop is a slender lever at the traditional spot on the left receiver wall. It pivots from the front so you can hold the rifle and operate it conveniently with one hand. It is designed so the rearward flung bolt force bears on the rear of the stop in the receiver wall, and not on the pivot pin.

Like the bolt, the forged receiver shows some muscle and the long tang is a deliberate feature: it minimises bolt wiggle at full extension. The jewelled bolt (not on all models) has a low lift of 60°, further enhancing its effortless simplicity in use. The stock is secured to the action by three

stout guard screws, one into each lug.

A removable box magazine holds three short action rounds and tapers at the top to feed cartridges in a straight stack system. This straight-up feed is smooth and reliable and is obviously influenced by Tikka.

The trigger, designed by T/C expressly for this rifle, is easily adjustable from 2½-6lb by reaching through the tang with the supplied hex-head wrench, without having to disassemble the rifle. Dry firing, I found the trigger wonderfully manageable at a crisp and consistent 3lb. A two-position thumb safety works smoothly and quietly, disengaging sear from trigger.

I added a Zeiss 2.5-10x50 Victory scope and a T8 moderator to the rifle. After zeroing the rifle without a problem, I achieved a ½in group off the bench. I was going to use the Icon for stag stalking on the hill and checked zero at 200 yards on arrival at the keeper's house. In windy conditions I still achieved an acceptable 2in grouping.

Out on the hill, however, I pulled my first shot. I was hanging over a 200ft precipice, on the Glen Doll beat of Balmoral estate no less. The stag filled the Zeiss scope. I held my

breath, aimed, and winged a bullet on its way but completely missed. Realising it wasn't such a great place to be, the beast changed ends and dashed down hill. I instantly changed position and followed the stag in the Zeiss scope. He paused mid-flight, looking back, unsure. I took a careful bead up the beast's front leg to the heart and lung region and squeezed off another round. This time the bullet ran true and the stag tumbled spectacularly, head over heels, down the hill.

"Aye, your second shot was better than your first one, laddie," murmured the stalker, Stuart Donald. It must've been my precarious position, on the edge of a 200ft drop, which had contributed to my miss. The second shot was right on the button, confirming the first was down to pilot error.

Disturbed by the shooting, another beast trotted into view. I deployed the rifle once more on the Harris bipod. Holding true on the beast's heart I held a half-breath and fired. My majestic monarch of the glen absorbed the bullet; clinically dead on his hooves, he stood stock still for a moment before tumbling forwards toward the first stag.

This rifle was a real pleasure to shoot. Fit and finish were first-class, as was the hand ability. The trigger was a joy and, fitted with the superb Zeiss Victory scope and T8 mod, it was as good a set-up as it gets. T/C has taken a considered approach and the Icon is brilliantly conceived. At £1,362 for a rifle of this quality, the Icon will surely prove to be a serious contender for a first choice stalking rifle. **PC**

Thompson Tool and Warren Centre joined forces in 1965 to form Thompson Centre Arms, well known for its black powder muzzle-loaders, hunting handguns and rifles. In 2007, it became part of the Smith & Wesson Holdings group. This gave the company access to higher R&D, budgets, not forgetting piggy-backing on a world-renowned name in firearms. 'Foundation for accuracy' is one of its strap lines, so when two rifles kindly appeared from importer Viking Arms, I was hoping they were as good as promised.

In this review I go into more detail on the company's Icon rifle. As soon as I lifted the Icon from its box, I warmed to it. Visually, the angular receiver looks modern, with a quality wooden stock and a sleek, chromed bolt handle and release lever. I could see that this rifle targets the mid-range Sako customer, as opposed to the many entry-level rifles that I have reviewed over the past three months, and first impressions were spot on.

Starting with the stock, made from field-grade walnut, it looks and feels like a beauty, aided by high-quality chequering around the pistol grip and forend. The low, straight comb allows for a good head position that suits the mobile hunter shooting off sticks or freehand shots in the forest. With its traditional build, the stock oozes quality as soon as it reaches the shoulder and allows the perfect grip for both hands. I have possibly handled too many synthetic stocks recently, and need to get out a bit more, but I like it. One observation is that the forend is a little flexible, with little clearance between the barrel and wood for a fully floating barrel design, which was surprising for such a great piece of walnut. On removal of the action and barrel, the integral aluminium 'interlock bedding system' is visible. This accepts the three recoil lugs from the action – apparently a superior design to the larger single lug.

Moving on to the one-piece steel receiver, as mentioned before, it looks different thanks to the left-sided angular, flat receiver with the 'Icon' logo pressed into its large face. Finished in a deep matt bluing, as opposed to the shinier barrel, the receiver facilitates a smooth sliding bolt that most makers would be proud of.

I really warmed to the Weaver-style bases, integral to the receiver, which allow a wide variety of mounts to be fitted. The large, heavy bolt has a jewelled finish that draws the eye to the action and is easy to strip with the tools supplied in the kit. It supports three locking lugs to the front, resulting in a short 60-degree bolt throw, with a cocking indicator to the rear. For ejection, there is a tiny extractor fitted to one of these lugs, aided by a further spring plunger. As previously noted, the sleek chrome release lever ('butter knife' design), handle and the angular design of the rear of the bolt give it a tactile feel and modern look. I will pass comment on the bolt handle later, but Thompson Centre offers alternative bolt handles from a weather shield knurled design to a classic knob style.

The Icon has an adjustable trigger from three to five pounds and with this rifle set to a firm four pounds, there was little creep. The adjustment is made simply by removing the bolt and, with the use of the special Allen key, turning the adjuster screw that sits in the top of the trigger assembly. The blade feels narrow and is protected by an aluminium guard, which doubles up as part of the magazine support chassis. For safety, there is a basic two-position lever to the right of the action. To lock the bolt, slide another small lever to the rear, located to the front of the main safety. This automatically releases when the safety is pushed forward to fire.

The three-shot polymer magazine feels a little low-cost and, in my opinion, lets the rifle down. To release it, a small, stiff lever (too small to locate quickly when wearing gloves) is located to the front, which allows it to pop out efficiently thanks to two side springs. It feeds well and, with a closed-off extracting port, top feeding is not an option, so you have to use the magazine on all occasions.

Lastly, the 24in barrel has the unique TC '5R' rifling instead of the six lands and grooves used by most barrel makers. This apparently enhances accuracy, and with a match-grade barrel, not forgetting the medium contoured profile, this has all the attributes of a high performance rifle. With a twist rate of one in 10in, I expect it may favour heavier ammunition.

Overall, I would describe the Icon as an elegant, well-built and modern-looking rifle that oozes quality, setting itself apart from many of its competitors – but how does it perform in the field? For the review, Zeiss kindly supplied a Victory Diavari 3-12x56T* with a Rapid Z reticle attached by some Weaver bases, and for ammunition, Viking Arms supplied some Lapua 150-grain SP ammunition – ideal for the deer stalking that I had lined up. A Harris bipod was only fitted for zeroing and accuracy testing.

After zeroing, the Icon shot to 1.2in at 100 yards, which I thought was disappointing considering the superior design of the bolt and barrel. I used a variety of different weighted ammunition and received the best results with a 165-grain bullet. I am sure that, with a little more investigation, the expected sub one-inch would be achievable. This is a light 7¾lb rifle, and in .308, muzzle lift and recoil were noticeable, but acceptable considering the absence of a moderator. The four pound trigger was nicely firm but predictable, with little creep, and when easily adjusted to three pounds, I sensed a little more creep, but it helped accuracy. The pistol grip is long and wide, and with the quality chequering, it felt comfortable to shoot.

With the bipod fitted, the gap between the barrel and the inner forend surface was more or less nonexistent. This could be a slight concern if the barrel was screw cut and a heavy moderator fitted, as this may have an effect on the point of impact. Off sticks and other firm surfaces, the rifle felt superb to shoot and, despite the medium-weight barrel heating up, accuracy did not seem to be affected.

The second rifle I reviewed is the Venture. Chambered in .243, it has been aimed at the competitive end of the market. There are many makes of rifles in its price range, so will it stand out from the rest?

The Venture model comes with a very lightweight grey synthetic stock with lighter grey rubber inlays around the pistol grip and forend, making it an easy stock to handle, especially in wet and muddy conditions. The butt has a soft recoil pad – no doubt useful for larger calibres – with a fair degree of flex on the forend, but not quite enough to touch the barrel.

The robust-looking action comes complete with integrated Weaver style scope mounts and a two-stage safety catch positioned to the right of the bolt, which allows the bolt to cycle when engaged. As for the bolt, similarly to the Icon it has three lugs, a 60-degree throw and is substantial and easily disassembled, though it is not as smooth as the Icon.

The trigger was set to three and a half pounds, but unlike the Icon it has a simple two-position safety without the bolt lock facility. The barrel is a standard lightweight hunting grade with a length of 22in, screw cut (1/2in UNF) to accept a moderator, with a one in 10in twist.

For the review, Swarovski kindly sent a range of Z3 scopes, so I opted for a compact 3-10x42 model with a 4A reticle. Once again, high quality Lapua 100-grain SP ammunition was supplied (MV 2,950fps), and Viking Arms provided the short and lightweight Swiss B&T moderator.

Once on paper, the first group at 100 yards was just under an inch, which was as expected, and the lighter 70-grain ammunition grouped a little better. Shooting the Venture, the pistol grip felt very comfortable, helped by the soft hand pads. With the bipod removed, it was well balanced when used for freehand shots. The forend was a little soft and flexed on the bipod – typical of most rifles at this price. The

small amount of trigger creep was acceptable; otherwise it was very crisp. The bolt was precise, smooth and felt tight throughout its travel, telling that the whole action is of a superior standard and finish.

As my wedding anniversary loomed, I thought a romantic weekend in Exmoor would fit the bill. Coincidentally, it is home to many West Country shooting estates, so with the Icon and my wife's camera gear secured in the car, off we ventured. Surrounded by some of the most famous pheasant and partridge shoots, such as Clovelly and Castle Hill, I met up with well-known stalker Paul Messenger of Beckland Game. Paul manages his own business as a sporting agent, acting for several local shoots together with his own shoots, along with access to duck, woodcock and snipe shooting. With regards to red, fallow and roe deer, Paul takes clients over several large estates in North Devon and North Cornwall. The Exmoor stags have a reputation for being some of the largest in the country, with an 18-pointer having been shot only two weeks before my visit. Paul is the current chairman and training officer for the

West Country branch of the BDS – not only is he busy, he also has a wealth of information on most aspects of country sports.

We set off into Biteford Woods, a plantation of sitka spruce surrounded by old oak trees that have been stunted and suppressed by the extreme weather of that part of the country. After a short, wet stalk, Paul spied a roe doe grazing in a narrow ride 60 yards ahead of us. Up came the sticks, then the rifle, followed by two very loud reports, one from the gun and one from Paul – he had forgotten about the Icon's lack of moderator. Good shot placement ensured quick and humane dispatch.

I enjoyed shooting the Icon thanks to its classic stock and modern-looking action. I was slightly disappointed with the accuracy, but with new rifles this is often the case, and they usually improve with use. The Achilles' heel of this rifle is its easily changeable bolt handle, as it cannot be gripped when cycling quickly – it looks nice and shiny but that's it. With an RRP of £1,200, it sits in the higher Tikka or Sako price range, and if you like something a little different, then this is your rifle. The Venture is a hard-working,

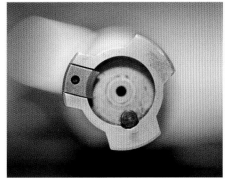

functional and accurate rifle, and at £779 it is just above the budget Savage, Ruger and Marlin models, not forgetting the Howa 1500s. It is a very competitive end of the market, and as they are all accurate, it is down to individual tastes, but it is great to have the choice. **TP**

### TC ICON

**Model tested:** Icon standard action in .308

**Price range:** £1,200

**Contact:** Viking Arms  01423 780810
**www.vikingarms.com**

# THOMPSON CENTER VENTURE

Thompson Center (TC) is not a well known brand in this country, so I was looking forward to receiving one in .204 Ruger from UK importer Viking Arms.

The Thompson Center 'Venture' has been aimed at the value end of the market (its standard retail price is £778) to compete against the Browning, CZ, Remington and cheaper Tikkas. This is a very competitive market, so I was looking forward to finding out what makes it stand out from its competitors.

The Venture model comes with a lightweight grey synthetic stock with lighter grey rubber inlays around the pistol grip and forend – making it a very easy stock to handle, especially in wet and muddy conditions. The butt end has a soft recoil pad – no doubt very useful for the larger calibres. For this review a bipod was fitted, giving it a fair degree of flex on the forend although not quite enough to touch the barrel.

The robust-looking action comes complete with integrated Weaver-style scope mounts and a two-stage safety catch positioned to the right of the bolt, which will still allow the bolt to cycle when engaged. As for the chunky bolt, it has a throw short of 60 degrees, can be easily disassembled by hand and seems rather smooth for a new rifle in this price range. Three lugs are used to lock it into the front of the receiver. To release this tight, well-fitting assembly, press a lever to the left of the action – it will come out easily. The tough-looking magazine is made of hardened plastic that holds three rounds and is released by an easily found metal clip, located to the front.

The trigger was set to about 3.5lb but, as with most TC rifles, a hex-headed key is supplied, allowing you to quickly adjust it to your needs. To do this, simply remove the bolt, locate a set screw that sits above the trigger assembly, and turn it to increase or decrease the trigger pressure. Refit the bolt and test it – it is that straightforward.

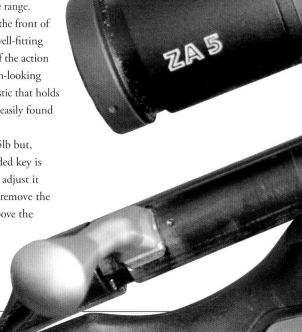

Other trigger adjustments can easily be made by removing the stock. For this review, I reset the pressure to 2.5lb. While there was a little trigger creep, it felt reasonably crisp – no problems there.

As for the barrel, it is a typical lightweight hunting grade with a standard length of 22in, screw-cut to accept a moderator. With a 1-in-10in twist, it should suit the heavier bullets. Another unique feature of most TC barrels is that they use '5R' rifling that uses five lands and five grooves, which apparently means the lands are directly opposite from the grooves. The manufacturer says this reduces damage from the bullet travelling down the barrel and maintains a more consistent chamber pressure. Furthermore, this increases accuracy – all rifles come with a guaranteed 1MOA accuracy at 100 yards.

So the Thompson Center Venture boasts impressive attributes on paper: an ergonomic stock, short-throw bolt, easily adjustable trigger pressure to suit most shooters, and a guaranteed accuracy of 1MOA. It was time to see if the field test would support these claims. For the review, a ZA5 Minox 3-15x40 with a BDC reticle was supplied with Millett mounts, which clamp onto the Weaver-lookalike base mounts.

Bearing in mind

this was a brand new rifle in the tiny, fragile .204 Ruger calibre, I anticipated problems trying to achieve 'out of the box' accuracy from the first shot. Mind you, other accuracy issues arose due to time constraints. On top of that, I had to put up with winds of a constant 7-15mph, sometimes gusting up to 20mph.

As with all my rifle tests, I only used the bipod as a support – I didn't use a rear support. This exactly replicates the position I would be in when out foxing or varminting in the field.

I used Remington 32- and 40-grain Premier Accutip ammo to push the little projectiles out at a blistering 4,200 and 3,900fps respectively. Once zeroed 0.5in high at 100 yards (200-yard zero), the 32-grain achieved a 1.5in group and the 40-grain 1.7in. After shooting 20 rounds, the groups came in to 1.25in. Bearing in mind that the wind was moving the rifle, this was not too shabby. I would expect to see 0.5in accuracy for this round in still conditions. Recoil was, as anticipated, very light. When I popped

on my large T8 moderator, it was hardly noticeable, with little or no effect on retaining full sight picture while taking the shot.

The pistol grip felt very comfortable to shoot with, helped by the soft hand pads. With the bipod removed, it was well balanced when used for freehand shots. As mentioned, the forend was a little soft, and when bounced on the bipod the gap between it and the barrel was easily closed – it nearly touched the barrel. The small amount of trigger creep was acceptable, and the trigger was otherwise very crisp.

When ejecting, be warned – these tiny cases will be thrown at least three feet thanks to an exceptionally efficient ejector. The bolt was very precise, fairly smooth and felt quite tight throughout its travel, telling that the whole action is of a superior standard and

## THE GROUPS CAME IN TO 1.25IN. BEARING IN MIND THE WIND, THIS WAS NOT TOO SHABBY

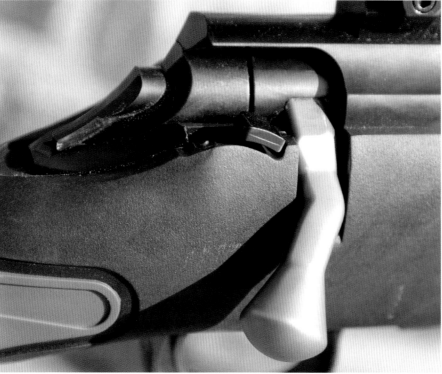

finish. You can see if the bolt is cocked by looking at its back end. As for the safety catch, however, on many occasions I found it would not return to the safety position after cocking. Maybe an adjustment was required, but the safety is something that needs to work every time.

A farming colleague of mine called to tell me he had lost three lambs the previous night. This was a great opportunity to test the rifle, as it was a bitterly cold night with a strong, icy, easterly wind.

Despite not seeing any foxes prowling around the sheep, I tested the .204 on a couple of rabbits from 100-175 yards using the Lightforce Striker lamp. Even though I was wearing gloves, the trigger was very pleasant and the bolt was easy to cycle. The magazine was simple to remove with one hand, but not the easiest to fill as it was very tight in the cold weather. The Minox scope's BDC reticle performed well for varminting, and the crosshairs were just the right thickness for night shooting.

Overall, this is a well put together rifle for the price. I would welcome the opportunity to test other Thompson Center rifles – they do produce rifles that are higher up the price scale, and that's where they really get tempting. As for the rifle in hand: If it was up against a low-end Tikka, CZ or Remington, would a perspective buyer take a gamble and move away from the well established brands? Pick one up, check out the action, tweak that adjustable trigger and you will be hooked. With a lifetime warranty and a guaranteed accuracy of 1MOA (1in at 100 yards), it is definitely a lot of rifle for the money. **TP**

### TC VENTURE

**Model tested:** Venture sporting weight in .204 Ruger

**Price range:** Around £800

**Contact:** Viking Arms  01423 780810
**www.vikingarms.com**

# TIKKA T3

Let me start by saying that when I test a new rifle, my thoughts are always slanted towards the practical aspect rather than the high-tech approach adopted by many. I have always believed that a substantial number of shooters and prospective rifle buyers want information that is applicable to the gun's use in the field, rather than technical descriptions. Another point I have heard made is that reviews never run down anything that is being tested. You may be assured that if I test a product – whatever it may be – and I really don't like it or something about it, I will say so. In the past I have bought items that have certainly not had their faults revealed by the reviewer, and I would not wish that experience on anybody else.

I bore that in mind when GMK sent me a Tikka T3 Varmint Blue in .223 Rem for testing. I personally own a Sako 85 and have been a fan of Finnish gunmaking for a long time. Read any of the shooting websites and you will see a steady stream of praise for the T3. Getting the rifle out of the box, it was easy to see why this rifle has become so popular.

The overall length was 40in with barrel length of 20in; with these dimensions it felt compact. The heavy barrel pushed the weight up to 7½lb without a scope or moderator, but owing to the overall dimensions the weight did not present a problem.

Being of the old school, I have to say I am not a great fan of synthetic stocks, but I can see the advantages to using modern materials. In our climate, possibly the two greatest benefits of the synthetic stock are its resistance to weather and the fact that it does not tend to warp. The stock on the T3 does feel a bit flimsy but – made from glass-reinforced polymer – it is undoubtedly stronger than it appears. The cheekpiece is nicely shaped and the pistol grip is slim, unlike many synthetic stocks. There does not appear to be a palm swell but the grip was comfortable, the wide forend is sturdy and the moulded chequering, like that on the neck of the stock, settles well into your hold. It takes a bipod with no distortion at all. Normally I don't use a bipod, relying on my Bushwear tripod, but I have to say the T3 lent itself very well to being used with one.

The heavy barrel, with its one in 12 twist (ideal for the lighter foxing rounds), is nicely finished, and the overall appearance is pleasing while at the same time being highly functional.

The magazine has come in for some criticism, as it's all-polymer in its construction. There have also been negative responses to the way the magazine protrudes below the rifle body. Well, yes

it does, but it is merely an aesthetic issue – in use it presents no problem – and if its critics really hated the look of it they probably wouldn't have bought it in the first place.

The concept of the T3 is that one size caters for all calibres. The long action, which is machined from a solid piece of steel, is the same for all calibres, and changes to the calibre are catered for by altering the magazine internals. The integral scope rails are best suited to Sako/Tikka optilock bases, which, with their polymer inserts, are by far the best to use with these two makes of rifle. They are not the cheapest but they are certainly the choice of many discerning shooters.

The trigger is a single-stage unit and is adjustable. Unlike some American rifles, these Finnish items have useable triggers straight out of the box. The test rifle tripped the tester at a shade over three pounds – not too far adrift – and showed no discernible creep. The magazine, which is released by pressure on a small catch situated at the forward end, allows the magazine to drop easily into your hand. The capacity is five in the single stack magazine with one in the chamber.

Sling/bipod swivels come as standard, as does the factory screw cutting for the moderator. The safety catch is the standard build: Forward to fire, rearward for safe. The usual red dot is displayed when ready to fire, as is the red indicator at the rear of the bolt showing that the rifle is cocked.

As I said earlier I am not a great lover of synthetic rifles, but in truth the more I handled the Tikka the more I got to like it. I suppose the word that sums it up is: 'Functional'.

Having done the descriptive piece, I was ready to try it out in the field. The first outing was to zero the rifle; the scope GMK had sent me was a Burris 3-9x50 Fullfield with the Ballistic Plex reticle. I had never used a Burris before but found that this one did the job well. It comes with a range finding facility as well as information relating to specific loads. At under £250 it's exceptionally good value.

Boresighting the T3 got it pretty well on target. It is always a bit tedious when you follow the 'shoot one and clean' method, which is essential on a new weapon to ensure a long and accurate life. Once I was on the A4 size target, another half a dozen shots started to show results. Groups of one inch or a fraction over were duly punched in the paper. For a brand new weapon, this is more than good enough to take it into the field. I am quite

sure that when 'shot in' the T3 would perform to a standard that would prove more than adequate for foxing. Home loaders (whose numbers are ever increasing) would, I am sure, be able to squeeze the groups even tighter.

A day or so after sighting the rifle in, I took it out on a beautiful evening to wait for one of the local foxes that had been giving a friend some grief. After a pleasant wait in the sun, Charlie appeared and most accommodatingly curled up and went to sleep 140 yards away. The first shot this Tikka fired in anger went straight through the fox's mouth, and its evening siesta became permanent.

There really couldn't have been a better test for this very practical rifle. The more I used it, the more its appearance and general feel appealed to me. Comfortable to carry and use, and easy to maintain, I really started to enjoy the T3 even though it's not dressed in wood! Although it is not one of the most expensive rifles out there, the phrase that probably sums it up is, in fact: 'More than fit for purpose'. **MP**

Before you say it, I know what you are thinking. This model of Tikka T3 is not really a traditional hunting rifle, what with all its adjustable gizmos, heavy barrel and bright laminated stock, but the Tikka Sporter concept has been around for many years. In Scandinavia, they are used for a range of shooting disciplines such as target, biathlon and hunting.

I managed to pick up an older Tikka M55 Sporter in .308 from the 2010 Game Fair for under £500, and used it for deer control and target practice out to over 800 yards with ½MOA accuracy. In 2011, the new T3 Tikka Sporter was launched, and after I badgered importer GMK to lend me one, my late Christmas present arrived, much to my delight.

The Sporter, in simplistic terms, uses the T3 Varmint model steelwork dressed with a high quality laminated stock, designed to shoot in all positions. The T3 range guarantees 1MOA accuracy and exceptional engineering, resulting in one of the most popular rifles in the UK.

The action and barrel are both finished in matt black. An integral dovetail scope rail accepts a wide range of optical mounts, together with screw holes to help fit Weaver-style rails if required. The bolt, with its twin locking lugs is, as

ever, simple and smooth to operate with a short, 70-degree throw. Combined with a large knob, it is a fast and effortless bolt to cycle. A standard extractor claw and plunger ejector system provide a reliable and proven ejection. To the rear, a cocking indicator is easy to see together with a two-position safety catch that locks the bolt when applied.

The single stage trigger is factory set to a heavy 3.75lb, but can be adjusted after removing the stock with the help of a hex-head key. As with most Tikkas, the trigger is crisp with little or no creep whatsoever, but if I was the owner, I would reduce it to just above 2lb, helping me shoot more accurately at long range. The trigger guard, as with the magazine, is made of high-density plastic, and is neatly enveloped by the laminated stock. The stock also drops down to cover the magazine, and with a capacity of six rounds (two mags supplied) it uses a single column feed with the release catch to the front.

The barrel is available in two lengths – 20in threaded to M18mm or 24in unthreaded – with a heavy profile and fully free-floating. This is ideal for target shooting, as the point of impact should not alter when the barrel warms up. This rifle has a twist rate of 1 in 8in, which is perfect for bullets over 50 grains, but a 1 in 14in is also available for the faster, lighter bullets.

So we have a proven, smooth and efficient action and a heavyweight barrel that I know will perform, but what about that stock? It is laminated wood with of a range of beige, dark grey and bright orange colours. A variety of spacers are supplied with the rifle, so the butt plate can be adjusted to increase or decrease the length of pull. The cheekpiece can be raised by over an inch, and moved sideways by just under ½in. To remove the bolt, the cheekpiece must be taken off using the Torx key, but there is a clever 'memory' screw that can be set to help refit it to a preset height. The pistol grip is smooth and recessed to allow the trigger finger to naturally curl around the stock. The thumb also sinks into the rear of the bolt area, making the whole handling experience an ergonomic dream. There is no chequering anywhere, and when it rains it is not the easiest of rifles to grip, but you can't have everything.

The forend is vented, wide and chunky with a good clearance from the barrel. There is also an eight-inch adjustable rail for the fitting of a variety of slings and with the correct fitting kit, a bipod (not supplied). However,

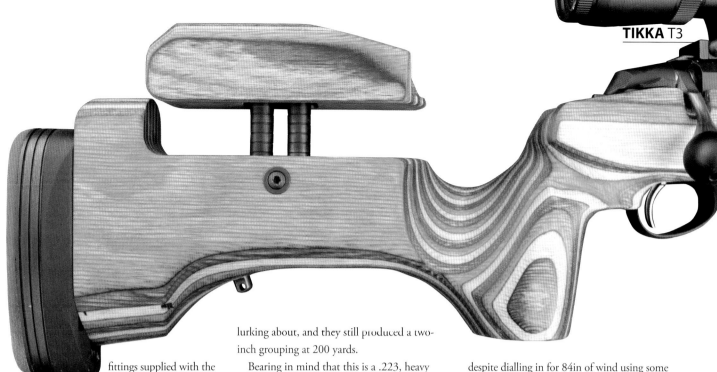

fittings supplied with the rifle include a T25 Torx key, QD clips and sling attachments.

Now for the interesting part of the test: How does it shoot? For the review, GMK supplied a Leupold 4.5-15x50 with a mil-dot illuminated reticle, secured with a set of Optilock bases and 30mm rings. Also supplied by Jackson Rifles was an ASE Utra Jet-Z Compact moderator. As for ammunition, I used a variety of weights and brands, namely 40-grain Federal Nosler Ballistic Tip, 55-grain Sako Gamehead soft point and some specialist rounds, Speer Gold Dot 64-grain, all supplied by GMK.

Once zeroed at 200 yards using a bipod, it was soon apparent that this was a very accurate rifle. With an unladen weight of 9lb (4.1kg), it gave me a stable platform to shoot off. I adjusted the butt pad and cheekpiece to the most comfortable position, allowing me to shoot groups of around 1.4–1.75in using all the different weights of ammunition. The best was achieved by the Sako 55-grain ammunition at 1.4in. I have some cheap military 67-grain stuff

lurking about, and they still produced a two-inch grouping at 200 yards.

Bearing in mind that this is a .223, heavy rifle, with a moderator and bipod, the recoil was negligible, and thanks to the smooth T3 action, it was a pleasure to shoot. The pistol grip fitted my hand well, aided by the enhanced palm swell, giving me complete and total control of every aspect of the shooting process. I've got to say it – I felt at one with the Sporter. At 300 yards, now in variable winds, it achieved under a 2½in grouping, telling me that this is capable of a consistent ½-¾MOA.

Not content with that, I, together with experienced riflemen Matt and Chris, cluttered off to Wales to test the Sporter at longer ranges at WMS, courtesy of Andrew Venables. The wind was blowing down the range from the right at 8-12mph, which can be testing for such small bullets. Chris took control and once the zero was checked, the 800-yard mark seemed like a fair challenge for a person with his rather annoying natural ability. Once the bullets were dialled in for a sizeable 212in (17ft) of drop using the superb target turrets on the Leupold scope, Chris managed to hit a 10in steel plate with most shots,

despite dialling in for 84in of wind using some higher quality match grade 77-grain ammunition.

Suffice to say, these shots are way beyond the range of responsible hunters, but they demonstrated the ability of the Sporter. Is it a hunting rifle, though – practical in the field or woodland? Before I come to a conclusion, I think the desire for better accuracy, and perhaps an increase in the popularity of longer-range varminting, has made the use of heavier rifles more acceptable. If you, like me, enjoy shooting anything from 50-yard foxes to 1,000-yard targets, the Sporter will suit you well. Lose the moderator and the rifle feels well balanced, and practical to shoot off sticks or resting the wide forend on something suitable.

This would make a brilliant varminting rifle, and with some careful homeloading, I reckon accuracy of around ½MOA could be achieved. Maybe it does look a little 'loud' when stalking, but frankly, I don't care. If I was a 'one gun' sporting rifleman who also enjoys range work, this concept of rifle would be well worth considering.

In my opinion it is really designed for the target market, but in Scandinavia, they have superb competitions based on a biathlon-style contest, where competitors also use this type of rifle for hunting. With an SRP of £1,645, it is available in a limited range of calibres and can only be bought by special order, but it demonstrates Tikka's ability to provide a personalised service to the all-round rifleman. **TP**

## TIKKA T3

**Models tested:** Varmint Blue in .223; Sporter in .223

**Price range:** Models from £935

**Contact:** GMK  01489 587500
**www.gmk.co.uk**

# VOERE 2155

s the 'K98 action' description dragged my gaze across the page of the magazine, I was sure that I had never come across Voere rifles before. This despite the Austrian company being in business for more than 60 years. It looked like it ticked all the boxes for being a real gem of a rifle, so I hunted down Global Rifle online and went about organising a rifle to test.

For many hunters, the ultimate world-conquering action can be found in the age-old K98 design. Voere builds all its fullbore rifles on reclaimed Mauser 98 actions, screened, tested, and refurbished before re-barrelling and re-stocking ready for the consumer. Given the volume of old Mauser based rifles available, and the expense entailed in producing brand new handmade actions, this process allows Voere to keep the cost reasonable.

After ogling the fine woodwork in the magazine article I'd been reading, I was a little disappointed by the rubberised synthetic stock base model that greeted me on opening the box. I have come around to synthetic stocks in recent years, but this one didn't do much for me. The rubber over-mould was like the Hogue stocks on a Howa, which I am a fan of, but the shape, Braille-like grips and hugely flexible forend were a bit of a turn off. Knowing that some fine-looking wood was also an option, I put my misgivings to one side and turned my attention to the action.

The familiar action design was exactly what I expected: Two locking lugs at the front of the bolt and a third at the rear, a strong oversized extractor claw and a solid controlled feed providing positive ejection of every case. On requesting more information from the manufacturer, I discovered that the Voere 2155 is built on reclaimed Santa Barbara Mausers. My own investigation uncovered that these were originally manufactured in Spain, and are almost identical to the Centurion Mauser actions. Both are near-perfect copies of the now obsolete Firearms International FN Deluxe action, with many of the components reportedly manufactured by the military arsenal in La Coruña.

One difference, however, is found in the manufacturing process, which in the case of the Santa Barbara entailed an investment casting

process. Today, the high-end Mauser 98-based actions are machined steel, providing a stronger, more refined build.

One of the best of these in modern production comes from Granite Mountain Arms. Indeed, the last I heard from Holland and Holland was that they too were ceasing to reclaim actions, as high quality K98s become harder to source, and instead now have actions built to their exacting specifications in Germany.

Taking a closer look at the bolt, I was surprised by the lack of refinement given the reconditioning. Voere is advertised as providing precision machining technology in another arm of the company, so it was hard to understand the unpolished surfaces on the action. It is interesting to note that Frank de Haas made similar observations on the original Santa Barbara action (Bolt Action Rifles, 4th edition).

Dry working the bolt felt like any classic Mauser 98. They are roomy to operate, but that is one of the reasons for their inherent reliability in all conditions. Certainly it had been vastly improved from its previous Spanish incarnation, with lapping and polishing along the bolt raceways and locking lugs.

As with most K98 based rifles, cycling rounds requires a firm forward stroke as the case rides under the ejector claw. On my first try, the Voere chambered with far more force than I was

expecting, and on inspection of the ejected case I could see why. An oversight on the magazine shoulders had left very sharp burred edges, which gripped the cases instead of letting them roll over. Five minutes with some wet and dry emery paper would fix the problem permanently.

Like the trigger, the safety is available in a number of different factory options. The wing safety that was fitted to the rifle on test is impractical for a scoped rifle, despite being cut down to accommodate scopes. Even with the medium-height mounts supplied, I was actually unable put it on safe. My advice would be to opt for the low rotary safety catch, which is nicer and quieter to operate. Other options are also available and worth looking at before deciding, including the ability to cock and de-cock the weapon with your thumb – a feature Voere has cleverly adapted to retro fit on Remington-based actions as well.

The fitted trigger was again the basic option. Described as a 'shotgun trigger' in their literature, there wasn't a great deal to love about the heavy, creepy break. The original Santa Barbara trigger was superior, and similar in design to a modern, fully adjustable Timney. I would go for the upgraded K98-MF Direct trigger unit, which shoots much nicer, though it will add another £115 to the rifle.

Taking the rifle to the range, I shot a variety of .308 Win rounds, including a few hand

loads. Starting with the supplied Hornady performance 150-grain ammo, the rifle returned a first group of three just on the 1.5in mark. After familiarising myself with the trigger, I did marginally better with subsequent groupings, but the poor sear release was hindering the rifle's ability to shoot. Pushing some 140-grain ammo down-range produced similar results, but the 170-grain Geco ammo I used didn't agree with the rifle, scattering holes across 2.5in.

Extending handloaded 150-grain heads close to the lands with neck-sized brass, I was able to close the groups to between 1 and 1.25in. This wouldn't be acceptable as a varminting rifle, but chambered in .308 Win, it isn't intended as one, and this performance will be more than adequate for most applications.

For those who want to own an original Mauser action rifle, the Voere does provide a viable option. It requires a bit of refinement, but with the available upgrades and a wooden stock, this could be a very serviceable rifle. Built on the famous K98 you can't go far wrong. **BP**

**VOERE 2155**

*Model tested:* 2155 in .308 Win

*Price range:* From £850

*Contact:* Global Rifle  01455 291100
**www.globalrifle.co.uk**

# WEATHERBY VANGUARD

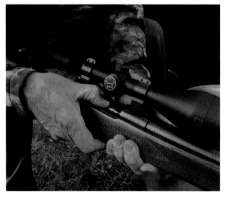

When I was young, and avidly read American and Canadian shooting magazines, the Weatherby ranked alongside such top names as Marlin and Ruger. So I was looking forward to seeing the Weatherby Vanguard 'in the flesh'. Would this mystical name live up to my boyhood dreams once it arrived on these shores?

Times have moved on, and the American gun-making scene now looks carefully at the wider market. On opening the box I was pleasantly surprised. The stock was finished in straight-grained walnut with a rosewood tip to the forend, and the cheekpiece on the Monte Carlo-type stock was nicely finished and comfortable in use. The chequering was sharp and well defined, and the stock was completed with a well-fitted rubber butt pad. There was some fibreglass bedding, and the overall fitting of the action and barrel to the stock was extremely good for a rifle in this kind of price range. Any chasing out of the forend had been nicely finished.

Sling swivels had been fitted, and the 24in barrel was screw-cut with a half-inch UNF thread. The screw-cutting was well executed, and the crown was quite deeply cut. The blueing was not heavy, but it was more than adequate. The twist rate is one in 12. The safety catch is a conventional 'forward for fire, rearward for safe' mechanism, and there is a cocking indicator at the rear of the bolt.

The manufacturers guarantee a 1.5 MOA at 100 yards. Although many would say this is not outstanding by modern standards, it is good enough in the field, and many of these rifles will do much better than this. Home loaders will, of course, greatly improve on the guaranteed figure.

The rifle is largely manufactured by Howa in Japan, a relationship that dates back to the 1960s. While Weatherby is associated largely with its two magnum calibres, .257 and .460, it has a much wider range available today.

The Vanguard resembles both the Remington 700 and the Winchester Model 70 – which

is not surprising, as the rifle was originally brought out to offer an alternative to those two icons. The magazine, which is of floor-plate design, takes five rounds; the trigger pull was excellent and broke crisply at just over three pounds. It was good to see that American rifles have addressed trigger pulls.

This particular rifle was on loan from Sportsman Gun Centre, which is now the distributor for Weatherby. I decided to test the combo deal Sportsman offers on this rifle, which includes the rifle, a scope (in this case a Redfield Revolution 3-9x50) and a Wildcat Predator 8 sound moderator. I was keen to try the scope, as it would be the first time I had got my hands on this particular make.

The whole outfit looked the part, but the real test would come in the field. Cleaning the rifle before testing showed a very good standard of finish, both internally and externally. Bore sighting the rifle at 50 yards got the Sako 55-grain ammo on the paper after a couple of rounds. From there I moved the target out to 100 yards, zeroing an inch high as usual. It only took three shots before I was on the money, so I switched targets to the excellent life-sized fox target copied from Robert Bucknell's Foxing with Lamp and Rifle. I put three shots in, and they did the

trick. I know I only tried one make of ammo, but I am quite sure this rifle is more than capable of producing even better results with factory ammo matched to it. Home loaders will almost certainly do better still.

The Redfield scope performed well, with a clean, sharp picture. I would have liked the turrets to have sharper, more well-defined 'clicks', but I am just being picky – this does not affect the actual performance of the scope. Redfield scopes are made by Leupold in Oregon, so you would expect the build quality to be well up to standard. Leupold has resurrected the old, established Redfield name, and this range of scopes will certainly have an impact on the market. Price-wise, it slots into the mid-range of a market that has an ever-wider choice to fit all pockets.

UK Custom Shop's Wildcat Predator 8 is well known to me, as I have used both the Predator 8 and the Whisper on my own rifles for some time now. Both are very well made and can be stripped down for cleaning. As usual, the test model performed perfectly, bringing the noise down to a very acceptable level. Also, although not small, this is one of the few mods that doesn't look totally out of place on a rifle.

What, then, were my overall thoughts on this set-up? I have to say, I am well aware that

there are those who say reviewers always 'big up' the test items. This is because there is not much point in reviewing rubbish. And most of what I get offered for test is truly of very good quality. This certainly applied to this outfit – I liked pretty much everything about it. The rifle felt right somehow – nothing pretentious, but a good-looking, functional rifle that gave the impression it would give many years of trouble-free service.

If I was looking for a reasonably priced rifle, I would certainly look very closely at a Weatherby, and probably end up buying one. Well made and well finished with plenty of attention to detail, it was a pleasure to test.

I also applaud Sportsman Gun Centre's decision to marry the rifle to the scope and moderator selected in the deal. This gives a practical, sensible and above all really usable rifle for foxing. Anyone coming into the sport and looking for a good set-up really wouldn't go far wrong with this one, especially at the combo price.

The rifle I reviewed was in .223, but Weatherby offers a full range of calibres to suit all needs. If time permits, I will take it out and see what Charlie thinks about it. **MP**

Weatherby as a company is best known for producing some of the most powerful hunting cartridges in the world, chambered, of course, in its famous Weatherby Mk V rifles. In the 1970s it introduced a line of rifles that would support the less powerful cartridges on offer, and brought to the market the Vanguard line. Like the Mk V, it was built by Howa in Japan, but the design was quite different. This allowed Weatherby to launch the Vanguard to the shooting public at a very affordable price level.

The rifle has enjoyed a lot of success over the years because it is seen as an excellent budget choice and still delivers solid build quality. It has always been one of the cheapest fullbore rifles available in the UK, and gives a lot of 'bang for your buck'. Now, the Vanguard has been relaunched after many years without any wholesale changes. After months of waiting, the Vanguard Mk 2 is finally here.

I have always been a big fan of Howa rifles, with their rock-solid and simple design. Given that the Weatherby Vanguard is almost an identical rifle, I had an idea of what to expect. I was, however, eager to examine the tweaks that had been made to modernise the rifle. Most importantly, all Vanguard Mk 2s now come with a 1MOA guarantee, bettering the 1.5MOA that was previously the standard. It would be interesting to see if the rifle

could live up to this on the range, especially considering these promises were being made about a rifle with such a low price.

The new stock is the first upgrade to become obvious on picking up the rifle. I was testing the basic synthetic model, and of all the entry-level rifles that have passed through my hands, this had by far the best stock. There is some awful injection-moulded rubbish on the market that is horrendous in both design and feel. It is an easy trap for manufacturers to fall into as they try to cut costs to offer the most affordable rifle on the market. Across the board, Weatherby has been careful not to fall foul of the common mistakes.

It may be a trivial point, but dropping the black in favour of a grey/green stock does make the rifle appear and feel more expensive than it is. In line with modern trends, Weatherby also opted for a hard-wearing rubberised material instead of chequering, inlaying it in a similar way to the synthetic stocks in Sako rifles. This is an excellent choice, providing optimal grip in even the worst conditions. Most importantly, however, the ribbed design of the forestock ensures rigidity, and prevents the terrible side-to-side flexing so common in cheap synthetic stocks. There is no doubt that for the money this is the best synthetic stock on the market.

Turning our attention to the action doesn't really provide any revelations. Those who are familiar with Howa rifles or the old Vanguard will find few alterations here. The action is a one-piece steel receiver, with a sturdy integral

recoil lug, drilled and tapped for mounts on top. The bolt has been refined marginally with a matt finish on the handle, and, unlike the Howa, has a knurled band around the bolt knob. Weatherby has also removed the rather tacky red 'F' and 'S' stamped on the bolt shroud, instead opting for black lettering – much more sensible.

The other noticeable difference between the two brands of rifle is the addition of flutes on the bolt shaft of the Weatherby. This helps to gather grit and dirt, while also carrying residual oil to lubricate loading. The twin lug design remains unchanged, providing push-feed loading, a push-bottom ejector and long, M16-type extractor. This is a tried, tested, simple and strong design that I found hard to fault.

The trigger on the Mk 2 has been vastly improved, offering a two-stage adjustable unit, with a three-position safety catch. Growing up with Weihrauch air rifles, I was spoilt with a

quality Rekord trigger from an early age, and really appreciated the two stages offered by the design. This is, however, rarely seen in fullbore rifles. I was surprised to find, firstly, that the Vanguard offered this, and, secondly, that the release was actually very good. American rifles have historically been fitted with heavy and really quite poor triggers. Although it would have been nice if the unit adjusted down another half a pound, I can't really complain, and wouldn't go to the expense of fitting an after-market trigger.

The overall finish of the rifle was good, with the bead blasted bluing on the metalwork particularly nice. The bottom metal is solid and functional, but didn't fit as flush into the stock as I would have liked. This model came with a drop plate, although a magazine upgrade is available, providing either a five- or ten-shot capacity. Sportsman Gun Centre, which imports Weatherby rifles, screw cuts all the models on arrival, making them ready to accept

the moderator of your choice.

It's not the lightest of rifles, but is perfectly manageable, weighing in at 7½lb. In the hand it feels quite chunky, owing largely to the flared forestock. My personal preference is for a slightly slimmer profile, such as that sported by the sleek lines of a Classic Steyr Mannlicher. However, everyone is different, and from a functional standpoint the wider bottom holds a bipod more securely.

The one major criticism I have of the rifle is easily rectifiable, though it is marginally frustrating that such details were not considered in the factory. Most rifles today come with free-floating barrels as standard, yet here we

see the stock firmly held in the barrel channel. Under the barrel, inside the stock, there is plenty of free space, but the channel edges and tip of the forestock touch along the entire length. It would have been easier to design the stock mould to give generous clearance. A small amount of time with fine emery paper will soon rectify the issue, and I would suggest doing this. With the substantial recoil lug and flat bottomed action, there is ample fixed area to support the generously profiled barrel.

As with any rifle, range results are important, but as I have said before, results have to be observed with caution, as it can take some time to find a load that

demonstrates what a rifle is really capable of. The Vanguard comes with a 1MOA guarantee using premium ammo, so this certainly bodes well. I didn't have time to work up hand loads before getting this review out – owing largely to the terrible weather that has tormented hunters and farmers – but a good selection of factory ammo allowed a fair test. Shooting from 150-grain through to 180-grain, the standout winner was the 162-grain and 168-grain A-Max from Hornady. With these rounds, the rifle was able to drop bullets into the promised 1MOA, although it was apparent that the rifle shot better when rested on a sandbag as opposed to a bipod. I am sure this

is down to the lack of free-floating barrel. There isn't a lot you can buy for £600 these days, and every penny will certainly be well spent for anyone who adds the Vanguard to their collection. This rifle really is superb value for money, and I am sure it will find favour with many shooters. **BP**

### WEATHERBY VANGUARD

**Models tested:** Vanguard in walnut .223; Vanguard Mk2 in .308

**Price range:** Models from £600

**Contact:** Sportsman Gun Centre
01392 354854
**www.sportsmanguncentre.co.uk**

# WHICH CALIBRE

Deciding on the ideal foxing, deer stalking, or big game calibre is no small task, but it is one all riflemen will have to ponder over more than once in their career. Most UK hunters will either be a foxer or a stalker, some will be both, and a big percentage will travel overseas to hunt on an annual basis. Taking hunters as a whole, most will have mixed sporting interests. For them, there is no one perfect calibre that can cover all quarries and eventualities.

If you want a one-rifle calibre choice for UK deer and foxing, it would have to be the .243 Winchester. Although I would hesitate at trying to tackle a big West Country red stag with a .243, I have shot a considerable number of hill stags with this calibre. For all UK species and the occasional safari, boar or moose hunt, I would probably choose a 6.5x55 Swedish, .308 Winchester or .30-06 Springfield. That said, the .300 Winchester Magnum is suitable for all UK, European and US game, plus it's a perfect

choice for all African antelope. For the regular travelling hunter, this calibre would be the ideal one-rifle choice as it is suitable for everything but the big five – though it could be considered a little on the large side for smaller deer species. One may encounter difficulties obtaining a variation for this calibre for UK deer, but there are a number of FAC holders who do possess it for stalking, so don't rule it out.

Foxing is the fastest growing sector of our sport, with specific kit increasing on a near daily basis. Known as varminting in the USA, it is a term universally applied to predator hunting, from coyotes to prairie dogs. I mention the US term because it is being used more and more to refer to fox and corvid control with centrefire rifles this side of the Atlantic pond. Though I have enjoyed a lot of foxing forays in my time as a keeper, my hunting history has traditionally been more oriented towards stalking deer and hunting big game. That said, I have been fortunate enough to spend time with some of

the great foxers, such as Bob Bucknell and Mike Powell among others, and learnt far more in a short space of time with these specialists than I ever thought possible.

This has led me to a number of my own conclusions on that most emotive issue of all, one's choice of foxing calibre. The list of suitable calibres is vast, even if not always practical. So I will stick to the popular favourites – and they are popular for good

# DO I CHOOSE?

reason and shouldn't be rejected just because "they are common," as I recently heard someone say at a show. The ubiquitous .22-250 Remington is a great choice, as is the .223 Remington, whose popularity has never really waned. Both, with the right bullet, will also double up for the smaller deer species. Of course the versatile .243 Win, stoked with some of the lighter loads this cartridge comes in, will do the job admirably. I doubt there is a big brand manufacturer who doesn't chamber any of the above, and as I have said, they are widely used across the world for varmint work. One further addition I have always had hankering for is the mighty .220 Swift. It hasn't the popularity others of its vintage do, but it is always in the conversation when foxing calibres come to the fore.

Leaving behind the firm favourites, there are some newer foxing calibres that are finding favour. Two come immediately to mind: the .17 Hornet and .204 Ruger. It's too early to tell, but they are quite the talk at the moment and becoming something of a sensation. Both of these calibres look excellent on paper and amazing results have been achieved with them, so they do deserve serious consideration. Time will tell if they have the qualities to retain their appeal in the long term, but all indications look promising.

The hunter planning a trip to Africa is going to be faced with a potentially bewildering decision as to what calibre of firearm to take with him. Of course, this will depend largely on what game he is expecting to hunt, and in what conditions and terrain he will be practising his sport.

Most first timers, and indeed the highest percentage of UK hunters going on safari will focus mainly on plains game, which will vary in size from the diminutive duiker to that giant antelope the eland and the giraffe. With the possible exception of the .270 for use on small and some medium antelope species, any .20 calibres mentioned elsewhere in this book would be inadequate for most antelope other than the very smallest. Indeed a minimum of .308

Winchester for medium-sized antelope is the ethical benchmark, with the .30-06 and .300 Win Mag better still for bigger species such as kudu and eland. The .300 Win Mag is on the borderline for use against giraffe, in my opinion, and I would always go for my .375 when tackling this species.

That brings us to one of my favourite calibres, and the one that would suit every huntable species in the world. The .375 is the minimum calibre for thick-skinned dangerous game such as the elephant, buffalo, rhino and hippo required by law in most African states for these quarry species. The big cats can be taken with smaller calibres, although for lion, in most countries, the minimum legal limit is the .375, and quite rightly too. A few would say the .375 is marginal for game like buffalo and elephant, but as Craig Boddington once said, "It

is on the right side of marginal". Better to use a calibre that shoots sweet and you can handle comfortably, rather than use a bigger shoulder-cannon that may affect your nerves and accuracy. Better a lighter bullet in the right place than a bigger one in the wrong place – your life, and that of your companions, may depend on it.

My contention that the British had, by the turn of the 20th century, created an array of calibres that would remain a yardstick by which all other calibres would be measured for the next 100 years is epitomised by the .375 H&H. Since it was introduced in 1912 there have been a whole variety of faster, flatter-shooting cartridges that hit almost as hard as the .375, but Holland's old battle horse has held its place as a stalwart of African calibres against this modern competition. In fact arguably, even today, it is a cartridge that has only been

marginally bettered, if it has been at all. The .375 H&H must be the most popular all-round calibre for the Dark Continent, and in many African countries the .375 is the minimum legal calibre for shooting thick-skinned dangerous game.

When it was introduced, the .375 came in either the flanged or the belted versions. Between them, they were possibly the most famous cartridges ever devised. The flanged or rimmed case was intended for use with double rifles or single loaders, while the belted option was for use in magazine rifles. When they came out their only real competition was the .450/.400 for doubles and the .404 Jeffrey for magazine rifles. The

.375 H&H has been a popular calibre in India, Alaska, and of course in Africa. Just about every manufacturer has made rifles for the belted rimless version of this prince of calibres, capable of killing any game species on the face of the planet. But please don't me sway you because it is my favourite – the .416 Rigby and .458 Winchester Magnum all have a strong following, as does the .470, and all should be considered.

Whatever the primary work your rifle will be employed to do – foxing, deer stalking, or hunting overseas – some calibres will do it better than others. To help simplify things, there are a few questions most hunters should ask before deciding on a calibre:

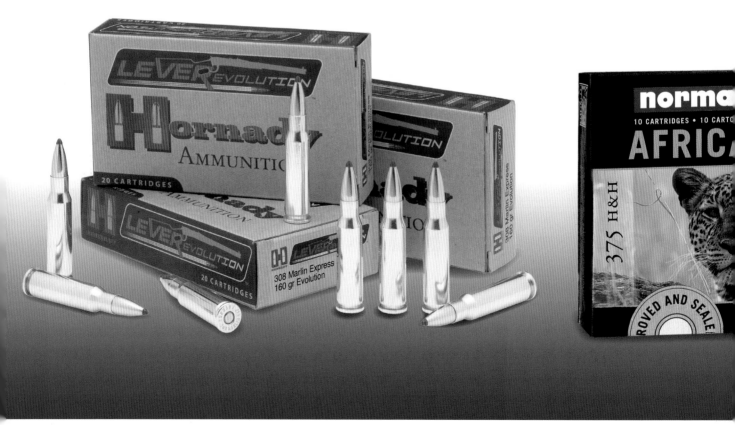

- What is the cost of ammunition?
- What is the availability of ammunition?
- Are rifles readily chambered in the calibre?
- What are the down-range ballistics and performance like?
- How long will my barrel last?
- Does it have enough stopping power for the principal quarry?

Perhaps a few hunters reading the following section may shake their head at the fact I have missed out their calibre of choice, but we need to keep the above criteria in mind and accept that a popular shortlist is a good platform from which to start one's quest for a suitable calibre.

This list is in no way intended to be conclusive. Today's available calibre options are far too extensive for that – but many can, in my view, be considered unnecessary. I have included most of the popular calibres that have ammunition readily available, and that is the very reason for staying away from the wildcat calibres. They are the subject of those who reload. Many do have slight advantages, but none I can see make that much difference in the field. Indeed some of them have been created out of vanity alone, and that isn't going to help fill the larder or put a trophy on the wall. Whatever your final choice, it will never replace accurate shooting, and that is the first consideration every ethical hunter should attend to. **PC**

# .17 CENTREFIRES

Today most shooters will be familiar with the .17 calibre thanks to the raging success of the .17 HMR, but until the advent of the .17 Hornet, few would have even heard of a .17 centrefire, let alone fired one. But many .17 concoctions have come in and out of fashion over the years, as wildcats and as commercially produced rounds.

The story starts back in the 1950s when wildcatting possibilities were boiling over the imagination of reloaders. One of the first was the .17 Hornet (Ackley), based on a necked down version of the .22 Hornet Improved, providing an accurate round with mild report and almost zero muzzle flip. Of all the .17s conceived in that era this was probably the most popular, with many varmint shooters marrying this little stinger with small Sako actions,

designed specifically to chamber rimmed cases such as the .22 Hornet and .218 Bee. Indeed the .218 Bee also saw the Ackley treatment, providing a case with larger capacity than the .22 Hornet, resulting in around 250fps extra muzzle velocity. The .222 Remington, .223 Remington and .221 Remington Fireball have all been used as parent cases for various .17 wildcat designs.

The .17-222 was a straightforward .222 Rem case necked down to .17, and although many other variations in shoulder angle and body taper spawned from this, it remained the most popular based on this case. It would throw a 25-grain bullet at virtually 2,600fps with around 17 grains of H4198. Then, the .17-223 was a similar concept to the .17-222, but with greater case capacity it could push out 25 grains

of lead at almost 3,900fps owing to an extra 5.5 grains of powder.

This wildcat became the basis the first commercially loaded .17 calibre, the .17 Remington, introduced in 1971. It has enjoyed steady sales throughout its lifespan, but has been held back by its exclusive varminting application. In this format the .17 centrefire was zipping along on the edge of the 4,000fps boundary, but paid the price with quick barrel wear and heavy fouling. In fact this put many hunters off the calibre in the early days. Badly made barrels and poorly designed bullets resulted in mid-flight disintegration or keyholing on the target just 15-20 shots.

Next, the more modern .17 Mach IV design. Conceived by Vern O'Brian in 1962, it took the .221 Remington Fireball case and necked it down with a 30-degree shoulder to take the little .17 bullet. In 2007 this wildcat cartridge was modified marginally by Remington, resulting in the aptly named 17 Remington Fireball. This proved extremely popular in the US, outstripping demand for the original .17 Rem. The case shoulder remained at 30 degrees, but OAL is slightly longer at 1.42in.

Delving into the ballistics, the advertised 4,000fps is more likely to be around 100fps less out your hunting rifle. This is still nipping along, with a 300-yard velocity around 2,200fps, delivering in excess of 235ft/lb of energy. To put this in perspective, the Fireball is delivering the same ft/lb at 300 yards as the ME of a .17 HMR, proving some considerable destructive power at these extended ranges (these stats are produced from a 24in test barrel).

Where it becomes interesting is drawing comparisons with the .204 Ruger. Remington load data indicates that the two have almost identical ballistics out to 200 yards, despite the .204 pushing a bullet twice the weight. At the 300-yard mark the .204 Ruger drops almost an inch less than the.17. It does this with almost three times as much energy and nearly half the wind drift, making one wonder if the .17 calibre is now redundant. Indeed, if I owned the .204 Ruger, I think the .17 Rem Fireball would be wasted space in the cupboard. It's now down to the new Hornet calibre to revive the fortunes of the .17. **BP**

# .17 HORNET

Their love of long-range prairie dog and rock chuck hunting makes this an interesting competitor. There is little doubt that the performance on these small mammals will be explosive, and of course the smaller bullets and minimal powder charge will make reloading as cheap as possible.

Where it will fit into the British market is an interesting question. There are plenty of varmint enthusiasts who see the HMR as acceptable for foxing, although I would have to disagree with this (though if used sensibly it makes an excellent back-up if the opportunity arises on a night out rabbit shooting). The step up in velocity offered by the Hornet may make it wholly more suitable for our vulpine nemesis. Indeed, tests at the launch showed considerably greater cavity damage when shooting into ballistic soap. We were unable to compare volumes, but the picture gives a reasonable idea. Only field tests will tell, and I will withhold judgement until then.

For handloaders it may indeed prove on par with or cheaper than .17 HMR ammo, although final prices have not been confirmed as yet. However, I can't see it being used as a serious rabbit controlling calibre for anything other than extended range shooting. I say this as I can't picture many people wanting to reload 200 rounds a night. The flipside to that, though, is that it is bound to be serious fun. I am very much looking forward to the first test rifle. **BP**

After emptying the Savage's four-shot magazine, I stepped back to let other journalists have a play with the new .17 Hornet. In conjunction with Hornady and Savage, Edgar Brothers had brought the very first .17 Hornet into the country, and everyone was eager to see how it performed at its launch.

Even without a moderator, the recoil was almost non-existent. It certainly was sweet to fire. Essentially we were looking at a necked-down .22 Hornet case, accepting the same V-Max bullet used in the formidable .17 HMR, only three grains heavier. With about 14 grains of Superformance blend, the 20-grain bullet achieves a muzzle velocity of around 3,600fps – some 1,000fps more than the rimfire. Doing the numbers on muzzle energy produces 600ft/lb, just over twice that of the HMR.

Speaking to Hornady's representative, we were informed that the trajectory was comparable to a 55-grain .223 Rem. Looking at the factory numbers certainly reflects this. Obviously the big drawback with any light bullet is wind drift, which will be in the region of 6in at 200 yards with a 10mph wind. This is about double a .204 Ruger (39-grain) but only a third of the drift on a .22 Hornet (30-grain). The same is also true of the improved wind drift in comparison to a .17 HMR: 5.8in versus 15.5in over 200 yards.

I was unable to complete any kind of accuracy tests at the launch, but I am informed they are readily achieving ¾in groups at 100 yards with factory ammo. We can assume, then, that the .17 Hornet will be as accurate as you can shoot it.

This is a calibre that has really been designed with the American market in mind.

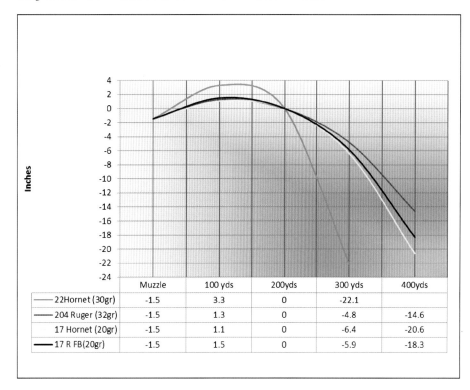

| | Muzzle | 100 yds | 200yds | 300 yds | 400yds |
|---|---|---|---|---|---|
| 22Hornet (30gr) | -1.5 | 3.3 | 0 | -22.1 | |
| 204 Ruger (32gr) | -1.5 | 1.3 | 0 | -4.8 | -14.6 |
| 17 Hornet (20gr) | -1.5 | 1.1 | 0 | -6.4 | -20.6 |
| 17 R FB(20gr) | -1.5 | 1.5 | 0 | -5.9 | -18.3 |

# .204 RUGER

Recent years have seen rising popularity in smaller, faster calibres, with the .17 HMR being the champion of rimfire innovation since the inception of the versatile .22LR. Foxers have gladly latched onto this super-fast rimmy, which packs a punch well beyond what its on-paper ballistics would suggest. I still have reservations regarding its use for larger quarry; that, on top of its sensitivity to wind drift and limited long-range capability compared to centrefires, means dedicated foxers will probably hold on to their .22-250s and .220 Swifts.

But there has been a new kid on the block for the past 10 years, waiting in the wings to knock the classic foxing calibres from the top of the pile. The .204 Ruger may just be the varmint shooter's dream cartridge. It shoots flatter than a .22-250 Rem, comes very close to the trajectory of the .220 Swift (the 39-grain in .204 Ruger is not shown but almost identical to the 32-grain), and resists wind drift better than either of its rivals in its 39-grain offering – some 1.5in and 7.2in less drift over 300 yards than the .220 Swift and .22-250 Rem respectively in a 10mph crosswind.

One of the big considerations for trigger-happy hunters has been how much powder is burned in larger-cased .22 centrefires. For the regular range user, this consideration often leads to more economical alternatives such as the .222 Remington; but as with anything, there is a compromise in ballistic capability. The .204 Ruger, on the other hand, seems to deliver pretty much everything the larger-cased calibres offer while requiring far less powder. Combine this with a milder report, softer recoil and longer barrel life than a .223, and it becomes a tasty alternative.

The new cartridge received the Shooting Industry Academy of Excellence award in 2004, not long after its introduction by Hornady and Ruger. At that time, Ruger claimed that the factory-loaded 32-grain round was the fastest commercially available cartridge in any calibre (Ruger may still maintain this, although I am not certain). This sweet little design is based on the .222 Remington Magnum case necked down to .20 calibre, bucking the trend in modern bullet design of 'short and fat'. Hornady, Remington, and Winchester currently produce brass for this calibre, although .222 Rem Mag brass is easily resized to accommodate it. Currently in the US, the .204 Ruger is the most popular of all of the .20-cal cartridges on offer, despite being the newest.

While low-profile cartridges like the .20 BR are normally more efficient than a tall and thin case, the .204 Ruger more than holds its own in the velocity department compared with any of the popular .20-calibre cartridges. Moreover, the .204 enjoys one huge advantage over all the other popular twenties: the availability of factory ammunition. We reloaders may scoff at the idea of buying factory fodder, but it's nice to know that the option is available for those who are still to have their eyes opened to the wonder of reloading.

So it's fast (very fast, at over 4,000fps) and has an impressive trajectory – but can it shoot? Everything mentioned to this point is of little use if you can't knock a beer can over at 100 yards. Well it doesn't disappoint here either. Factory ammo regularly produces groups just over 0.5MOA, with handloads pulling this into 0.25MOA with efficient repetition.

It is, however, a very light bullet, and this shows when it comes to crunching downrange energy. Whereas the .220 Swift is still punching over 1,000ft/lb at 150 yards (40-grain), the .204 is already well bellow that with around 870ft/lb for the 39-grain bullet, and 740ft/lb for the 32-grain bullet. Compare this to the underused 55-grain .243 Winchester, whose 1,300ft/lb delivered at 150 yards makes the .204 look like a mild irritation. Granted, this is for a heavier bullet, but when it has a superior trajectory to the 39-grain .204 (not shown in graph) and equal wind drift, it does make one wonder whether the .204 is redundant.

The .204 Ruger is an interesting, quirky calibre that would be a joy to own, but has limited practical application. It is too expensive to use on vermin other than foxes, and a .243 will do the job more efficiently with considerably more versatility. On the other hand, it is very sweet to shoot, and easy on the powder stocks. Would I buy one? If there is room in the cabinet, then maybe I will. BP

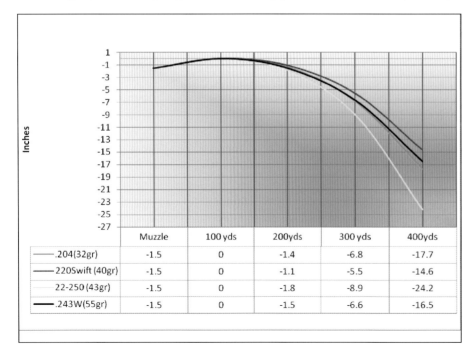

| | Muzzle | 100 yds | 200yds | 300 yds | 400yds |
|---|---|---|---|---|---|
| .204 (32gr) | -1.5 | 0 | -1.4 | -6.8 | -17.7 |
| 220Swift (40gr) | -1.5 | 0 | -1.1 | -5.5 | -14.6 |
| 22-250 (43gr) | -1.5 | 0 | -1.8 | -8.9 | -24.2 |
| .243W (55gr) | -1.5 | 0 | -1.5 | -6.6 | -16.5 |

# .22 HORNET

The .22 Hornet's popularity has waned in the last decade. Will its direct descendant, the new .17 Hornet, prove more enticing? With smaller and faster calibres very in fashion it seems like a recipe for success.

Unlike most centrefire cartridges used today, the .22 Hornet has a rimmed case. It started life as the black powder .22 WCF, developed in the 1920s at the Springfield armoury. A decade later the cartridge was standardised by Winchester, and within a few years most manufacturers were chambering it.

Although the .22 Hornet quivers in the shadows of modern high-velocity small-bores, in its day it was a pioneering king. This reign was, however, short-lived, as the introduction of the .218 Bee surpassed the Hornet's ballistics as a result of greater case capacity.

With a reputation for superb accuracy, the .22 Hornet was seen in some parts as a 'wonder bullet'. With negligible recoil but substantially greater energy than a .22LR, the Hornet allowed those who wielded it to push the boundaries of its capabilities. Filtering into Africa, it never really saw use as a major game calibre, but its manageable nature found favour with farmers, and it was used to hunt everything up to kudu.

Of course, when careful head shots, or well-placed engine room shots on plenty of open ground were employed, it was very

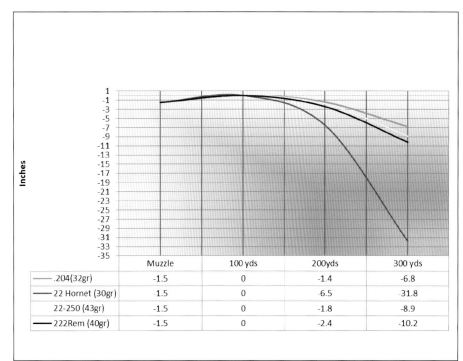

| | Muzzle | 100 yds | 200yds | 300 yds |
|---|---|---|---|---|
| .204(32gr) | -1.5 | 0 | -1.4 | -6.8 |
| 22 Hornet (30gr) | -1.5 | 0 | -6.5 | -31.8 |
| 22-250 (43gr) | -1.5 | 0 | -1.8 | -8.9 |
| 222Rem (40gr) | -1.5 | 0 | -2.4 | -10.2 |

effective. The problem was that there was almost zero room for error. The tiny amount of internal damage caused long bleed-out periods, allowing game to travel great distances before succumbing to the wound. So it was banned for use on larger game in Africa, across America and Europe.

It also suffered from later comparisons with the .223 Rem and .22-250 Rem, which

of course shoot the same .224 bullets – and there is no questioning the fact that these bigger-cased cartridges are more effective in almost every way. The only things that are left going for the humble Hornet are reduced recoil, lighter rifles and a less greedy rate of powder consumption.

Thanks to the .17 HMR, the Hornet is unlikely to be used for longer-range rabbiting. With ME well below the required 1,000ft/lb for shooting deer, its only UK application would be the pursuit of foxes, but I'm not convinced. There's no comparison with the higher velocity, larger cases – when it comes to down-range killing ability, the .22 Hornet is left dead in the water.

It seems that as far as the Hornet is concerned, times have moved on. Even compared with the .222 Rem, the Hornet lags some 350ft/lb behind in ME. Compare it with the .204 Ruger and it will punch almost 500ft/lb less. The trajectory issue is clear to see – the bullet drops at 200 yards what most cartridges will show at 300 yards. In its day the cartridge must have been a marvel, but in today's hunting world I see little practical application. Could its newer .17 incarnation be the facelift this cartridge needs? Only time will tell. **BP**

# .22-243 MIDDLESTEAD

I recently looked to build a semi-custom rifle for foxing. My calibre choice followed in the footsteps of many foxers – I settled on a .22-250 Rem Improved, which enjoys great ballistics while having longer barrel life than the faster .220 Swift. But in the process of researching which calibre to chamber my foxing rig in, I came across a curious and relatively unknown calibre, which I think is worth sharing.

I have only ever met one person who owned a .22-243 Middlestead, and he could do nothing but sing its praises – although he was reluctant to tell me how many barrels he had gone through over the 10 years he had owned it. That aside, it was an awesome bit of kit, with an impressive ballistic spec.

As can be deduced from the name, it's based on a .243 Win case necked down with a 30-degree shoulder to .224, firing the same bullet as a .220 Swift. It pushes a tiny bullet at velocities that exceed 4,000fps, which can have detrimental effect on both your barrel and your wallet, with a lifespan unlikely to exceed 1,500 rounds. I guess that's the price you pay for such flat trajectories.

It is not a calibre you will find on a gun shop shelf, and I don't believe any ammo manufacturer has ever loaded it, making the .22-243 a real wildcat. Although pre-formed brass is also absent from the reloading catalogues, it is easily

formed by running .243 brass through a .22-243 Middlestead die and trimming to length as necessary. Also, owing to the greater case dimensions of this .243 derivative, a .22-250 can quite readily be rechambered to .22-243 spec.

Given the pedigree of the .243 Win, it's not surprising that necked down to .224 it produces

some truly excellent accuracy. Printing tiny groups will be no issue if the shooter and rifle are up to it.

Most of the material I read about the calibre suggested that even the .220 Swift would be eaten up and spat out by the larger-cased .22-243, but the tests I did showed very little advantage. In fact, when firing comparable reloads side by side, any separation was merely academic. I spent some considerable time manipulating powder, bullet and case variables in QuickLoad and QuickTarget, but only once loading bullets above 70 grains was there any advantage worth noting. I was slightly disappointed by this, having initially thought it might be a superior round to the longstanding varmint favourites. If you just want to shoot 70-grain rounds, you would be far better off with a straight .243 Win, providing greater versatility.

Given the special chambering requirements and lack of factory ammo or brass, I think I would stick with the .220 Swift. I am normally the first to latch on to a quirky calibre, preferring to try something a bit more imaginative. But I can't think of a good reason to own this calibre. With more time spent tweaking the loads it could be made to surpass the .220 Swift, but any benefit is far outweighed by the inconvenience of the calibre. An interesting round, but one that can stay on the bookshelf. **BP**

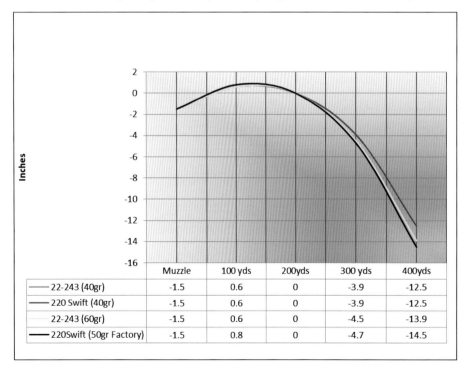

| | Muzzle | 100 yds | 200yds | 300 yds | 400yds |
|---|---|---|---|---|---|
| 22-243 (40gr) | -1.5 | 0.6 | 0 | -3.9 | -12.5 |
| 220 Swift (40gr) | -1.5 | 0.6 | 0 | -3.9 | -12.5 |
| 22-243 (60gr) | -1.5 | 0.6 | 0 | -4.5 | -13.9 |
| 220Swift (50gr Factory) | -1.5 | 0.8 | 0 | -4.7 | -14.5 |

# .22-250 REM

In 2013 I supplied a series of articles for *Sporting Rifle* magazine in which I endeavoured to find the 'ultimate foxing calibre'. Though I handed many of the calibres up for consideration to my friends and colleagues, I took the .22-250 Rem on board myself – indeed, this is what my Howa 1500 foxing rig is chambered in. The treble-two-fifty can definitely be described as a sweet shooter. It's not as gentle as a .222 Rem or the smaller cased calibres, but a moderated rifle fitted with a varmint barrel will hardly recoil, with sight picture easily maintained between shots. It's a soft shooter, but you are very aware that a lot of energy is hurtling down-range.

In terms of terminal performance, the .22-250 Rem is superb. I am yet to have a fox do anything other than drop on the spot when the person behind the trigger does their bit. Shooting homeloads of 55-grain Nosler Ballistic tips, there is only occasionally an exit wound, with the internals blended into a claret soup. It tends not to be a particularly fussy

calibre either, with loads fairly easy to tune, and most accepting an array of factory fodder. It is also inherently accurate, with my own rifle putting pretty much any ammo into ¾in, and homeloads into a five-pence piece at 100 yards.

Ballistically, it's not the most impressive, but then it's not far off either. There are some benefits to this, though, with barrel life better than the short-lived Swift. Loaded to sensible levels of around 3,600fps, you're looking at a 300-yard drop of just 5in when zeroed 0.88in high at 100 yards. With that you will tackle almost any situation you will encounter at night. Obviously wind has to be taken into account, and that will be the limiting factor of the .22-250 Rem.

In terms of our list, it is one of the more expensive calibres, but choice certainly won't be a problem. Neither will finding the rifle you want, as every manufacturer worth their salt will chamber at least one model in .22-250 Rem. I can't see me ever replacing my foxing set-up in .22-250 Rem. **BP**

# .220 SWIFT

"Fastest production cartridge ever made" was the title held by the .220 Swift for more than 65 years. Today it is superseded by the feisty .204 Ruger, although according to Hornady and Federal data, shooting equal 40-grain bullets will still put the older .220 Swift on top by some 350fps. Launching 40-grain Nosler B-Tips, the .220 Swift comes factory loaded at 4,250fps, although I know of handloaders taking it over 4,500fps.

Introduced by Winchester in 1935, offered in the company's Model 54 bolt-action rifles with the 6mm Lee Navy as a parent case, the concept came from Grosvenor Wotkyns two years earlier, when he necked down the .250-3000 Savage case to produce a high-velocity light calibre.

The name is somewhat misleading, as it shoots the same .224 diameter bullets loaded in the .22-250 Rem, making available a wide range of weights to the hand loader. However, as with the .22-250 Rem, a standard factory twist rate of 1 in 14in lends itself to the lower end of the weight spectrum, placing it firmly as a varminting calibre. Until relatively recently, laws in England and Wales prohibited the use of small .22 calibres on deer, but given the opening up on muntjac and Chinese water deer, the .220 Swift may well find an increasingly diverse use.

The key here is using suitable bullets, as many factory loads were originally designed for rapid expansion with very thin jackets. Even so, reliability on larger game can be erratic due to the variable bullet integrity of small calibres at such high velocities. They do not tolerate hitting any substantial bone structures, calling for careful shots, and is the primary reason for its restriction to smaller species. Furthermore, the meat damage when shooting small deer is colossal even when only hitting ribs, giving unsatisfactory results if you want to fill your freezer. I see the .220 Swift as a varmint calibre first and foremost, while also providing the capability for other small game species. Be in no doubt though, its killing ability within these categories is quite exceptional.

Like most of the super-fast .22 calibres, the .220 Swift is very accurate, with many believing it to be the most accurate ever invented. I cannot confirm or deny this, but given how well a .22-250 Rem can shoot, I am sure any difference is merely academic.

The point blank range is quite incredible. Zeroed at 250 yards, it will put the 40-grain

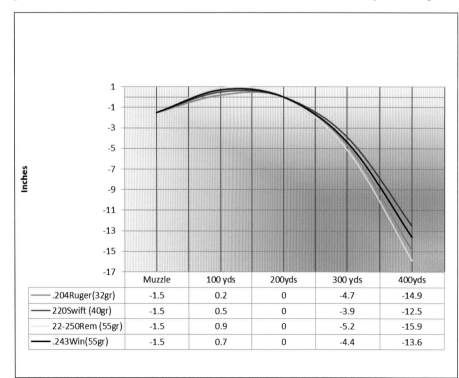

bullet 1.5in high at 150 yards and -1.5in at 275 yards, shooting well inside a clay pigeon sized target. At 300 yards the drop is just 3.2in. The graph shows a clear trajectory advantage over other available factory rounds. The comparison puts the ME of the Swift third in line with 498ft/lb at 400 yards, marginally behind the heavier .22-250 Rem (although in the same bullet weight it will surpass it).

It is interesting to note that the .243 Win 55-grain delivers some 200ft/lb more at 400 yards, although this is with 15 grains more weight. However, according to factory data, with 55 grains apiece the .243 would still be delivering around 100ft/lb more.

If you own a .22-250 Rem, I wouldn't be quick to replace it with the .220 Swift, as the price you pay for the extra performance can be very short barrel life. Moreover, I am becoming increasingly aware that the .243 Win shooting a 55-grain bullet is an amazing little combination, albeit with a fair amount of recoil. **BP**

| | Muzzle | 100 yds | 200yds | 300 yds | 400yds |
|---|---|---|---|---|---|
| .204Ruger(32gr) | -1.5 | 0.2 | 0 | -4.7 | -14.9 |
| 220Swift (40gr) | -1.5 | 0.5 | 0 | -3.9 | -12.5 |
| 22-250Rem (55gr) | -1.5 | 0.9 | 0 | -5.2 | -15.9 |
| .243Win(55gr) | -1.5 | 0.7 | 0 | -4.4 | -13.6 |

Inches

# .223 REM

It is probably fair to say that the .223 Rem wouldn't be as popular as it is today without it being a military calibre. Like the .308 Win, the availability of cheap ammunition and rifles certainly helped establish the calibre in the sporting world.

There is no doubt that the .223 Rem is very popular as a foxing calibre. As you would expect, there is a vast selection of rifles chambered in .223. Off the shelf ammunition selection is good, and, of course, you can obtain very cheap military surplus ammo as well. Being non-expanding, it can't be used for hunting, however it does provide a cheap way of getting a lot of practice in. Having said that, of the mil spec ammo I have fired, I have never found any to group particularly well in a hunting rifle. This is most likely due to the clash between rifle twist rate and the loaded bullet weight.

Shooting the .223 Rem is a very calm and understated affair. When moderated, there really is very little fuss, and I have never had any trouble getting factory ammo to shoot well. Shooting with a very modest muzzle velocity, barrel life is generous. It's unlikely most hunters will ever shoot out a rifle in their lifetime, unless doing a serious amount of range work. The same cannot be said for some of the other calibres. It's not the flattest shooter, and a 55-grain bullet will need a full inch and a half at 100 yards to drop on target at 200 yards. Once you're comfortable with that, it becomes second nature. At night, most shots will be up to 200 yards, with a much smaller proportion past this, so the drop beyond isn't too much of an issue as long as you're aware.

Possibly one of the most convenient points of this smaller calibre is that you can get away with having a much shorter barrel than, say, a .22-250. Cut a .22-250 down to 18in and you will be wasting a lot of performance. You can get away with it when it comes to the .223 Rem, and that makes shooting in and out of a vehicle much more convenient.

I would say finally that, although the calibre kills the vast majority of foxes outright, every now and then you will get them running on a way. Obviously this could happen with any calibre, but it is more noticeable with the .223 Rem than a .243 Win or .22-250 Rem.

*Phil Chapman, grouse keeper*

# 6MM VARIANTS

I had set out to explore the .220 Russian, given that it forms the parent case of many of the modern 6mm benchrest calibres. However, on putting pen to paper, I realised that for many dedicated hunters, this range of calibres falls outside those commonly found in factory rifles. Indeed, the closest most people will come to a 6mm BR, 6mm PPC or .220 Russian would be the well-loved .243 Winchester (hardly comparable to the ethos behind the world record-breaking 6mm). So I thought it may be beneficial to look at the history of the calibres falling in the 6mm benchrest class before following on in future articles to take a deeper look at possible hunting applications.

## ARRIVAL OF THE RUSSIAN

The .220 Russian actually began its life as the 7.62x39 Soviet, a cartridge that has been the Russians' official military medicine since the end of World War Two. This had limited use for the sporting rifleman, and found its niche mainly in the use of semi-automatic weapons (most notably the AK-47). In the late 1950s this case was necked down to form the .220 Russian, firing a 5.56mm bullet with similar ballistic properties to the .223 Remington, and found support among deer and varmint hunters alike. By 1965 it was produced by Sako, and this is where the story really starts.

Although there are few people today who still shoot the original .220 Russian, the super-accurate modern concoctions based on this case have found their way into the record books, as well as becoming a staple of modern benchrest shooting.

## FROM AK TO BR

The 6mm PPC was developed by Louis Palmisano and Ferris Pindel in 1975 – PPC standing for Pindel-Palmisano Cartridge – as a necked up version of the .22 PPC, which in turn found its parent case in the .220 Russian. The 6mm version dominates the 100-200 yard Group BR scene, and is regarded by many as the most accurate round ever invented over such distances. This is attributed to the small flash hole and primer pocket, combined with the short, fat shape of the case, conducive to efficient combustion and chamber behaviour.

The cases are easily formed directly from .220 Russian brass, which the vast majority of shooters source from Lapua. However, Sako standardised the calibre in 1985, allowing pre-formed 6mm PPC brass to be purchased. Today they have been joined by Norma, but the brass tends to be considerably softer than Lapua, and will not stand up to the repetitive reloading of 'hot loads'. Most 6 PPC competition chambered rifles will not shoot the Sako versions, as they are marginally larger than the original. On request from the 6 PPC inventors, the standardised cases carry the USA tag after the calibre headstamp, in order to distinguish the two.

This calibre soon started to find its feet among varmint shooters, and a number of 'off the shelf' manufactures such as Sako, Kimber and Cooper Firearms began chambering rifles. The most commonly used bullet weights are in the 60-70 grain region, which offer 3,200fps MV and 1,481ft/lb ME with Sako factory loads. The trajectory is listed as +1.5in at 100 yards with a 200-yard zero, following on with a 7.2in drop at 300 yards.

## FROM 6MM PPC TO 6MM BR

If the 6 PPC is king of the short ranges, then the 6 BR takes over from 300-1,000 yards in terms of accuracy. Many of the characteristics that make the 6 PPC an inherently accurate and efficient calibre are also found in the 6 BR, although it takes its parent case from the 6mm Remington Benchrest cartridge. This gives it slightly greater case capacity, and hence the extra down-range 'oomph' and accuracy beyond 300 yards. Like the 6 PPC, the 6 BR is responsible for a hoard of world records, dominating 300-600 yard competitions. It is also known as the 6mm Norma BR.

This is in no way a complete overview, but it does give a bit of background for the two most common 6mm benchrest calibres. The 6 BR has fathered calibres such as the Dasher, 6 BRX and 6 BRDX. The .220 Russian also forms the parent case for the .220 Beggs and 6mm Beggs, both of which are outstanding rounds in their own right. We also have the lesser-known 6mm X (20-degree shoulder) and 6 XC (30-degree shoulder), but I will save this very interesting calibre for another month. **BP**

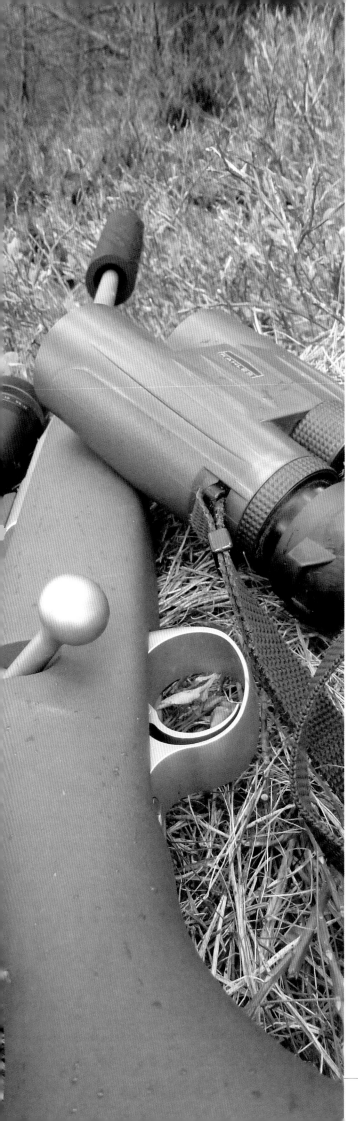

# .243 WIN

Like a large proportion of UK hunters, my first full-bore rifle was in .243 Win: a second-hand Sako 75 (a joint firearm held between my dad and me). This was to be our primary rifle for several years, before moving on to the 7x57 some years later. The calibre was of limited consideration – I knew little about it and was more concerned about getting a half-decent rifle. But before long I was shunning the 'default' pair of .308 Win and .243 Win, chosen by many to tackle the UK deer spectrum. I saw it as following the herd. Obviously rifle availability was a big part of this, and it was self-fulfilling, as more people made a calibre decision based on off-the-shelf rifle opportunity.

I would say things have changed a bit now, and hunters have become more savvy. Custom rifles have never been so popular, and with that comes a calibre choice as long as time. Having said this, after shooting many rifles and calibres, I have come full circle and returned to the stalwarts of modern UK hunting. My last rifle buy was a .243 Win Kimber Montana.

The .243 Win takes it parent case from the .308 Win. An efficient, short-action design, the .243 Win was a breakthrough in terms of factory-loaded ammunition. It allowed hunters to shoot one calibre for a large spectrum of quarry, with moderate recoil and excellent down-range trajectory. The 6mm bullet proved accurate and, as we have seen in the likes of the 6mm BR, this was just the beginning of its potential.

Loaded as low as 55 grains, and factory loaded to 105, it makes an excellent foxing calibre while offering good knockdown power for small and medium-sized deer. For hand loaders, tapping into the long-range potential of the 115-grain bullet is available but rarely investigated. Loaded with the lightning-fast, 55-grain varmint bullet, it easily surpasses the performance from a .220 Swift.

I have found the 87-grain bullet an excellent compromise to cover foxes and smaller deer species. Running out at around 3,200fps, you are looking at a 300-yard drop of six inches with under an inch high zero at 100 yards. This excludes one from hunting the bigger UK deer species, in which case you will have to step up to 100 grains. The 105-grain Geco is excellent for this, being a relatively inexpensive choice while still providing good accuracy with suitable carcase performance.

The new 95-grain Superformance from Hornady is ballistically fantastic, but sadly can't be used at home on red deer as a result of legislation on bullet weight. In terms of long range accuracy, many hunters will be pleasantly surprised by how good the .243 Win is, and my rifle is the most accurate I have ever owned, dropping bullets into less than 2in at 400 yards.

Interestingly, the .243 Win was intended as a long-range varmint cartridge, with barrel twists reflecting this. Soon people realised that the calibre could be used for much more than this, leading to where we are today.

It is tempting to say the .243 Win could be the answer to all, but be cautious. Beyond lightweight foxing loads, bullet selection for quarry type is important. At the top end of the .243 Win capabilities, it is a little underpowered, and placement has to be good. That is why some estates insist on calibres larger than .243 Win when stag season comes around. It does offer tremendous scope, if used with some thought and attention. **BP**

# .257 ROBERTS

I have never been one to follow the crowd, and I've steered clear of the common .243 Win, .270 Win and .308 Win chosen by most hunters. There is no imagination in that, even though – the overrated .270 Win excluded – they may be the logical choice. When I went looking for a new calibre to slot into the dominant position usually reserved for a .243 Win, I wanted a calibre that showed a bit of lateral thinking, and that could hold its own from foxes to red deer.

I initially thought I had the investigation sewn up with the .25-06, but in the process of looking into .25 calibre options, I stumbled across the .257 Roberts. I have to admit I had never heard of the calibre before, but on discovering it was based on a necked-down version of the 7x57 case, I was immediately interested.

The original cartridge design was chambered in custom rifles as far back as 1928. Remington released a commercial version in 1934, altering the shoulder angle from 15 to 20 degrees.

In the early years, the widespread use of old military 7x57 actions for .257 conversions held the calibre back. The ageing constructions of old actions meant pressures had to be kept down to ensure safe operation, so factory ammo was generally under-loaded. This issue was addressed in the 1980s with the introduction of the .257 Roberts (+P), allowing factory loads to reach their full potential. But the real question is: How does it compare to other options?

It's important to decide what we are pitting it against. A friend of mine said the .257 Roberts doesn't match up to 6.5mm cartridges. That may be true, but I think it is the wrong comparison to make. In the UK we have no real need for the punching power of bullets above the 120-grain mark. While the 100-grain .243 Win is often seen as too light for bigger

deer species and the .308 Win a bit of overkill, I see the .257 Roberts as a sensible mid-point.

The output from QuickLoad puts the 75-grain .257 Roberts 1.7in flatter at 400 yards than the equivalent for the .243 Win. Even the 117-grain bullet in the Roberts has 1.6in on the 100-grain .243 at the same range, only losing an inch to the 115-grain .270 Win. In terms of wind drift, the 117-grain Roberts tops the table with a 0.4MOA edge over the rest, while its down-range energy almost mirrors the .270 Win once out to 300 yards. The stats are very favourable, while the calibre shows a break from the crowd and a flare of imagination. I can't think of a good reason not to buy one. **BP**

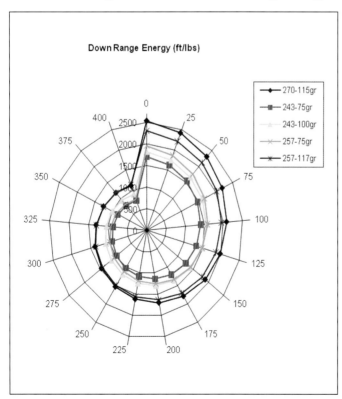

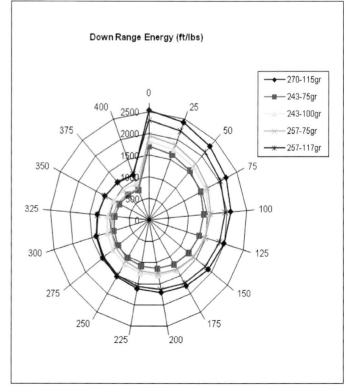

# 6.5x47 LAPUA

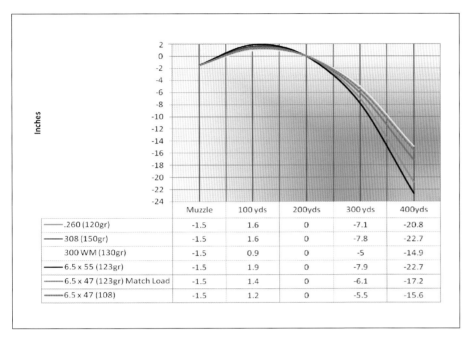

| | Muzzle | 100 yds | 200yds | 300 yds | 400yds |
|---|---|---|---|---|---|
| .260 (120gr) | -1.5 | 1.6 | 0 | -7.1 | -20.8 |
| 308 (150gr) | -1.5 | 1.6 | 0 | -7.8 | -22.7 |
| 300 WM (130gr) | -1.5 | 0.9 | 0 | -5 | -14.9 |
| 6.5 x 55 (123gr) | -1.5 | 1.9 | 0 | -7.9 | -22.7 |
| 6.5 x 47 (123gr) Match Load | -1.5 | 1.4 | 0 | -6.1 | -17.2 |
| 6.5 x 47 (108) | -1.5 | 1.2 | 0 | -5.5 | -15.6 |

Lapua is one of those companies that never stops innovating. It is well known among reloaders for producing some of the finest brass around, and can boast a long list of international shooting medals courtesy of Lapua components. Lapua is responsible for possibly the most accurate ultra-long distance calibre ever invented – the .338 Lapua Magnum – and more recently took the target shooting world by storm with the introduction of the 6.5x47 in 2005.

I have long been a fan of the 6.5mm bullet, having had the opportunity to use the fantastic and popular 6.5x55 Swedish from a young age. The excellent ballistic properties of the 6.5mm bullet are no secret, and have also been tapped into commercially in the form of the .260 Remington. Armed with the historical success and a definitive move by target shooters away from the .300 calibres to the 6.5mm bullet, Lapua and Swiss rifle maker Grunig Elmiger AG set about producing the most efficient and accurate round possible.

The result was a shorter, fatter case than the 6.5x55, but with similar base diameter and overall case length to a .308, which allows easy conversion from short actions previously chambered in calibres where a .308 is the parent case. This followed in the footsteps of specialist benchrest rounds such as the 6mm BR, allowing a more efficient burn of power

while using a small primer in the squat case. However, unlike some of its 6mm benchrest brethren, it didn't suffer from magazine feeding problems, and barrel wear was much less pronounced. This super-accurate, easy-feeding, soft-recoiling, high-BC round suddenly became not only an option for target shooting, but also a very exciting prospect for hunting.

With Lapua's reputation and the fact that the round was specifically designed to compete in European 300-metre CISM competitions, the 6.5x47 Lapua had a lot to live up to. It most definitely did not disappoint. The strong case design allowed home loads to easily exceed factory ammo velocities, producing superior down-range ballistics to similar calibres such as the .308. It did this with minimal fuss and noticeably less recoil, making it stand out for the 'practical' rifle matches so popular in the USA.

One of the beautiful characteristics of this superbly efficient calibre is the ease of working up a load. Mixing combinations of bullet weights and powder showed remarkable accuracy across the 123-grain, 130-grain and 139-grain bullets, using RL15, H4350, Varget, and N550 as propellants. Of the 50 or so combinations I tested, only around 10 per cent were marked out as "poor accuracy". It is however all relative, as "poor accuracy" was assigned to the loads that exceeded 0.5MOA.

Most will print tidy groups between 0.25 and 0.5MOA given a quality rifle set-up. With a tailored benchrest rig, groups under 0.2MOA are possible.

How does it stack up in a side-by-side comparison? On velocity, all the calibres listed in the graph leave the muzzle at 2,750-2,950fps, with the exception of the .300 Win Mag, which achieved a nippy 3,500fps. With match components, the 6.5x47 can produce as much as 2,350fps at 400 yards – some 300fps more than the rest and only marginally less than the .300 Win Mag. It must be noted here the bullets used in the comparison are similar but not identical, and this is across a range of representative bullet weights. If using bullets suitable for hunting, the ballistics in terms of wind drift, down-range energy, velocity and trajectory sit neatly between the 6.5x55 Swedish and the .260 Remington. A little load tweaking easily makes it mirror the .260.

Zeroed at 200 yards, the 123-grain bullet will comfortably take care of any deer species in the UK, dropping bullets along a vertical string of 3.5in from muzzle to target out to 250 yards. With the 139-grain load, it would be well placed for small to medium antelope in Africa, and similar-sized deer species in America. I am yet to read any data on heavier bullets being tested, such as those used by the Swedish concoction. It was originally designed to shoot the low- to middle-weighted bullets, so until I do some of my own testing, I cannot comment on how well it eats anything in excess of 139 grains.

From a practical hunting point of view, the 6.5x47 scores higher than the other 6.5s on barrel wear, recoil and powder consumption, but it is unlikely that a standard hunting rifle will be able to take much advantage of the superb accuracy. If I was target shooting, it would be my first choice, but when it comes to hunting, I don't think I will replace my 6.5x55. **BP**

# 6.5x55 SWEDISH

I have always been a fan of the old European calibres. There is a good reason they have stood the test of time, and they come from a period where velocity was not the beginning and end of every conversation. The 6.5x55 is one of those good old moderate calibres.

The European convention for naming calibres always makes life easy for comparison purposes and, as we can see here, this calibre is in the same territory as the infamous 7x57 Mauser. Along with the 7mm bullet, the 6.5mm offers superb ballistics, with high ballistic coefficients providing an ideal combination of trajectory, wind deflection, down range energy and hunting performance. There are a number of modern cartridges that have taken advantage of this recently, with the .260 Rem, 6.5 Creedmore and 6.5x47 Lapua arriving in quick succession. All these new calibres are trying to replicate what the 6.5x55 already offered, but in a shorter action with more efficient case designs. From a hunting point of view, there is very little to separate them.

The 6.5mm bullet really came into use after 1886, when a number of European countries began experimenting with new military cartridges such as the 6.5x52. After a joint Norwegian and Swedish venture into designing the new calibre, Norway adopted the 6.5x55 in 1894 – although the involvement of the former was sadly lost in

the sands of time. Today it is known as the 6.5x55 Swedish Mauser, owing to the Mauser rifles adopted by the Swedish military.

As with most military calibres, the easy availability of rifles and ammo helped to make the calibre a popular choice for the sporting shooter across Europe. While most European calibres had been unable to find success in America, the 6.5x55 did, although its following waned with the introduction of the .260 Rem.

The 6.5 Swede is an excellent calibre for UK shores, covering the full spectrum of game we have available. With most rifles barrelled with a 1-in-8 twist as standard, they are most usefully loaded from 120-140 grain, although the lighter 90-grain would make for an excellent foxing option. It is renowned for its mild recoil and down range performance, and the long 140-grain bullets offer excellent penetration.

This calibre is fondly spoken of by almost all who use it, but don't think it's a magic pill. This is a modest cartridge and, although trajectory is perfectly acceptable, don't expect it to compete with faster modern designs. Accuracy is exceptional, and it is perfectly capable of taking red deer and dropping all but the biggest African antelope with ease. Although somewhat underpowered for moose and bear, it will do the deed in the right hands.

Shooting 140-grain Hornady A-Max handloads at 2,700fps results in a 1in high zero at 100 yards, with bullets landing smack on the money at 175 yards. Out at 200 yards it will land a shade over an inch low, and at 300 yards you are looking at a drop of just under 10in. 250 yards shows a drop of less than 5in, which would mean a top shoulder shot for a roe – perfectly manageable for 95 per cent of stalking situations.

The 6.5 Swede delivers everything a stalker in this country needs. It would make an excellent choice for anyone choosing a new calibre. **BP**

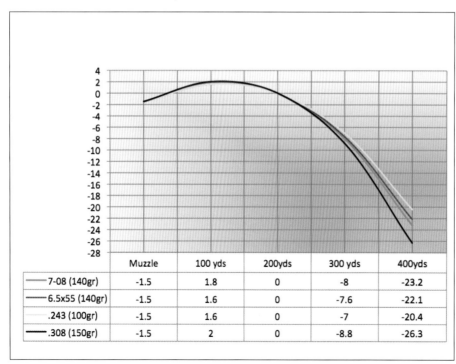

| | Muzzle | 100 yds | 200yds | 300 yds | 400yds |
|---|---|---|---|---|---|
| 7-08 (140gr) | -1.5 | 1.8 | 0 | -8 | -23.2 |
| 6.5x55 (140gr) | -1.5 | 1.6 | 0 | -7.6 | -22.1 |
| .243 (100gr) | -1.5 | 1.6 | 0 | -7 | -20.4 |
| .308 (150gr) | -1.5 | 2 | 0 | -8.8 | -26.3 |

# .260 REMINGTON

It comes as no surprise that so many manufacturers have tried to harness the awesome ballistics of the 6.5mm in their own concoction of brass housing. It is one of the most versatile, accurate and manageable bullet diameters ever to have been chambered. Indeed, the virtues of its favourable ballistic properties have been described here before. I will not repeat these, but will instead evaluate if the .260 Rem is a worthy addition to the already crowded queue of calibres hoping to be the ultimate answer to the 6.5mm bullet.

Essentially the .260 Rem is a commercialised answer to the 6.5-08 Wildcat cartridge. Launched by Remington in 2007, the calibre was held back initially by the availability of quality brass. Home-loaders soon found a satisfactory solution by necking up Lapua .243 brass or necking down .308 Lapua brass. The extra prep time was worth it for the results, but this didn't help non-loaders, with off-the-shelf ammo hard to come by.

Since then, life has been made considerably easier with Lapua recognising the need for dedicated, high-quality .260 Rem brass. In March this year, Hannam's Reloading started importing the first batches. I have been testing it since its arrival, and it is quite possibly the most high-tolerance and consistent brass I have ever used. This is hardly surprising given the calibre's rise through the target shooting world, with many shooters trading in their .308s for the new kid on the block.

Thankfully it is no longer a preserve of reloaders, as several ammo manufacturers now produce loads for the .260 Rem, including Remington and Federal. In the hunting world the uptake has been a bit slower, although it is enjoying increased use across Europe.

The .260 Rem does not have it all its own way, however, as the introduction of the 6.5x47 Lapua and Hornady's 6.5 Creedmoor cartridge have provided the inquisitive shooter with something of a dilemma. The bottom line is that in practical hunting terms, there isn't a hair between them. Sure, the 6.5x47 factory loads are down about 150fps on the others owing to the smaller case capacity. They can, however, be loaded to greater pressures, and handloads soon bring them back in line.

Until recently my personal preference would have been to opt for none of the above, and instead chamber a hunting rifle in 6.5x55 Ack Imp. Above 140 grains, the larger 55mm case has a marked advantage, but I never load rounds above this in the 6.5mm Swedish. If I want to punch 160- or 175-grain bullets, I reach for my 7x57 Mauser. I have a mountain rifle build in the planning stages for next year, and I am pretty sure now it will be a short action chambered in .260 Rem. Why this over the others? Simply because I have had the chance to load it at some length, and the brass is superb and readily available. **BP**

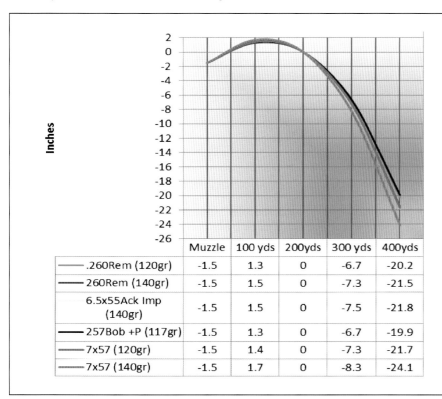

| | Muzzle | 100 yds | 200yds | 300 yds | 400yds |
|---|---|---|---|---|---|
| .260Rem (120gr) | -1.5 | 1.3 | 0 | -6.7 | -20.2 |
| 260Rem (140gr) | -1.5 | 1.5 | 0 | -7.3 | -21.5 |
| 6.5x55Ack Imp (140gr) | -1.5 | 1.5 | 0 | -7.5 | -21.8 |
| 257Bob +P (117gr) | -1.5 | 1.3 | 0 | -6.7 | -19.9 |
| 7x57 (120gr) | -1.5 | 1.4 | 0 | -7.3 | -21.7 |
| 7x57 (140gr) | -1.5 | 1.7 | 0 | -8.3 | -24.1 |

# .26 NOSLER

## WE ARE NOT TALKING THE ABILITY TO POINT AND SHOOT A CROW OUT TO 415 YARDS, BUT IF WE UPSCALE TO BIGGER GAME, THE APPEAL STARTS TO BECOME CLEAR

It's not often I write here about calibres I have no experience of. I have, for the most part, always endeavoured to gain some knowledge in the field, or at least have a close source who has used the calibre to a substantial extent. But this calibre certainly merits an investigation for pure interest's sake. At the SHOT show in Vegas in 2014, Nosler presented not just a new rifle, but also an enticing new calibre: the .26 Nosler. You will have to forgive me if the information on it is a little scant at the time of writing, but it grabbed me as something special, so I wanted to give you a peek into its possibilities.

After watching the Hollywood-style YouTube video at www.26nosler.com, I started to dig. On paper it was very impressive, with the headline of "dead on to 415 yards". That seemed like quite a claim – could it really be true?

First, we need to define exactly what Nosler means by 'flat'. As anyone who knows a little bit about bullet trajectory will already realise, this claim can't possibly mean the calibre shoots in the same place from muzzle to 415 yards. The comparisons Nosler helpfully

provides refer to kill zones, which would allow the .26 Nosler to shoot within a 10in circle out to 415 yards with a 350-yard zero. This would result in having a 4.93in high zero at 200 yards and 3.4in high zero at 100 yards. So we are not talking the ability to point and shoot a crow out to these ranges, but if we upscale to bigger game, the appeal starts to become clear. To give an idea of the comparison, with the .26 Nosler and .270 Win pushing a similarly weighted 130-grain bullet zeroed at 200 yards, the Nosler would drop 5in less at 400 yards.

Delving deeper, we can see that this is achieved by pushing the 6.5mm 129-grain bullet with a muzzle velocity of 3,400fps, offering down-range energy at 400 yards

of over 2,000ft/lb. Slightly more than a 180-grain bullet from a .300 Win Mag, and 500ft/lb more than a .308 Win loaded with a 165-grain bullet.

Fitting a standard .30-06 length action, Nosler, like a number of other ammo manufacturers in recent years, has designed its new cartridge around the inherently accurate, high BC 6.5mm calibre bullet. This, however, is different in its intended application to other similar calibres, with the .260 Rem, 6.5x47 Lapua and 6.5 Creedmoor all short-action calibres focusing on compact efficiency. Indeed, the .26 Nosler is very much upscaled, taking its parent case from the .404 Jeffery, blown out and necked down.

That should give you some idea of just how much powder is being used to propel this relatively small projectile. The .26 Nosler is even faster than the acclaimed 6.5-284, used to win so many long-range competitions. This doesn't, however, mean it is better by default. There are a number of faster calibres of similar vein available in the Weatherby range, and still the 6.5-284 finds favour.

It is hard to speculate about just what the .26 Nosler will deliver, but there are a few aspects worth bearing in mind. As already alluded to, it burns a lot of powder to push a bullet that is very small in comparison to the load, and this combination usually results in a short barrel life. On top of this this, currently we are only going to see the calibre loaded with a 129-grain bullet (based on initial reports). In any case, this will not stop handloaders from experimenting, and it is always enthusing to see the continued development in new cartridges. Nosler is clearly pushing the boundaries in a part of the market that has been quiet for a while. I just can't wait to get my hands on it for a play. **BP**

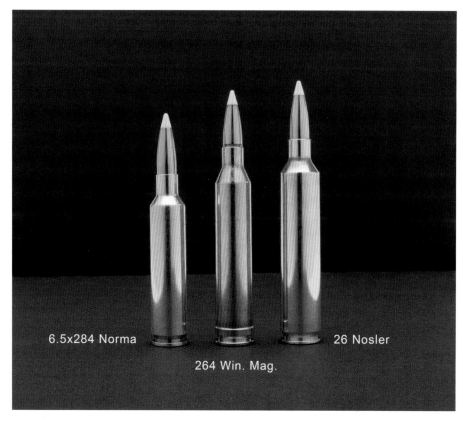

6.5x284 Norma

264 Win. Mag.

26 Nosler

# 7MM-08

I have always thought that the .308 Win case is proportionally perfect to look at. The dimensions are pleasing to the eye, and the performance and popularity of the round speaks for itself. So it is little wonder that this case was necked down to 7mm to take advantage of the array of superb projectiles available in this bullet diameter. Remington introduced the 7mm-08 in the 1980s, but it could hardly lay claim to ownership as the 7mm-08 wildcat had been in use since before 1958. There is nothing fancy about the commercial offering either – it is simply the original .308 Win case necked down to take a 7mm bullet.

Although Remington claimed the 7mm-08 "was the first 7mm round designed for use in short actions" (Frank C Barnes, Cartridges of the World), this overlooked the fact that the .284 Winchester had been on the go since 1963. I will include no more mention of the .284 here, as it will be suitably discussed next month. It has prompted me to plan a custom rifle in the calibre, so it is not to be missed.

Today, most manufacturers offer a handful of models in 7mm-08. It was quickly taken up by silhouette shooters keen to take advantage of the superior ballistics over the .308 Win. The 7mm-08 exhibited a flatter trajectory and less wind drift, while benefiting from the .308 Win's inherent accuracy and long barrel life.

The table below shows the performance of the two calibres, taking a 168-grain Berger

VLD (BC=0.486) 7mm-08 and comparing it to a 170-grain Sierra MK (BC=0.496) from the .308. For long-range delivery of bullets greater than 150-grain, the 7mm-08's advantages are pretty clear. The difference in retained energy at 1,000 yards is surprising, with 7mm-08 delivering over 150ft/lb more than the historically chosen long-distance calibre. Combined with the reduced drop and wind drift evident in the table, it is obvious to see why shooters partaking in precise long-distance silhouette shooting were quick to trade in their outclassed .308 Winchesters.

It is true, however, that the .308 is capable of pushing much heavier bullets at faster velocities than the 7mm-08, bringing the ballistic coefficients back in line. The trade-off here is recoil – most people would not want to shoot many rounds of the 210-grain projectile required to match the ballistics of a 175-grain 7mm. This would equate to something like 17 per cent more recoil if the bullet is pushed at the 2,800fps required to equal trajectory and wind drift (percentage and figures produced by Bryan Litz, Applied Ballistics). I hasten to add that this would not be a safe load in most instances, and is merely to illustrate the point.

Obviously recoil isn't of great consideration to hunters, with most rarely firing more than two shots in an outing. If you are a fan of range days, however, the 7mm will offer a whole world of pleasure and comfort round after round.

But what of the other 7mm rounds? We could not talk about the 7mm-08 without mentioning the 7x57 Mauser. The two produce similar ballistics to one another with the lower- to middle- weight bullets, although the slightly larger case capacity of the old 7x57 makes it more versatile than the relatively new kid on the block. Once we get to 170-grain and above, bullets have to be seated quite deep in the 7mm-08, further reducing case capacity. The 7mm-08 doesn't have the grunt required to shoot those heavier bullets to the same standard as the 7x57, with MVs 100-180fps less. Having said that, up to 160 grains the two calibres are pretty much on par, although the more efficient case of the 7mm-08 makes for tighter long-range groups.

The 7mm bullet is without a doubt my favourite all-round calibre. Choosing the case to send that fantastic projectile down-range is where it becomes a matter for serious contention. For me, the short action and accuracy benefits over the 7x57 don't quite make up for the reduced performance in the heaviest bullet weights. However, that may be because my rifle sees extensive use in Africa as well as the UK. Does it mean that the reign of the .308 Winchester should now be over? Probably not, but if factory rifle and ammo production were equal, and they had been launched around the same time, I would bet that most hunters would have reached for smaller 7mm-08 off the rack in the gun shop. **BP**

# .280 REMINGTON

The .280 Remington has never gained the same attention as the well-used .270 Winchester. It is, however, a potentially superior cartridge.

Introduced in 1957, it was originally chambered in Remington model 740 semi-automatic rifles. For this to function correctly, the cartridge was only loaded up to 50,000psi, resulting in less than impressive performance in sporting rifles. Conversely, the .270 Win was loaded up to 54,000psi, producing faster velocities than the .280 Rem. Because of this, the .280 was poorly received.

Another detrimental factor was the successful launch of the 7mm Rem Mag, which went on to become one of the most popular 7mm calibres in America. Despite the .280 being loaded in most Remington rifle models, it failed to gain much attention. By the 1970s, the ammunition

was on the verge of going out of production. It wasn't until the 1990s that the calibre began to gain some traction, as hunters realised its potential benefits. This spawned a gun writers' battle, as two camps emerged professing the virtues of the .280 Rem against the well established and much loved .270 Win.

The concept for the .280 Rem was taken from the wildcat 7mm-06, necking down a .30-06 case to accept .284 bullets. The case shoulder was bumped forward by 0.05in to prevent it being loaded in rifles chambered for a .270 Win. Although you won't be able to chamber a .280 Rem in a .270 Win, the opposite is possible.

It is accepted that the 7mm bullet provides excellent ballistics, but of all the ammunition on the commercial market in 7mm, the .280 Rem is towards the bottom in the popularity stakes. The initial reasons for this have been

discussed, but it is difficult to understand why it is not used more.

The first sensible comparison is with the 7-08 Rem, a similarly designed calibre using the .308 Win as the parent case instead of the .30-06. With a 200-yard zero, the drop to 400 yards is just over 3in less with the .280 when shooting the same 140-grain Nosler Ballistic Tip. It does this with an extra 217ft/lb of energy, as a result of the 350ft/lb more ME produced from the larger capacity round. This translates into 190fps more muzzle velocity, coming in at 2,990fps, while the 7-08 Rem pushes out 2,800fps.

The .280 Rem has superior performance against its arch-rival. The 7mm projects a 140-grain bullet with the same trajectory as the .270 Win shooting a 130-grain. Consequently, an extra 167ft/lb is delivered at 300 yards. The .280 Rem is also able to shoot much heavier bullets.

What is interesting is how it shapes up against the 7mm Rem Mag. Shooting the same 160-grain bullet, the Magnum delivers only 1.7in less drop at 400 yards, with the .280 Rem zeroed 0.2in higher at 100 yards. Down-range, the extra velocity equates 133ft/lb extra energy at the same distance.

It seems that the .280 Rem outperforms most other 7mms available, and isn't a million miles away from the 7mm Rem Mag. It is softer to shoot, and has proved to be extremely accurate. It makes one wonder why the calibre isn't more popular. Ammunition and rifles are now available in the Ackley improved version of the .280 Rem – this is surely worth looking at. **BP**

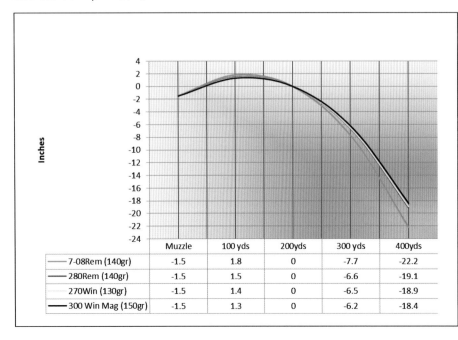

| | Muzzle | 100 yds | 200yds | 300 yds | 400yds |
|---|---|---|---|---|---|
| 7-08Rem (140gr) | -1.5 | 1.8 | 0 | -7.7 | -22.2 |
| 280Rem (140gr) | -1.5 | 1.5 | 0 | -6.6 | -19.1 |
| 270Win (130gr) | -1.5 | 1.4 | 0 | -6.5 | -18.9 |
| 300 Win Mag (150gr) | -1.5 | 1.3 | 0 | -6.2 | -18.4 |

# 7x57

The 7x57 (or 7mm Mauser, or .275 Rigby) is most famously known as an elephant calibre, but it started life as a military cartridge in 1892, designed by German firm Mauser. It was adopted by the Spanish military, initially chambered with 173-grain bullets, but its adoption by other governments saw a range of new weights loaded from 139-grain upwards.

The calibre played a number of pivotal roles in military conflict, such as in 1898, where a 700-strong Spanish defence at San Juan Hill inflicted more than 1,400 casualties on a 15,000-strong American force. The Americans'

conclusion was that such losses were solely because of the superior firepower of the 7x57 over their newly adopted .30-40 Krag. They replaced it shortly afterwards.

In the Boer War, the British found themselves ballistically outclassed by the 7mm Mauser. Their old cordite-based .303 rifles were no match for the Boers' more powerful, flatter-shooting rifles. Realising the disadvantage, the British went on to produce an upgraded version of the .303, using the more modern smokeless powders.

Its popularity extended across Latin America, Europe, and into Serbia. In 1907 John Rigby & Co rebranded it as the .275 Rigby. Although it is still a popular calibre in parts of Europe, it is becoming increasingly difficult to find rifles chambered in 7x57.

It is probably fair to say that it was cemented in hunting history by W D M Bell, who was an advocate of accurate, mild recoiling rifles. His meticulous study of shot placement for shooting elephants allowed Bell to collect an enormous amount of ivory; most attributed to a well-placed shot from his 7x57 loaded with 175-grain solids.

With this momentum and the already widespread use, the 7x57 became a default choice in Africa, and over its lifetime the 7mm Mauser has taken every large land mammal on earth.

Despite having been designed more than 100 years ago, it remains one of the most well-balanced cartridges ever invented. Being able to cope with bullet weights from 110 to 190 grains makes it adaptable to most hunting situations.

I have found the 120-grain bullets to be particularly effective on roe deer-sized species, providing impressive down-range energy and trajectory with minimal recoil. Loaded with Sierra Pro Hunters, in modern rifles it is possible to churn these out at just over 3,000fps, which equates to a trajectory path 1.1in high at 100 yards, -0.6in at 200 yards, and a perfectly manageable -3.4in at 250 yards. This even makes it a feasible option for foxing – indeed it was my primary set-up until I bought a .22-250 Rem. Loaded with 140 grains, it'll serve you well for most game in Europe, America, and medium-sized plains game in Africa. With a zero 1.3in high at 100 yards, a 250-yard shot will drop four inches. With handloads the 120-grain, 140-grain and 160-grain bullets shoot very accurately, and even the 175-grain magnum tips – travelling at a much slower 2,300fps – will shoot into just over 1.25in with ease. Armed with the 160-grain or 175-grain options, you will be well equipped to tackle moose and eland with a well-placed shot.

I have referenced the 7x57 in comparisons before, but feel there is little point here. It will be outclassed by modern magnums on almost every account, but that doesn't really matter. The 7x57 has nothing left to prove – it has worked exceptionally well for over 100 years, and there's no reason to think anything has changed. **BP**

# 7MM REM MAG

The arrival of the 7mm Remington Magnum in 1962 conveniently coincided with Remington's new and improved Model 700 series – a design which has stood the test of time, and to this day remains one of the most popular and versatile actions around. This fast, long-range calibre was by no means a new discovery, as its introduction and subsequent take-up by other manufacturers was some 40 years behind the .275 H&H, which had graced hunting rifles since 1912. Although this calibre was discontinued in 1939, future wildcats – including the 7mm Rem Mag – took inspiration from the calibre's ability to accurately shoot a 175-grain 7mm bullet with a high muzzle velocity and a flat trajectory.

The 7mm Rem Mag is most at home in open country, plains, and mountains, where long-range shots and substantial down-range energy delivery is essential. It is undoubtedly the standard by which all long-range big game calibres are judged, and enjoys a healthy following, with few rifle manufacturers not chambering the calibre in one of their models.

The graph shows rather impressively that with Federal factory ammo, the 7mm Rem Mag delivers a hefty 160-grain bullet at 300 yards with just a seven-inch drop, following on from a 200-yard zero. Compared to the 708 Remington, the 7mm has a clear two-inch advantage, despite the 708 Rem being loaded with a bullet 10

grains lighter. Extend the range to 400 yards, and we can see 6.7in less drop. It achieves this with a whopping 1,778ft/lb, after leaving the muzzle with 2,989ft/lb of energy. Putting this in perspective: The 7mm Rem Mag will deliver a 160-grain bullet at 400 yards with energy almost equal to a 100-grain .243 Win as it leaves the barrel. That's some serious clobber.

The wind-bucking ability of all three 7mm Magnums mentioned below is almost identical, with less than two inches separating them at 600 yards. With a manageable 4.5in drift over 300 yards against a 10mph wind, the 7mm Rem Mag gives the hunter very little excuse for not landing a decisive shot with every trigger pull. A quick scan of some of the USA-based websites lets you appreciate just what the calibre is capable of – many shooters boast of taking deer at 500 yards. I would never suggest that this was ethical, but it does illustrate what is possible. To add to its credentials, it was also used for some time as a sniper round by America's secret service, although it has now been superseded by the .300 Win Mag.

On the downside, the 7mm Rem Mag produces some rather unpleasant recoil unless dampened with a muzzle brake, in which case you will end up deaf. But that's where a moderator comes in – it does wonders for this hard-kicking cartridge, transforming it from a mere one-night-stand into dating material. As with all heavy-recoiling calibres, moderation

has the tendency to pull groups in, and makes for a much more pleasant and accurate load development experience.

Like many of its magnum brethren, the 7mm Rem Mag also suffers from relatively short barrel life and hungry powder consumption. Throat erosion will start to become noticeable after around 1,500 rounds, with barrel life generally between 1,500 and 3,000 rounds depending on the load of ammo and make of barrel. That said, unless you are using your rifle for a lot of range days, this could quite easily stretch to 15 years of happy hunting.

The big question is: How does it compare to other 7mm Magnums? There is no denying that a straight comparison across wind drift, energy, trajectory, and velocity puts the 7mm Rem Mag at the bottom of the list. But the differences are barely worth mentioning. The Weatherby Magnum may be superior on paper, but its advantages are outweighed by even more severe recoil and shorter barrel life. To this end, and due to the greater availability of rifles in the 7mm Rem Mag, the Weatherby has never quite enjoyed the same success as Remington's offering.

The much newer kid on the block, the Winchester Short Magnum, may just throw a spanner in the works. The jury is still out here, and it has not gained the same popularity despite proving to be more accurate for long-range shooting. As always, you have to ask yourself just how far you are going to be shooting game at. Out to 300 yards, which is generally accepted as the furthest distance for an ethical shot, there isn't a hair between the calibres. What may be a swaying factor is the far superior availability of rifles and ammo for the Remington. **BP**

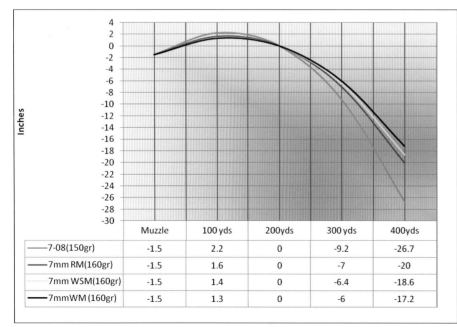

| | Muzzle | 100 yds | 200yds | 300 yds | 400yds |
|---|---|---|---|---|---|
| 7-08(150gr) | -1.5 | 2.2 | 0 | -9.2 | -26.7 |
| 7mm RM(160gr) | -1.5 | 1.6 | 0 | -7 | -20 |
| 7mm WSM(160gr) | -1.5 | 1.4 | 0 | -6.4 | -18.6 |
| 7mmWM (160gr) | -1.5 | 1.3 | 0 | -6 | -17.2 |

.300 H&H

Every now and then I get an email from a reader of one of my articles in the sporting press, requesting a review on a rifle or a particular article. One of the most memorable came from a Mr Wheeler, enquiring if I could take a look at the .300 Holland and Holland. From his mail it was clear he was a massive fan of British-designed calibres, so I decided to delve into the calibre, also one of my favoured cartridges of old.

The origins of the .300 H&H may be surprising to some, starting life in 1925 as a .375 H&H case. Already enjoying the runaway success of its .375 belted magnum, Holland and Holland necked its own cartridge down to .30 cal, producing the .300 H&H. During the development there was a lot of secrecy, with the design patented by the company. As a proprietary cartridge, no other gun manufacturer was allowed to chamber a rifle in the calibre without permission from H&H. Indeed, there were even restrictions on the manufacturer of the ammunition without consent.

Initially this stunted the success of the calibre, with only those able to afford the princely sum for an H&H custom rifle able to take advantage of the new calibre. At the time ammunition was loaded by Kynoch, but the performance was a little lacklustre compared to its potential, equalling that offered by the .30-06 Springfield. Today Kynoch still loads ammunition, but with modern powders.

In the late 1920s Holland and Holland decided to release the patent rights, allowing all rifle manufacturers to chamber the calibre. Even then it took another decade before any interest was shown beyond the upper class. It took a 1,000-yard win at the Wimbledon cup by an American shooter for people to take notice.

Within a few years Winchester had jumped on the success of the calibre, offering its famous model 70 in .300 H&H and .375 H&H. The cartridge was now at the fingertips of the general hunting public. Powder development helped get more out of the casing, and soon the calibre was seen to have an advantage over other market offerings. It was ideal for bigger game and long-distance targets.

Holland and Holland's .30 cal continued to gain an increased following in America and at home, with many hunters destined for Africa opting to make use of the British-designed cartridge. Soon other ammo manufacturers developed their own cartridges to muscle in on the success, with the .300 Weatherby Magnum launched in 1944. By the 1960s the now-famous .300 Winchester Magnum was launched, pretty much spelling an end for the .300 H&H over the pond. As is inevitable with the marketing power and weight of American brands, within a decade the Winchester Magnum had reduced the H&H's reach to a shadow of its former levels.

Today it still sees some use, but it is rare to find a rifle chambered in the calibre. Mostly it is used by those nostalgic about the old cartridges and British design. That said, even pitted against modern cartridges it still offers excellent performance. Compared to a .30-06, a 180-grain bullet drops over 2in less at 400 yards with a 100-yard zero. Muzzle energy is also substantially more, with an extra 400ft/lb. Compared to the .300 Win Mag it's a bit of a reverse story, although the gap is much smaller. In truth there isn't a great deal between them, but ammo and rifle availability of the .300 Win Mag makes it the more popular choice.

The .300 H&H was a pioneer, pre-empting what modern cartridges could offer. For America's large game, and antelope in Africa, it is still an excellent choice. Featuring in books from Capstick to Hemingway, it reminds me of what made Britain great. If I have the chance to get my hands on a nice rifle chambered in 300 H&H, I will need a good reason not to buy it. **BP**

# .300 WIN MAG

The .300 Win Mag definitely falls into the long-distance cartridge category, but it also encompasses some very favourable properties, making it a superb all-round calibre. It has no shortage of followers, counting our own editor and Mike Yardley among them.

Launched some 38 years before the Winchester, the highly respected .300 H&H Magnum had covered similar ground, seeing widespread use across Africa and winning the 1,000-yard Wimbledon Cup in 1935. The blown out and shortened case of the .300 Win Mag sports a much steeper shoulder than the .300 H&H. The body of the case was stretched by some 0.12in over equivalent calibres, and although unconfirmed, it was speculated that Winchester oversized the case to allow rifles already chambered in .30-338 and .308 Norma to be easily reamed out to fit .300 Win Mag dimensions.

In any event, the .300 Win Mag has seen global success, seeing extensive use as the calibre of choice for those reaching shots required on antelope in the open plains, or cross-canyon targeting for perilously perching sheep and goats. It truly is an excellent sheep calibre, if not the best. Equally, it provides adequate energy to cope with the biggest bears, pushing a 180-grain bullet with 3,500ft/lb muzzle energy. It also exhibits more than acceptable varminting capabilities, using the flat-shooting 130-grain head (rising just 0.9in for a 200-yard zero, with a five-inch drop to 300 yards).

Today it is hard not to feel that the calibre has been outclassed ballistically by the .300 Weatherby Magnum and more recently the .300 Rem Ultra Magnum. The numbers are quite telling. Taking the same 180-grain bullet with factory loads in all three calibres, we see the .300 Rem Ult Mag drop 5.6in at 300 yards, compared to 6.2in and 7in for the Weatherby and Winchester respectively (based on a 200-yard zero). Over 400 yards the Remington trumps the Winchester by over four inches, delivering considerably more down-range energy at 2,400ft/lb – 200ft/lb more than the Weatherby and 600ft/lb more than the Winchester.

This all sounds great in theory, but the laws of physics mean you can't squeeze out all that performance without having to pay for it. The equal and opposite reaction to this down-range magic is felt by the shooter in the form of some seriously unpleasant recoil. Unless you enjoy feeling like you have been worked over with an iron bar the morning after, this will not be the rifle to take for a date at the shooting range.

So where does this leave the .300 Win Mag? Although it appeared to have been swept away by the new-fangled cool kids on the block, this owed more to testing on paper than in the field. Given a 260-yard zero, the .300 Win Mag will still shoot inside a six-inch kill zone out to 300 yards. You will gain a few more yards with the Ultra Mag, sure, but even at out at 350 yards we are only talking a 1.5in advantage. Serious advantage is only seen in ultra-long range shots, which have questionable ethics at any rate. The .300 Win Mag provides an excellent compromise, with a level of accuracy that was never in question. **BP**

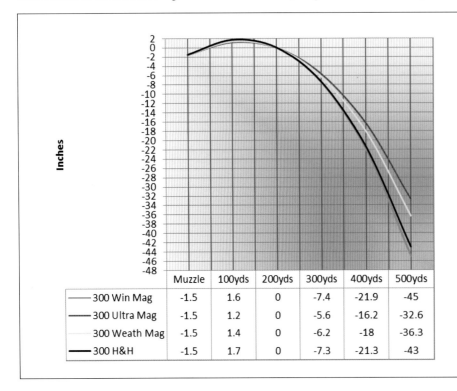

| | Muzzle | 100yds | 200yds | 300yds | 400yds | 500yds |
|---|---|---|---|---|---|---|
| 300 Win Mag | -1.5 | 1.6 | 0 | -7.4 | -21.9 | -45 |
| 300 Ultra Mag | -1.5 | 1.2 | 0 | -5.6 | -16.2 | -32.6 |
| 300 Weath Mag | -1.5 | 1.4 | 0 | -6.2 | -18 | -36.3 |
| 300 H&H | -1.5 | 1.7 | 0 | -7.3 | -21.3 | -43 |

# .30-06 SPRINGFIELD

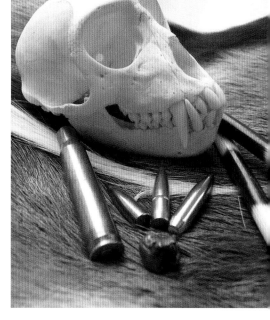

More 7.62mm – or .308 – bullets have been fired than probably any other calibre. Not only is it used currently by the US military in the 7.62x51mm NATO round, it was also used in the .30-06 Springfield service rifles adopted in 1906 for many combat roles, including long-range sniping. During World War Two America also supplied arms and ammo in .30-06 to many Allied countries, including Great Britain. The British military used the 7.62 NATO until it was replaced by the arguably less effective .223 Remington. I believe plans are now in motion to go back to the 7.62 due to Remington's inferior performance in Afghanistan.

As far as sporting calibres go, the .308 is one of the most popular of all, leading to a vast array of bullet weights and designs. The .30-06, however, has been somewhat left behind in the modern world of calibre choice. Seen as dated and less effective compared to modern Magnums, this hugely successful calibre deserves serious consideration from hunters in every country, including the UK. Indeed, the usefulness of the calibre is reflected in the fact that every major manufacturer offers rifles chambered in .30-06.

The extensive history and reloading options for the .30-06 make this an exciting calibre to tinker with. Seen by Frank C. Barnes as "undoubtedly the most flexible, useful, all-round big game cartridge available to the American hunter", its hunting credentials extend back to its introduction via a bolt action rifle, the Remington model 30, in 1921.

Seen for decades as the standard by which all other big game cartridges should be judged, it's perhaps surprising to find that it performs very well even when pitted against more modern rounds.

For all antelope, deer, goats, sheep, black and brown bear, this 180-grain offering is judged by experienced hunters to be able to cope with virtually any hunting conditions. In the past it was used for dangerous game in Africa, including lion, buffalo, and leopard, on a regular basis (although a 220-grain bullet was more widely used for the biggest and most dangerous game). Despite this, many countries ban its use on big game today – probably a sensible move for all but the most experienced hunter.

A 175-yard zero proves the most useful for the 180-grain bullet, equating to a 1.4in-high zero at 100 yards. Coincidentally, this is also the zenith (highest point) of the trajectory above line-of-sight (using Federal ammo with a Nosler partition bullet). According to Federal, this drops a 200-yard shot 1.2in below the aim point, with all shots out to that range within a 2.6in kill zone. This is very respectable.

The trajectory data also shows virtual mirroring of the 150-grain .30-06 and .308

Win out to 200 yards, with the 06 falling less rapidly beyond the zero range, gaining 1.6in on the .308 at the 400-yard mark. With exactly the same bullets used, the BC and SC are obviously identical, but the extra 100fps muzzle velocity of the .30-06 carries the bullet marginally flatter at the extended distances. On the other hand, the larger case is packing more powder, around four or five grains, for the 150-grain bullet load depending on powders – making for a more expensive shooting experience and greater recoil.

What is not shown on the graph is how the super-fast (3,400fps) 110-grain bullet load compares to similar bullet loads from other calibres. Running it alongside the widely used .270 Win shows that the .30-06 only starts to noticeably drop off from the .270 after about 300 yards. This despite the .270 packing an extra 100fps muzzle velocity.

So what use is the .30-06 to the modern-day UK hunter? Well, albeit at a stretch, it covers all bases. It is a little heavy for foxing, and can't boast the laser straight trajectory of a .220 Swift, but on other hand you can't hunt a bear with a 50-grain bullet, not if you want to stay alive. The 110-grain bullet will adequately take care of any deer in the UK, while heavier options give you scope for varying conditions, foreign travel and wild boar. In spite of this, it doesn't do anything the .308 Win can't do cheaper, and in some cases more accurately. Although both were used for NRA competitions, competitors soon changed over to the more efficiently burning, shorter-cased .308 Win, because of its consistently superior accuracy (as much as two or three times better).

For hunting, however, this is largely irrelevant. So if you don't want to follow the crowd, and don't mind paying a little extra for the ammo, then embrace an old favourite with a long shooting heritage, and choose the .30-06. **BP**

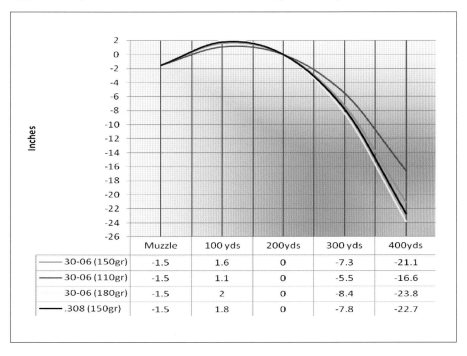

| | Muzzle | 100 yds | 200yds | 300 yds | 400yds |
|---|---|---|---|---|---|
| 30-06 (150gr) | -1.5 | 1.6 | 0 | -7.3 | -21.1 |
| 30-06 (110gr) | -1.5 | 1.1 | 0 | -5.5 | -16.6 |
| 30-06 (180gr) | -1.5 | 2 | 0 | -8.4 | -23.8 |
| .308 (150gr) | -1.5 | 1.8 | 0 | -7.8 | -22.7 |

# 7x64 BRENNEKE

Most gun nuts will know the satisfying feeling gained from slowly building your perfect rifle collection. I was on the search for a new rifle to fulfil longer-range expeditions for bigger game. I didn't want a calibre as brutal as the 7mm Rem Mag, so I knew I would have to look elsewhere.

The 7x64 Brenneke was born in 1917, but started life rather unsuccessfully as another calibre invention of the now renowned Wilhelm Brenneke. Backing up to 1912, we were given the 8x64 (comparable to today's 8mm-06 wildcat). It was designed to be a ballistic upgrade of the military issue 8x57. There were ballistic advantages, but the complications of war meant it didn't gain traction – the German military stuck with the 8x57. Brenneke continued his development and by 1917 he had necked down the 8x64 to take a 7mm bullet. This time he was on to a winner.

The calibre didn't get much interest in the US, but back home it found a strong following to rival the 7mm Rem Mag. The 7x64 is one of very few calibres that were produced by American manufacturers despite having very little demand in the US. With a similar case design to the .30-06, it resembles the capabilities of the .280 Rem and offers virtually identical ballistics to the .284 Winchester. Unlike the 7mm Rem Mag, the 7x64 is not belted. It will fit a standard length action, though, as it is almost the same overall length. The Remington, however, will outperform it, and this

is the reason for the US preference for its America-born 7mm.

In Europe it was seen as a major development, with substantial increases in muzzle velocity and corresponding improved ballistics over the established 7x57. The older calibre saw widespread and popular use, not just across Europe but also in Africa. What the 7x64 offered was something familiar, yet faster, flatter and harder-hitting. The choice was easy.

A rimmed version was brought out to cater for those using lightweight, single-shot mountain rifles, as well as the combination rifle/shotguns

particularly popular in Germany. The 7x65R is, for all intents and purposes, an identical round.

Hunters are spoilt for choice with bullets, like with other 7mm calibres, though factory loads don't facilitate the true versatility. Here we will take the middle ground to give a good comparison with the better-known market contenders.

Unsurprisingly, the flattest trajectory prize goes to the 7mm Rem Mag, with MV 170fps faster than its European cousin. But firing exactly the same bullet gives just a two-inch advantage at 300 yards. For the reduced performance, the 7x64 is noticeably softer to shoot, as well as being kinder on throat erosion. Compared to the .308 Win, the 7x64 has quite a bit more poke, delivering just under 300ft/lb more energy at 300 yards. Looking at the trajectories you will see that comparing the 7x64 to the .308 Win is a bit like the difference between the 7mm Rem Mag and the Brenneke.

As is often the case, few new things are an original idea. The 7x64 Brenneke proves this, coming decades before Remington introduced its .280 Rem. With the ballistic benefits of the 7mm bullet, and case capacity allowing almost identical stats to the .280 Rem, the 7x64 is a convenient stopgap between calibres based on the .308 Win and the heavier recoiling magnums. As major European gun makers also chamber it, I think I have just found the new calibre that will be joining the family. **BP**

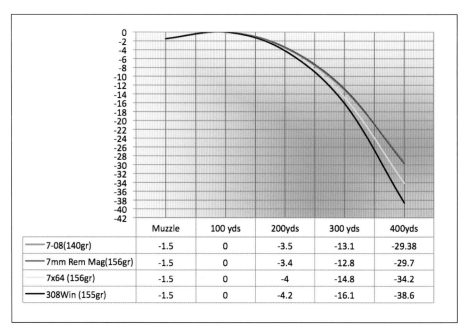

| | Muzzle | 100 yds | 200yds | 300 yds | 400yds |
|---|---|---|---|---|---|
| 7-08(140gr) | -1.5 | 0 | -3.5 | -13.1 | -29.38 |
| 7mm Rem Mag(156gr) | -1.5 | 0 | -3.4 | -12.8 | -29.7 |
| 7x64 (156gr) | -1.5 | 0 | -4 | -14.8 | -34.2 |
| 308Win (155gr) | -1.5 | 0 | -4.2 | -16.1 | -38.6 |

# .303 BRITISH

"You do realise nobody uses those any more? Devan, is that the best you could do for your Scottish friend?" Chuckling, the Afrikaans farmer scoffed at the primitive action and open sights on the old .303 rifle. It had long been an ambition of mine to use a truly old rifle and calibre, so after a few adjustments on the range I was off after warthogs.

This interesting calibre has a lifespan of almost 114 years, even though it rarely sees use today. Adopted as a military calibre in 1988, the .303 British (which is actually a .312 bullet) saw widespread use across two World Wars before being superseded by the 7.62 NATO (.308 Win) in 1957.

It started life as a black powder cartridge before the arrival of smokeless powders. This allowed around 1,860fps from a 70-grain compressed load and a 215-grain round nose bullet. Four years later, the propellant was upgraded to cordite, which allowed increased velocities. By 1910, the bullet weight had been dropped to 174 grains, increasing speeds further and bringing them more in line with the kind of velocities we would recognise today. This Mk VII round travelled at around 2,440fps and remained in this format until it was discontinued for military use. (Velocities and stats obtained from Frank C Barnes, 'Cartridges of the World' 8th ed.)

It was also this calibre which was used to develop the first expanding ammunition, known then as Dum Dum bullets. Around the 1890s in the Dum Dum arsenal in India, Capt. Bertie Clay experimented with exposing the lead core at the point of the bullet. The mushrooming effect this caused saw a staggering increase in effectiveness. By the time the MK VII evolution came around, the bullet design had moved on considerably from the full metal jacketed version, constructing the lighter bullets with fibreglass or aluminium tips.

Soon after its arrival it became a sought-after calibre for sporting purposes. It saw use on every species imaginable, from tigers in India to crocodiles in Australia. The enthusiastic take-up of the round will undoubtedly have been as a result of easy availability of ammo and rifles, but nonetheless it performed well. This was despite most hunting in the early years of the .303 British being done with jacketed, non-expanding rounds.

For many years the only sporting loads available were 215-grain solid and soft points, although some factory ammo shooting 150 and 180 grains did come on the market later. Handloaders were eventually able to take advantage of much lighter heads and higher velocities than factory production.

Today there are few manufacturers who chamber the .303 British, or indeed make ammo for it. This is understandable when comparing the stats on the 215-grain bullet with its modern equivalents. However, in lighter bullet weights its performance is surprising – it chucks the 180-grain head down-range with a trajectory not a million miles from a .308 (which has an advantage of about 3in at 300 yards). It achieves this with about 2,500fps MV and 2,520ft/lb ME. This is 100fps and just over 250ft/lb less than the .308, largely owing to the higher case pressures possible.

Kynoch still makes .303 ammo, loading the traditional 215-grain bullet. Using the stats chart, it is easy to see its shortcomings in today's hunting world, but for the handloader using lighter bullet weights, it still has potential for those who wish for a taste of the Empire. BP

# .30-30 WINCHESTER

I had always disregarded under-lever rifles as a plinkers: they shoot a centrefire cartridge and put plenty of lead down range, but who would really would take an under-lever hunting? They see much more use in the States though, and unless you are some sort of wannabe cowboy, surely buying an under-lever was only for the curious. Well, that's what I used to think. However, it wasn't a Yankee experience that changed my mind, it was a trip to Africa.

With a day spare, some friends gathered for a session at the range. We burnt a lot of gunpowder, shooting everything from a .45 pistol to a .300 Win Mag at 600 yards. Among the lot was a newly-acquired under-lever rifle chambered in .30-30 Winchester. It was my first time using one, and what tremendous fun it was. Surprisingly accurate, I was slowly converted to the idea of using it for hunting. It would definitely make a superb rifle for pigs, whether warthogs and bushpigs, or even driven boar.

The .30-30 calibre I used dates back to 1895 where it first appeared in Winchester's catalogue. It was America's first smokeless powder hunting cartridge, loaded with a jacketed bullet. Originally chambered in the under-lever Winchester model 94, it was

advertised as the .30 Winchester Centrefire (.30WCF). When the same calibre was chambered by Marlin, the name was changed to the .30-30 smokeless, with the extra '-30' referring to the standardised load of 30 grains of the early smokeless powders. Later, these variations were combined to leave the name .30-30 Winchester.

It became apparent that this new cartridge offered superior ballistics to the black powder cartridges hunters had been using. The flatter trajectory made it a more reliable killer than

the bigger, more popular calibres, simply because it was easier to place the bullet where you wanted it. It was not without critics though, as many saw the relatively light 160-grain bullet as too light for America's bigger game.

Part of its success was undoubtedly due to the easy shooting under-lever platform it was available in. This provided a compact, fast-shooting, lightweight rifle, producing comfortably moderate recoil. Perfect as a saddle carbine, it was a calibre that could be used by men, women and children alike.

The performance of the .30-30 is unlikely to impress many hunters on home soil, especially in the trajectory department. Zeroed at 200 yards, a 150-grain bullet from a 30-30 will rise over 3.5in at 100 yards, whereas the equivalent .308 Win would be less than 2in. The drop at 300 yards would be a full 16in, whereas the .308 drops less than 8in. Energy delivery is also lacking by comparison, with a ME of just 1,900ft/lb compared with almost 2,700ft/lb from a .308 Win.

Initially I couldn't see the .30-30 as having much application. It worked in the past, but then so did a spear and blow pipe, and few people use those now. I was, however, too hasty to dismiss it completely, as although I can't see anyone jumping to the .30-30 Winchester as a first choice for deer, it makes a superb close-range pig rifle where quick shooting is required from a compact, manoeuvrable platform. **BP**

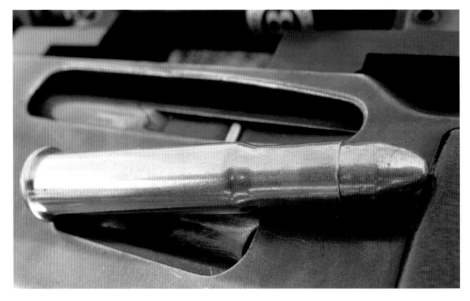

# .270 WIN

I have to admit from the off: I have never been a big fan of the .270 Win. I always saw it as a lot of fuss and bluster for what it offered down-range. My first experience of the calibre was in the infancy of my fullbore rifle career, shooting a number of rifles on one cold range day. Among these were some of the original Mannlichers made so famous by historic African expeditions, along with an old .375 H&H, a well-used .222 Rem BSA, and a Parker Hale .270 Win. I came away from that day with no affection towards the .270 Win. There are some calibres, such as the 7x57 and 6.5x55, that are just endearing. You feel like you want to shoot them more, just to feel the explosive combination of gunpowder, brass and lead again. The .270 Win did not do that for me. I couldn't see why it was so popular.

Today, it still isn't a calibre I would readily add to the gun collection – but I have certainly learned a lot since that first experience. My mates in Africa have a running joke when it comes to the .270 Win, saying it's the calibre that wannabe hunters come to hunt with. Indeed I saw this for myself on a number of questions. They tended to fit a bizarre stereotype: arriving straight from Johannesburg in a suped-up Toyota Hilux with the latest rifles and optics, knives as big as swords, .270 Win, and if they were really in the with cool kids, they were also sporting the ridiculous blue camo that some hunters insist on wearing. It was always amusing to see these guys – but it doesn't give you an insight into the calibre itself.

Turn the clock back as far as 1925, when Winchester launched the 130-grain .270 Win to the hunting public, and we see the beginning of a story that is anything but the success the calibre became. Instead of taking the industry by storm as expected, the calibre soon went quiet, more than likely owing to the popularity and availability of sporterised .30-06 Springfield rifles on the market.

Then, from the ashes, in a way I doubt any gun writer has ever done since, the famous Jack O'Connor rescued the calibre. It has always been unclear to me whether O'Connor was actually working with Winchester, but either way I am sure the company did what they could to encourage his promotion of the .270 Win. It is hard to deny that its early rise in popularity can be almost solely attributed to one man.

O'Connor went on to take a large spectrum of game from around the world with the .270 Win, although his wife, who was also an avid hunter, used a 7x57. During those years more and more hunters chose the calibre as a good all-round solution to North American game.

But as time wore on, we began to see cracks in the.270 Win. Most of these came in the form of excessive meat and skin damage owing to the high-velocity nature of the calibre. Some hunters began to note that although O'Connor had successfully used the calibre on big American game, it was far more suited to open range country on lighter game. Indeed the 130-grain bullet was woefully inadequate in the cold light of day when it came to efficiently hunting bigger species. Velocity was only going to count for so much. There is a certain point when you need bullet weight to penetrate and kill.

You cannot deny that the .270 Win has proved incredibly successful, and to this very day, even in the UK we see .270 Win chambered rifles leaving gun shops on a regular basis. The Forestry Commission, certainly for a time, used it as its calibre of choice, and it was the 'go-to' calibre of the hill stalker for many years. That said, I doubt it would have been elevated to such heights without the help of Jack O'Connor. Certainly if we compare it to other calibres available today, I would suggest that the day of the .270 Win has probably passed; even a 150-grain .308 Win offers superior down-range energy. I have hunted with the calibre, fairly extensively in Africa, and I would take a slower, heavier calibre over it every time. That said, each to their own. **BP**

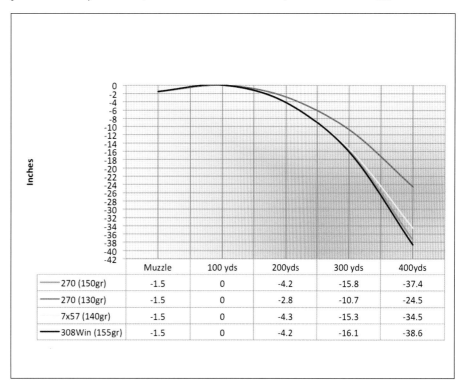

| | Muzzle | 100 yds | 200yds | 300 yds | 400yds |
|---|---|---|---|---|---|
| 270 (150gr) | -1.5 | 0 | -4.2 | -15.8 | -37.4 |
| 270 (130gr) | -1.5 | 0 | -2.8 | -10.7 | -24.5 |
| 7x57 (140gr) | -1.5 | 0 | -4.3 | -15.3 | -34.5 |
| 308Win (155gr) | -1.5 | 0 | -4.2 | -16.1 | -38.6 |

# .308 WIN

I was racking my brains, trying to think of a calibre I hadn't covered yet in my Calibre Hunter column for *Sporting Rifle* magazine. Thne it hit me. I realised I'd missed an obvious one: the venerable .308 Win. It has been used on more than a few occasions as a benchmark for other calibres, but I hadn't written about it in its own right. As I was on the verge of joining those wielding this truly international cartridge, I thought it was about time I put pen to paper on possibly the world's most successful calibre.

As most people are aware, the .308 Win we use for sporting purposes leads a Jekyll and Hyde existence. On one hand we put lead down-range in pursuit of game, and target shooters make use of the excellent accuracy to punch paper at some impressive ranges. On the other, the 7.62 NATO arms our allies and our enemies the world over. There has certainly been a lot of bloodshed using the .308 Win in military theatres.

The history of the calibre is complex. It began life as a research request from the American government to the Frankfort Arsenal. They wanted to achieve similar power and range capabilities to their already established .30-06 Springfield, but in a smaller, more compact case. Reportedly some 10,000 prototypes were made before settling on the 'T65', which itself went through modifications over a number years before the final case design was agreed in 1949. Further testing continued until 1954 before the cartridge was standardised as the 7.62x51 NATO.

Pressure from the commercial world, and speculated leaks in case design, saw the chief of ordinance give Winchester the permission to use the cartridge in its rifles, and hence the .308 Win was born. But Winchester was not riding solely on the back of research completed for the government-funded contract. Indeed, in the preceding years they had begun their own development, testing the .30-80 WCF in the early 1950s. Standing these cartridges together, it would be hard to see the difference, and by all accounts it was a successful project chambered initially in Winchester's Model 80 rifles. However, from the limited information available, the calibre ceased to be a concern about the same time as Winchester was given permission to brand the .308 Win. It seems that having taken it to the concluding phases, it was easier, and one assumes more cost-effective, to run with a design that had been through years of development and testing, with the backing of the American government. The plus side was that the availability of ammo and rifles in the future, owing to its military application, would help propel the cartridge to heights they could only have dreamt of otherwise.

The hunting world owes a lot to the development of this cartridge, which was one of the first that really went for compact efficiency. Previously, the focus tended to be on packing more powder in bigger cases, and little time had been spent trying to achieve similar performance from a smaller cartridge. The .308 Win led the way with this ethos, and more than 50 years on, we see the same push in modern calibre designs.

Personally I have always shied away from the .308 Win. I saw it as the default no-imagination choice of so many hunters, although I would take nothing away from its capabilities. Time has morphed my view, however, partly as a result of testing so many .308 Win rifles in my journalistic career. The ease of use, ammo availability, undeniable accuracy, and sheer choice with regard to rifles and reloading makes the .308 Win hard to ignore, especially when considering the scope of game that can be taken with it. Certainly in the UK, there is nothing it cannot handle, and for the most part, loaded with the correct bullet weight and type, the calibre will tackle most game around the world. **BP**

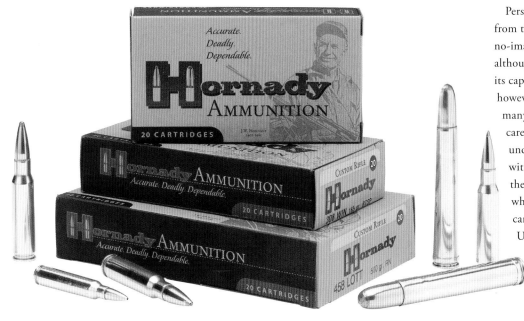

# .308 NORMA MAGNUM

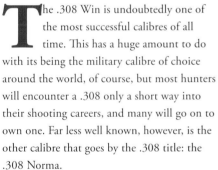

The .308 Win is undoubtedly one of the most successful calibres of all time. This has a huge amount to do with its being the military calibre of choice around the world, of course, but most hunters will encounter a .308 only a short way into their shooting careers, and many will go on to own one. Far less well known, however, is the other calibre that goes by the .308 title: the .308 Norma.

Norma's version was introduced in the USA in the 1960s. It started life a couple of years earlier as the .358 Norma Magnum, loosely based on the .338 Win case. Today most calibre launches are done in conjunction with rifle manufacturers, but back then Norma had to rely on the calibre being picked up by interested gun makers. Two manufacturers took the plunge, with Schultz and Larsen as well as Husqvarna chambering models in the .358 Norma.

By 1960 Norma had taken the .358 and necked it down to accept the vast array of .308 bullets available, producing a new calibre to join the already well catered range of .300 Magnums on offer. It was very similar to the wildcat .30-338, which as the name suggests took the .338 Win and necked it down to .308. Comparison can also be drawn with the much

older .300 H&H, which has featured in these pages before, and saw extensive use across the globe in its day, especially in Africa.

Cartridge dimensions allowed the .308 Norma to be re-chambered in any action that would fit a .30-06, while having slightly more case capacity than a .300 H&H. Advertised at 3,100fps muzzle velocity, this was later amended to 2,950fps.

Through the early 1960s it picked up steady momentum among shooters over the water, but began its decline before it had truly established itself. The .300 Win Mag was largely to blame, as it was soon picked up and chambered by Remington after its launch. Today the .308 Norma is rare, despite being an excellent calibre that is still well respected in the right circles.

As you would expect from Norma, this is a well designed cartridge whose performance makes it ideal for medium game. Just like the .300 Win Mag, it is a very flexible calibre, and can be used successfully across a wide range of game, making an excellent all-round calibre covering everything except dangerous game.

Talking of comparable performance is almost irrelevant because they are all so similar. The .300 Win Mag will push out the same bullet weight with marginally more velocity, but the difference is nothing to get excited about.

This translates to slightly less drop down range – although this is not reflected in the graph because the data (below) uses slightly different bullet designs.

The bottom line is that it's all but impossible to split the .300 H&H, .300 Win Mag and .308 Norma in any meaningful way. So why isn't the .308 Norma more widely used? Well, given the lack of chamberings in factory rifles, the question really answers itself. With availability of rifles and ammo being an issue, I think I would stick with Winchester's offering, even as interesting as the Norma would be as a talking point. **BP**

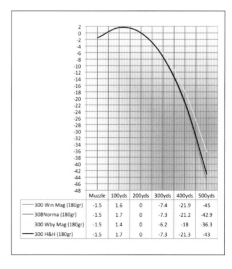

| | Muzzle | 100yds | 200yds | 300yds | 400yds | 500yds |
|---|---|---|---|---|---|---|
| 300 Win Mag (180gr) | -1.5 | 1.6 | 0 | -7.4 | -21.9 | -45 |
| 308 Norma (180gr) | -1.5 | 1.7 | 0 | -7.3 | -21.2 | -42.9 |
| 300 Wby Mag (180gr) | -1.5 | 1.4 | 0 | -6.2 | -18 | -36.3 |
| 300 H&H (180gr) | -1.5 | 1.7 | 0 | -7.3 | -21.3 | -43 |

# .338 WIN MAG

The .338 Win Mag was introduced in 1958, based on a necked-down version of the .458 Winchester, and saw its first appearance in the Winchester Model 70 'Alaskan' bolt-action rifle. It was designed with the heaviest of North American game in mind – to be able to grass the biggest moose with ease, and tame the most ferocious bear with calculating efficiency. Indeed, it lived up to its on-paper potential, and although initially slow to gain popularity, its success spread halfway around the world to Africa, where it became widely used for larger plains game. Although it also bagged considerable numbers of dangerous game – dispatching buffalo, lion and leopard with little fuss – the minimum calibre restriction of .375 in many countries prevented the calibre from being widely used for anything beyond plains game. Among professionals, its ability to drop big buffalo has never been in question, especially after Barnes introduced the 300-grain soft nosed bullet in .338 at 2500fps. This was serious ballistic medicine for these bovine brutes. Interestingly, the heaviest bullets loaded by Federal for the two calibres (250-grain for .338 and 300-grain for .375) show that although the muzzle energy of the .375H&H is some 570ft/lb more than the 50-grain lighter .338Win Mag (4,502ft/lb and 3,929ft/lb respectively), both deliver downrange muzzle energy at 200 yards of around 2950ft/lb.

The potential of the .338 calibre was quickly tapped into by Roy Weatherby, the dean of 'velocity at all cost' syndrome, when introducing the .340 Weatherby Magnum in 1962. This surpassed the original design's MV by some 150fps in the 250-grain offering. However this was largely a pointless exercise, and achieved very little except compound the short- to medium-range bullet failure problems at the time, which were due to the bullet construction being unsuitable for muzzle energies in excess of 4,000ft/lb. Impressive muzzle and downrange energies are of little use if penetration is inadequate.

This temporarily held back the calibre, before brass and gunpowder

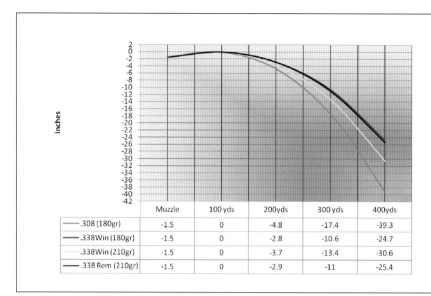

| | Muzzle | 100 yds | 200yds | 300 yds | 400yds |
|---|---|---|---|---|---|
| .308 (180gr) | -1.5 | 0 | -4.8 | -17.4 | -39.3 |
| .338Win (180gr) | -1.5 | 0 | -2.8 | -10.6 | -24.7 |
| .338Win (210gr) | -1.5 | 0 | -3.7 | -13.4 | -30.6 |
| .338 Rem (210gr) | -1.5 | 0 | -2.9 | -11 | -25.4 |

was married with Nosler Partition bullets, allowing its popularity to surge again. Soon the major manufacturers piggybacked onto an accelerating following, adding the .338 Win Mag to model lines from Remington, Savage, Sauer, Sako and Tikka.

Comparing it directly to other offerings, it is unsurprising to find that with the extra case volume and higher MV, the 180-grain .338 Win Mag sports a considerably flatter trajectory than the same bullet weight in .308 Win Mag, falling some two inches less at 200 yards.

What is most evident from the graph is the ability of the newer and arguably improved Remington Ultra Magnum to blast a 210-grain bullet downrange with an almost identical trajectory as the 180-grain Win Mag. Like the even more modern .338 Lapua Magnum, Remington's version pushes a hefty 250-grain bullet at almost 3,000fps, and benefits from a case design without a belt, which is said to provide better head-spacing and longer case life. Furthermore, the impeccable accuracy of the .338 Lapua Magnum blows the older

Winchester .338 out of the water as far as far as printing groups on paper is concerned.

So the question really is: Has the .338 Win. Mag. become redundant? This is answered by asking another question: Do people now regularly shoot game at 500-600 yards? The answer to that is no. The newer versions of the .338 are long-range calibres, and do an excellent job at it. But considering the game that would be hunted with such a calibre, and that 200 yards will probably be the longest shot taken nine times out of 10, this is probably unnecessary overkill. Analysing the graph again shows little advantage at this range, and I would suggest that the calibre still remains a potent option to this day, enjoying a respected reputation in the US and across Africa.

The recoil of the older design is noticeably less than the more modern variations, but unmoderated it is unlikely you would like to spend a day firing it on the range. Having said that, it is perfectly manageable for most people, with 1¾in groups regularly achieved with off-the-shelf rifles.

Regulations on minimum calibres aside, the .338 Win Mag may just be the most usable and versatile calibre around – certainly a serious contender for North American big game. ⊞

# .338 LAPUA

Despite the .338 Lapua being a relatively recent addition to hunting vocabulary, it has actually been on the go since 1982. Its life began as a request by the US Marine Corps to Research Armaments Industries for the development of a long-range rifle for sniper applications. With this, it became the first rifle to be developed solely for military target shooting; previously, sniper rifles had essentially been modified hunting rifles. This initially produced a .50 calibre version, which is still used today, along with a .300 Win Mag version, which allowed for an interchangeable barrel in .308 Win.

The .300 Win Mag didn't fulfil army penetration requirements, so they continued their research, intent on projecting a heavier bullet at the same kind of velocities. Initial tests began using the .378 Weatherby Magnum case necked down to .338, but the design caused a multitude of feeding problems. They then turned to a well-known big game calibre as the parent case, taking the .416 Rigby down to .338. The new calibre was born as the .338/.416, loaded with a 250-grain Hornady HPBT bullet.

This still didn't satisfy the US military – owing, it is believed, to the bullet choice. As contract deadlines grew nearer, Lapua was approached to help finish development of both the case and bullet. By 1985, final test products were shipped to the United States Army. A year later, the calibre went on to win the 1,000-yard Navy Rifle competition, but military selection parted company with the design, instead opting for a .50 calibre version.

With the lack of a potential government contract, Lapua was left with the remnants of the new .338. With management of Lapua opting to continue with development, the first test rifles were built on Sako L61 and Weatherby Mark V actions. The case dimensions underwent minor alterations, resulting in it being shortened by almost 2mm. The internal structure was also strengthened to withstand higher chamber pressures. Although it had started life some years before, the overall changes were substantial and a new cartridge was born.

The first mass-produced version of the .338 Lapua came from the now famed Accuracy International. It was soon followed by Sako, chambering the cartridge in its renowned TRG-41. At the time AI had the British military contract to supply sniper rifles, but the .338 Lapua was not included in this list. This came later, in 2008, when the first batch of L115A3s arrived in Afghanistan to help curve the insurgents' enthusiasm. Today most Western armies use the awesome power of the .338 Lapua in their sniping armoury.

It was never designed to be a hunting rifle, but as with many things in life, its original purpose doesn't stop people from experimenting.

Although it is far more at home in a Barrett, in 2011 Weatherby offered its Mark V in .338 Lapua with a 26in barrel and built-in muzzle break. This was, of course, intended for the long-range hunting that is so popular in America. There are now a number of other manufacturers chambering hunting rifles for the cartridge, including Savage, H-S Precision and McMillan.

As is the trend with smaller, flatter, faster calibres, the .338 Lapua had the same treatment as the .284 Winchester, with a 6.5-338 wildcat version coming into existence sometime after. This produced some spectacular ballistics, although information is difficult to find. Lapua gives stats of a 139-grain bullet producing muzzle velocities of 3,780fps. By comparison, the acclaimed 6.5-284 would project the same bullet at about 3,000fps. Of course, barrel life is something that has to be whispered quietly, as you're likely to change your socks less often.

The .338 Lapua is unlikely ever to be considered as a viable hunting calibre in the UK, although it is being used for long-distance target shooting. As you might expect, though, the Americans haven't shied away from harnessing the impressive ballistics on live quarry. Of course, there are ethical considerations at play here. The application of the .338 Lapua tends to be for super long-range hunting, where 1,000 yards is often passed. This aside, it is interesting to note, if only academically, what can be achieved.

Accuracy is in no doubt, with it already proving itself on human-dimensioned marks at ranges over a mile on a regular basis. The practicalities of a hunting rifle do prove tricky, mainly owing to the long barrel required to get the most out of this large-cased calibre. Loaded with slow burning powder, it needs a full 26in of barrel, which makes for an ungainly rifle when fitted with a moderator. You will need strong arms too, with even the lightest rifle weighing 9.5lb. That said, you will be glad of the weight when it comes to shooting it, and a moderator or muzzle brake is a must. **BP**

# .375 H&H

For anyone on the verge of a trip back to Africa, I think it only appropriate to take a look at possibly the most iconic and widely-used calibre in Africa: the venerable .375 H&H. As the legal minimum for dangerous game in many countries, it is often the default choice. The H&H will happily tame an elephant with a well-placed brain shot, but stops short of being overgunned if you intend to hunt antelope with the same rifle. Most manufacturers today chamber the .375 H&H, and ammunition is readily available. Importantly, you won't have any trouble getting your hands on it in Africa. There are, however, other .375 contenders, so how do they stack up?

The .375 H&H started out in 1912, making it a century this year since Holland & Holland breathed life into this belted, rimless magnum. The case itself has since been used in numerous wildcat incarnations, as well as some of the famous Weatherby Magnums.

The calibre was warmly embraced in Africa. The great writer and hunter John 'Pondoro' Taylor rated it the best medium bore for hunting in Africa, but it is not restricted to the land of lions and leopards – it has been widely used in North America too.

One of the most notable cartridge developments comes from Weatherby. Like most of the cartridges from Weatherby, everything is bigger and faster than the original. It does mean more recoil, and, in their smaller calibre magnums, considerably less barrel life.

The case was a blown-out and improved version of the H&H, delivering around 200fps more muzzle velocity. This allowed increased potential in the lower bullet weights, with the 270-grain soft nose replicating .30-06 trajectories. Conveniently, it is possible to shoot standard H&H ammo in a rifle built for the Weatherby cartridge, providing a safeguard should you run out of ammunition in the depths of the bush – you will always get your hands on the old-timer.

In this century, the .375 saw a radical reinvention as far as commercially available cartridges are concerned. Hornady got together with Ruger in 2006 to develop the .375 Ruger, designed specifically to shoot in standard length actions. They did this by removing the long tapered body in favour of a shorter, fatter case with a sharper shoulder, allowing it to be fired from .30-06 size actions. Though the case is shorter, its case capacity is greater, providing a performance edge on the old man of the .375

line-up. Having said that, this is only true when shooting the 270-grain bullet, and even then the difference is marginal.

Although the H&H 270-grain bullet's trajectory is not shown on the graph, the 400-yard bullet drop is -24.3in – just 0.9in more than the Ruger. When it comes to the 300-grain bullet, the difference between the two is all but non-existent, though if you want to split hairs the H&H is actually marginally superior. The Weatherby Magnum, by contrast, wipes the floor with the competition, pushing a 300-grain bullet out with the same trajectory as the other two calibres shooting the 270-grain. You don't get this performance for nothing though, so expect another 10ft/lb of recoil.

Despite the greater performance of the Weatherby, and shorter action option of the Ruger, I think I would probably follow in the footsteps of the great African hunters; after all, the H&H was good enough for them. **BP**

# .416 RIGBY

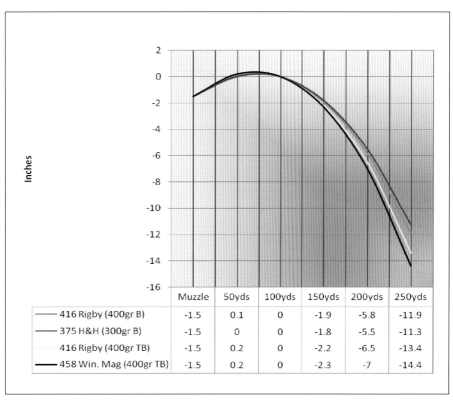

The .416 Rigby is a true African calibre, and has deservedly earned a fine reputation over the last 100 or so years. Introduced by John Rigby of London in 1911, the proprietary cartridge was originally designed for his Mauser-actioned rifles, and quickly garnered wide acclaim for its impeccable reliability on dangerous game. It was seen as a 'medium big bore' calibre by the renowned African hunter (cum poacher) John Taylor, who stated that, for a magazine-fed rifle, "there is no finer or more satisfactory weapon for all-round use against dangerous animals than the .416". Nearly a century after its creation, it is still heralded as one the great big game calibres.

Accessibility to the calibre and continued success was bolstered in 1989, when Federal Cartridges Co. added the .416 Rigby to their premium product line. Three years later, Ruger also tagged onto the success of this respected calibre, offering it in their rifle models. The combined backing of these two giants in the gun world gave the established .416 Rigby another boost, and sucked the wind from the sails of the newly introduced .416 Remington Magnum.

Despite another rival arriving on the market in 1989 in the form of the .416 Weatherby Magnum, the .416 Rigby still held its own against the younger, faster rounds; the .416 calibre was used for close-quarter work, so little advantage was to be gained with the flatter long-range trajectories of the more modern variations. The Weatherby and Remington Magnum versions were both based on a belted case, which was seen among professional hunters as a mistake, as the sleeker lines of the Rigby cartridge resulted in smoother feeding through the magazine.

The lower breech pressures produced with the hot African climate in mind (around 40,000 cup as opposed to upwards of 50,000 cup with the .416 Rem Mag) also meant that the Rigby round avoided sticky extraction on very hot days – a concern expressed by Frank C Barnes in Cartridges of the World. Unsurprisingly, it is also the case that the .416 Rigby is much more forgiving to fire than the other two.

As far as comparisons with similar calibres go, the .416 Rigby boasts some impressive figures. Out to 200 yards the graph shows very little difference between the .416 (400-grain Barnes) and the .375 (300-grain Barnes), despite the .375 being 100 grains lighter. Even out to 250 yards there is only a difference of 0.6in, with a 11.9in fall, which goes some way to explain the shooting world's long-standing love for the round's ballistics. The 400-grain (Trophy Bonded) also compares favorably to the same bullet weight in the .458 Win Mag, falling a full inch less at 250 yards.

The bottom line is that zeroing an inch high at 100yds will keep a 400-grain .416 Rigby trajectory within a two-inch kill zone out to 170 yards, with manageable bullet drop out to 200 yards – well beyond the distance most shots are taken with these large calibres. Considering that groups close to MOA are possible with the right factory ammo, this makes the .416 Rigby one of the most accurate 'big bore' calibres.

Analysing the sectional density confirms the impressive history for use on dangerous game, showing a 400-grain bullet with an SD of .330, which is greater than a 405-grain bullet from a .458 Win Mag at .276 (remember: the greater the SD, the greater the penetrative capability). With the SD of the .375 at .305, it shows, relatively speaking, just how poor the .458 is.

With a muzzle velocity of 2400fps, the .416 Rigby pushes out a mean muzzle energy of 5117ft/lb, some 619ft/lb more than the .458 Win Mag, which also has a slower MV (just 2250fps). The lighter .375 also delivers around 600ft/lb less ME, even with the increased MV of 2600fps. To give some perspective, a 100-grain .243 round delivers 1800ft/lb of ME.

With dangerous game calibres it is as much about having a tried and tested reputation as it is about number crunching ballistics. When your life is on the line, your calibre of choice has to perform, and almost 100 years of near-faultless service has proved – beyond doubt – that the .416 Rigby can do just that. For a large calibre it has pleasing trajectory and impressive penetrative and killing credentials, with perfectly manageable recoil, allowing for very accurate shooting by big bore standards. It is surely the perfect choice for dangerous game. **BP**

| | Muzzle | 50yds | 100yds | 150yds | 200yds | 250yds |
|---|---|---|---|---|---|---|
| 416 Rigby (400gr B) | -1.5 | 0.1 | 0 | -1.9 | -5.8 | -11.9 |
| 375 H&H (300gr B) | -1.5 | 0 | 0 | -1.8 | -5.5 | -11.3 |
| 416 Rigby (400gr TB) | -1.5 | 0.2 | 0 | -2.2 | -6.5 | -13.4 |
| 458 Win. Mag (400gr TB) | -1.5 | 0.2 | 0 | -2.3 | -7 | -14.4 |

# .450 RIGBY

Though it carries a name festooned in ancient calibre history, it will come as a surprise to many that the .450 Rigby is actually a relatively new cartridge, launched by Rigby in 1995. This came almost 100 years after it introduced the .450 Nitro Express.

It was an elephant hunting trip by Mr Paul Roberts, the owner of John Rigby and Co, that led to the development of this cartridge. He landed a well-placed lung shot with a .416 Rigby, and the elephant cow moved on a considerable distance before succumbing to several more shots. Disappointed with the performance of his round, Paul immediately started a fevered post-hunt discussion with his PH. He concluded that the extra weight and bullet diameter would be beneficial for taming the planet's largest land mammal.

Ultimately, the solution was tidy. By necking up the .416 case to .458, the already generous capacity would be able push a 480-grain bullet with moderate pressure at 2,400fps.

Given that Rigby already manufactured many rifles for the highly regarded .416 calibre, simply necking up this cartridge required minimal additional manufacturing expense or design development.

There are, however, a few downsides to using the already established brass. For one thing, it is terribly inefficient with modern powders. It also requires the use of magnum-length actions and non-standard magazine widths to accommodate the fat cases. Powder consumption is also a consideration.

According to QuickLoad, the .450 Rigby requires 96.8 grains of N550 to push out a 500-grain Woodleigh at 2,271fps. With a .458 Lott, similar velocities can be achieved with the same bullet and 76-grain N530. However, the Rigby does allow for far greater performance if the recoil can be handled, punching out 500 grains of copper and lead at 2,427fps with a 103.5-grain load of N550. It does this with considerably less chamber pressure than the Lott – 57,838psi compared with 62,141psi – yet sends the same bullet down range at 156fps more.

On paper, the recoil of the Rigby does seem punishing. For the comparable loads above, the .450 pushes back with 79.6ft/lb worth of recoil. Cranking a 2,427fps load out of the Rigby escalates this considerably, packing an unpleasant 91.4ft/lb of recoil. For those who are unacquainted with calibres of this size, the recoil of a .243 Win will be around 8.8ft/lb.

Despite this colossal difference, the .450 Rigby is surprisingly manageable. I remember being stunned on squeezing off the first round at just how easy it was to handle this large calibre. I wouldn't describe the recoil as severe – more like exhilarating. Unlike some big calibres that kick you abruptly with head-snatching violence, this was more of a long, hard push. Needless to say, I had already become a fan at this point.

With reliable and smooth cycling due to the rimless case, moderate pressures and availability of excellent .458 bullets, the Rigby has already forged itself an enviable reputation in what is a very short space of time. Welcome to the .450 Rigby – a modern great. **BP**

# .458 LOTT

I could feel the rich African dirt filling my flared nostrils. The musty smell signalled a heartening return to a land of great wonder. We were in the heart of elephant country on the edge of Kruger Park, on a mission to dart a big elephant bull for a radio collar replacement. As I watched the vets and game guards milling around, I was drawn to the lead warden with rifle slung over his shoulder. This was the first time I had seen a .458 Win, and it lead me to look into the .458 Lott.

The Lott was designed in 1971 by the knowledgeable and affectionately described 'gun nut' Jack Lott. Based on a blown out and shortened .375 H&H case, it was noticeably longer than its predecessor, the .458 Winchester Magnum. Jack Lott definitely had the inadequacies of Winchester's .458 in mind when he set about producing a new calibre, and wanted to ensure that the same lacklustre performance was not repeated. A close encounter with a Cape buffalo in Mozambique encouraged him to produce the perfect big game calibre.

Having sustained injuries during the altercation, Jack wanted something more powerful. The original issues were that the cartridge was too small to produce desired velocities and the powder clumped in the compressed charge.

Deciding there was no issue with the .458 calibre, Lott established that he needed to design a new case to launch the bullet at greater velocities to increase down-range energy. With the blown out .375 case trimmed to 2.8in, Jack achieved a 0.3in increase in case length over the Winchester. This allowed greater powder capacity and removed the need for such a compressed load.

A major benefit was that any rifle chambered in the new .458 Lott would also be able to fire the original .458 Winchester. This meant that any rifle chambered in the Winchester could quite easily be re-chambered to the more modern calibre with very little work. The only occasional problem was that the longer calibre did not fit the magazine, which required mag-well modifications. At the time, ammunition had to be custom made, so the advantage of being able to use the old .458 Winchester as a back-up undoubtedly added comfort.

The Lott version of the .458 grew in popularity. Recognition of the improvements soon came about, with A-Square beginning to load ammunition in 1989. In the 1970s Winchester was forced to resolve the powder clumping issue: the load of the .458 Winchester was reduced to remedy the problem (resulting in even lower exit velocities and widening the gap between the two cartridges). No doubt this helped the Lott further. Eventually, the calibre was standardised by SAAMI specifications. According to its records, this was issued on 06/04/1998. Although the standardised spec dictates a gradually tapering case, some manufacturers loaded a marginally improved version with a ghost shoulder to aid greater bullet retention under heavy recoil.

The Brno ZKK 602 was chambered to take the .458 Lott, and the calibre became imbedded in the world of African big game hunting. Today it is a standard used to compare all other calibres.

The .458 Lott is truly at home in Africa. Ammunition is no problem for this load – a number of big brand names produce Jack's beloved .458 Lott. The table below shows the performance comparison. BP

| CALIBRE | BULLET | MV (FPS) | ME (FT/LB) | DROP AT 100YDS WITH 50YD ZERO |
|---------|--------|----------|------------|-------------------------------|
| .458 Win | Barnes Banded Solid | 2050 | 4667 | -0.8 |
| .458 Lott | Barnes Banded Solid | 2300 | 5875 | -0.3 |
| .470 NE | Barnes Banded Solid | 2150 | 5133 | -0.7 |

# .470 NITRO EXPRESS

There are a handful of calibres that everyone associates with Africa. The 7x57, made famous by WDM Bell, is probably the first to roll off anyone's tongue. Although the .30-06 is widely used as well, Africa can hardly lay claim to a calibre used extensively the world over.

As we peer up the calibre scale and pass the benchmark .375 H&H, we get to the heart of African calibre territory. Some of these big dangerous game calibres have featured here before, but the .470 NE is probably where most hunters' thoughts land when we talk about African doubles.

Introduced in 1900 by Grant and Lang, the .470 NE is possibly the most popular of all the Nitro Express calibres. Seen primarily in double rifles, it was adopted by most of the big British gunmakers of the day. It is probably fair to say that the Nitro Express calibres transformed big game hunting in Africa, but the .470 was not the first.

As far as I can tell, the Nitro Express era started in 1898 with introduction of the .450

NE from John Rigby. In 1907 designers' hands were forced into producing something bigger when the British government banned the .450 in India and Sudan, where there was tribal unrest. With these restrictions, most settled on a halfway house between the .450 and .500.

Although Westley Richards and Holland & Holland came up with their own concoctions, only the respected gunmaker Joseph Lang released his calibre unrestricted to the trade, to be chambered by whoever wished. It is primarily for this reason that the .470 NE saw such an initial surge in uptake, and it quickly made it across the water to the land where it was intended to be used. Later, the calibre's reputation was given a further boost as John Rigby decided to adopt it in their own rifles instead of re-designing their own.

There is no doubt that the .470 NE is a tremendous big game calibre, and given the large number of guns chambered in .470 NE, ammunition is never a problem to get hold of. In terms of performance, the only reservation I have come came from John Taylor in his book African

Rifles and Cartridges. Here he expressed minor concerns over penetration on a small number of occasions, but this was put down to bullet design rather than an inherent issue with the cartridge – this was not a repeat of the .458 Win problems. Today .470 NE ammo is available with a variety of loaded bullets, including the exceptional Woodleigh Weld-Core, so bullet performance won't be an issue.

Ballistically, most of the stats will mean little to most UK hunters. It is a colossal calibre, and true big game back-up. It may be surprising for some to find that despite being a massive 500-grain projectile, a zero at 50 yards will only drop the bullet half an inch at 100 yards, and this is probably further than you will ever need to use such a calibre. Just in case, though, at 150 yards it drops a very manageable 3.7in, which for a back-up body shot on big game makes for an aim-and-shoot affair.

In the words of the great John Taylor, the .470 NE is "splendidly balanced cartridge in every way." It is one of the great African big game calibres. **BP**

# .500 JEFFERY

My first taste of a 'big calibre' dappled at the fringes as my 19-year-old self absorbed the unapologetic recoil of a .375 H&H for the first time. Though it is undoubtedly a versatile and acclaimed calibre, it cannot truly be classed as a 'stopper'. To venture into the romantic realms of the truly big African calibres requires a shoulder of steel and an unflinching steadiness in the face of inevitable recoiling punishment. Here, I present to you the iconic .500 Jeffery.

Spawning from German origin, the .500 Jeffery started life as the 12.7x70. Designed by Richard Schuller, it was first commercially advertised in 1923 as the 'Schuller Model Jumbo Rifle in the Schuller calibre .500'. Describing the calibre in British nomenclature instead of the normal German metric system was unusual, and is possibly what caught the attention of W J Jeffery around 1927. That year it launched as the .500 Jeffery, joining the already established line of Jeffery's cartridges. In subsequent years this gave many people the impression that this legendary calibre had been the brainchild of Jeffery. This was not so.

An interesting quirk in the design resulted from Schuller building his first rifles on standard Mauser 98 actions, using the large volume of surplus military rifles available. To fit the smaller bolt face, the case design had to be altered, re-batting the rim. This was seen by a number of notable African

hunters, including Tony Sanchez Arino, as a considerable compromise.

In fact, there was a serious reason for the misgivings towards this change. Owing to the undersized rim, the bolt face would occasionally slip over the case when trying to chamber a round from the staggered column magazine of the K98. The result of this was inevitably a jam, as the bolt face cut a groove down the side of the round. Schuller solved this problem with an extended single column mag, but sacrificed the controlled

feed with further chamber modifications, according to Tony Sanchez Arino.

Pulling the calibre apart exposes ballistics most UK hunters will struggle to fathom. Packing a 570-grain Woodleigh soft point, the modest 2,200fps MV smacks home a staggering 5,050ft/lb at 100 yards. The trajectory is also surprisingly manageable, dropping only 2.4in at 150 yards for a 100-yard zero. It will fall to -7.1in at 200 yards, but it's important to remember the situations and species being hunted with this goliath of the calibre world. It's not intended for rolling over dik dik at 250 yards. For the professional hunter with a client, the .500 will doubtless be launched at around 20-30 feet, considerably closer if Murphy is on watch. It is unquestionably a stopping calibre, and is the kind of companion you want to be wielding if you're in the sticky stuff. It's just up to the hunter not to miss.

For the amateur dangerous game hunter, this will be too much gun. Lighter, more comfortable calibres will likely be more accurate and useful. You will be comforted, however, to have a back-up .500 Jeffery in your corner just in case. Paraphrasing the great John Taylor to conclude, the .500 Jeffery 'is immensely powerful, yet very easy and pleasant to shoot'. Coming from the godfather of African calibres, the endorsement says all that's needed. **BP**

# .600 NITRO EXPRESS

Designed by Jeffery in 1903, the .600 Nitro Express was the largest and most powerful commercial hunting calibre in the world until 1988, when it was surpassed by the staggeringly powerful .700 NE. The .600 NE was designed solely for those 'back against the wall' situations, specifically with elephant in mind. When the trunk tucks and ears clamp back, the bravado of flared lugs, stomping dust and head-shaking trumpets will cease, leaving only cold steel and gunpowder for company. It is here, somewhere in limbo between the merciless African bush and five tonnes of hulking grey mass, that the .600 NE calls home.

Loaded normally in double rifles, it provided the maximum stopping power possible, inevitably flooring anything that stood within range. This was a close-quarters, explosively recoiling juggernaut killer, slamming even the most highly pumped, high-speed charging elephant to the ground.

It has been argued that this calibre is excessive. That was certainly the feeling among professional ivory hunters of that iconic era. As a working tool for day-to-day hunting, it is largely impractical, not only in recoil but in also in weight. Firing it on the range is an unpleasant affair, and there will be few people keen to shoot it more than twice. Of course, in a hunting situation with adrenalin pumping, this is far less noticeable.

I would have to say that even for elephant cropping, the .600 NE would not be high on my list of calibre choices. It really is a round for emergencies. As the ultimate back-up rifle, it is probably impossible to better. Clients on the quest for jumbo would certainly be comforted by the fact that their PH was wielding two tubes of .600 Nitro, especially if their ticket through the pearly gates comes under immediate threat of collection. If the .600 doesn't stop it, nothing short of an anti-tank round will provide any improved odds.

It was made famous by the American PH Mark Sullivan, who released a number of DVDs focused on dropping charging dangerous game with his .600 NE double rifle. The ethics and circumstances of these films are highly questionable – indeed, his methods led to him being kicked out of the SCI in 2010. However,

the footage does demonstrate the devastating effect of the cartridge.

By virtue of the calibre's mammoth proportion, rifles were heavy. In the region of 16lb, it is not the kind of rifle one could wield all day, and instead must be carried by a gun bearer until the shooter follows up wounded game in the thick brush. According to John 'Pondoro' Taylor, who happened to be an avid supporter of the .600 NE, a "professional ivory hunter should either have a .577 or .600 in his battery, although he may only want it once or twice in a twelvemonth." He did not, however, see it as necessary for the amateur sportsman.

With modern components, the .600 pushes out a 900-grain Woodleigh FMJ at 1,866fps and 6,959ft/lb ME. This equates to 106ft/lb of recoil – a full 10ft/lb less than the heavier load. By comparison, a 9lb .375 H&H shooting a 300-grain bullet has about 39ft/lb recoil. Interestingly, the load offered by Kynoch today mirrors the heavier load, with MV of 1,955fps and an extra 641ft/lb ME.

This is a calibre for the professional, and even then it will be overgunning 99 per cent of the time. That said, in the other 1 per cent it can be the difference between life and death. BP

# RECOMMENDED READING

**A Foxing Life with Gun and Rifle**
By: Mike Powell
Published by: Blaze Publishing
ISBN: 978-0-9549597-4-6
£19.95

Mike Powell's life has, in one way or another, run parallel to that of the fox. From running a fox control business and keepering, to making a living from selling their skins, the fox has always been present.

Today, Mike passes on his knowledge of the fox and details his dealings with Charlie over the course of his life in the new book: *A Foxing Life with Gun and Rifle*. The book traces Mike's early years in foxing, before delving into the various methods open to fox controllers, revealing his own hints and tips and discussing how these have evolved over his time hunting this wily predator.

**British Deer Stalking Bible, 2nd ed.**
By: Peter Carr
Published by: Blaze Publishing
ISBN: 978-0-9549597-8-4
£19.95

The *British Deer Stalking Bible* became a sell-out and an essential addition to the stalker's library. This revised second edition has been extended and modernised with updated photography, recently released stalking equipment, an additional hunting story, and a new preface from the author.

Adding to the practical use of the book, there is a significant section on rifles, optics and other necessary paraphernalia. It isn't all-inclusive and was never meant to be, but it has been compiled from the author's own experience and that of fellow professionals who have tried and tested the kit in the field.

**Hornady Reloading Manual 9th Edition**
Published by: Hornady
£39.99 (£34 from virtualnewsagent.com)

Reloaders will find the 9th edition *Hornady Handbook of Cartridge Reloading* an invaluable resource, with 900 pages covering all the newest Hornady bullets. Cartridge additions include the .17 Hornet, .327 Federal, .356 Winchester, 5.56 NATO, 416 Barrett and 505 Gibbs. There is also expanded data on more than 20 favourites like the .223 Rem, .300 Whisper, .308 Win, .25-06 and many more.

In addition to comprehensive reloading charts, this manual provides in-depth explanations of internal, external and terminal ballistics. Coupled with the Hornady online calculator, shooters will have the tools they need to replicate the environment where they plan to shoot.

**The Sporting Rifle: A User's Handbook**
By: Robin Marshall-Ball
Published by: Quiller
ISBN: 978-1-8468905-5-0
£25 (£21.50 from virtualnewsagent.com)

Marshall-Ball has split this engaging book up into three main segments: 'The Rifle', 'The Sport' and 'Rifle Ownership and Use'. There is a wealth of information to be found in the appendices, too, with useful contacts, a summary of the law surrounding rifles and their use – a topic handled with a rare clarity – and a comprehensive set of ballistic tables.

The book then gets going into a comprehensive guide of the many varieties of sporting rifles available to today's shooter. From the custom-made double-barrelled rifles of London to the entry-level workhorses of Russia, Marshall-Ball has all the knowledge you'll ever need.

**The Sporting Rifle Book of Foxing**
Published by: Blaze Publishing
£6.99 (£6 from virtualnewsagent.com)

An essential guide to foxing in the UK, the *Sporting Rifle* book of foxing compiles the collective knowledge of the best foxing scribes in the country as they told it to *Sporting Rifle* magazine. Luminaries including Mike Powell, Howard Heywood, and Pat 'The Warrener' Carey all contribute their best advice and foxing stories. Every part of the foxing calendar is covered, from cubbing time to harvest, with baiting tips, lamping, night vision and even daytime foxing all covered in depth. On top of that, there are sections on the best foxing rifles and ammunition, moderators and more. In all, this is a truly comprehensive collection of foxing expertise and hunting tales.

**Wild Boar: A British Perspective**
By: Steve Sweeting
Published by: Blaze Publishing
ISBN: 978-0-9549597-3-9
£19.95

Wild boar expert and big game hunter Steve Sweeting's new book *Wild Boar: A British Perspective* is a stunningly detailed look at the role wild boar has played throughout the history of hunting since the time of the Celts. Yet it's not just a historical document. From fieldcraft, ballistics, shot placement, to gralloching and cooking, Steve has penned a comprehensive, all-in-one guide to the wild boar and the best ways to hunt it.

Whether you're a seasoned boar shooter, or looking for information on how to do it safely and humanely, this is the perfect read.

All books available now from:
# www.virtualnewsagent.com